Secret Witness
The Steele Murder Case

A true story of murder
and saving grace in Ohio.
After years, her silence
is broken.

Carol J. Kilbane Byler

Gazelle
PRESS

Mobile, Alabama

ISBN 978-1-58169-418-5
For Worldwide Distribution
Printed in the U.S.A.

Gazelle Press
P.O. Box 191540 • Mobile, AL 36619
800-367-8203

As a messenger of restoration

I dedicate this book

to the many hurting women

who are reading it.

I pray they find

God's redeeming love.

Table of Contents

Acknowledgments

I want to thank foremost my Lord and Savior Jesus Christ for having His hand on me and never giving up on me, knowing I would one day surrender to Him. For sparing my life and helping me to become the godly woman I am today. You did restore the years the locusts had eaten. I seek no credit for this book. I give You all the credit for making this possible.

Thank you to my church family, who have supported me over the years.

Thanks to my two favorite men in my life, my wonderful sons, Ryan and Kevin, for supporting me with my story. You accepted me as Mom and never judged me for my past. I did the best I could under my circumstances. Our survival wasn't easy, but with the help of God, we made it. The Kilbane name changed with the two of you. I am proud of the young men you have become. You didn't follow your dad's or my footsteps.

Joseph, my husband, thank you for believing in me and accepting me regardless of my past. For saying to me, "It was the love you had for Jesus that attracted me to you, not your past. You are a new woman in Christ, I don't look at your past. Just like Jesus doesn't bring it up to you, neither will I."

The following acknowledgments are not in a particular order:

Faith, thank you for being my spiritual friend and sister in the Lord. For walking me through the most difficult times of my life. For taking my children and I into your family and making us a part of yours. Thanks for inspiring me to write this book and for all your wonderful helping in getting me started.

Thanks to my only sister, Barbara, who always supported me and told me I needed to write. I love you, sister pister.

My brother, Richard, who has gone home to be with the Lord. I am thankful I got to share the Lord with you.

Thanks to my daughter, Lynn, for our wonderful reunion. I pray that one day you will find it in your heart to be friends. Thanks for the grandchildren.

Thanks to my stepchildren, Tara and Sherry, for allowing me to be a part of your dad's life. Thanks for all my wonderful grandchildren.

Thank you, Dawn, for being a wonderful daughter-in-law and wife to my son Kevin and my grandchildren.

Thank you, Sandra, for being in my life all these years as we remain friends. Thank you for searching for my daughter.

Thanks to all my friends and family who always believed I could get this done.

Thanks for all the people who helped me edit my book over the years: Faith W., Kathy H., Rachael O., Tara W., Carie R., Mary Jane W., Sarah C., Leslie T., and the writers group.

Rachael H.—it was no accident we met. Thank you for making the final draft ready and for working so hard. You were an answer to my prayer.

I also want to thank my agent, Keith Carroll, who helped me make this all possible.

There is no way I could list everyone. You all know who you are, and I want to thank you from the bottom of my heart for all of your hard work and encouragement in making this book a reality.

I want to finally thank all those in the justice system for doing your job. I fought you at first. I am so glad I could come back years later and show you I am not the same person I was in 1977. You too could see that someone had to have changed my life.

Owen, I want to thank you for being in my life. If it weren't for you I could not be able to write this story. We were young, and I take responsibility for my part in our journey. My prayer is that one day you will experience the freedom I have by accepting Jesus into your heart.

Thank you, everyone, for taking the time to read my story. Pass it on to others who will be blessed by my message.

—*Carol J. Kilbane Byler*

Secret Witness

Silence hung in the packed courtroom. Curious faces of unfamiliar people stared at me as I clutched my six-week-old son, Ryan. I could feel their eyes burning holes into my back as I stood facing the judge. I wanted to melt deep into the floor. I desperately needed to hide from their probing glares and run from this life that had gotten so terribly out of control. The criminal secret I had kept for years was about to be revealed.

"It is obvious from the acts of the defendants that there is a collusion to prevent this woman from testifying," said Carmen Marino, the Cuyahoga County Prosecutor. His face flushed as he aggressively spit out these words in an effort to force me to testify. "She knows who conspired to kill Marlene Steele! She knows who did it!"

Billed by the local newspapers as "one of the most sensational homicide cases in Ohio," the scandal had attracted the curious for years. The media coverage promised the courtroom would be packed—there wasn't an empty seat in the courtroom.

As the media and the spectators had watched me bring Ryan to the courtroom, I could not help but wonder what they were really thinking of me. I hope they viewed me as a good mother and a loving wife, and yet I suspected I was being judged for the course my life had taken.

If only I could break away from this terrifying nightmare! I was in a web of entrapment, and keeping silent with the truth was my crime.

Judge Robert L. Steele from Euclid, Ohio, was on trial for his wife Marlene's murder. The prosecution labeled me a "central figure." County Prosecutor Marino claimed I was one of their secret key witnesses. They had taken me from my home and held me in protective custody, kept secret from the defense. They claimed it was necessary to protect me. They wanted me to testify against Ryan's father, Owen Kilbane, my common-law husband. Owen was also a defendant on trial for Mrs. Steele's murder.

My attorney, Thomas Shaughnessy, was determined that I would never take the witness stand. Mr. Shaughnessy desperately needed to keep me off the stand, no matter the cost. My testimony would irreparably harm their case and possibly send the defendants to prison for life.

What was I worried about? I thought, trying to reassure myself. These were some of the top criminal lawyers in town. Surely, their expertise would keep me from having to take the stand. They knew how to work the system to keep their clients out of jail.

"Don't worry, Carol," Shaughnessy assured me quietly. "Wives cannot be forced to testify against their husbands."

"She can't take the stand," Shaughnessy objected. "They are married. Here's the paper to prove it. Carol is Owen Kilbane's wife. Their conversations are privileged. They renewed their original vows recently."

Without a doubt, I was now the focal point within this murder trial. There was a strong possibility I might have to testify concerning a statement I had given to an FBI agent a few years earlier about my knowledge of Marlene Steele's murder.

The jury was asked to be removed from the courtroom. They were not allowed to hear the dialogue flying back and forth between Shaughnessy and the prosecutors. The argument was whether Owen's and my relationship was one of husband and wife or pimp and prostitute. For the first time, my past dealings with Robert Steele in prostitution were about to be made public. I was in the middle of a battle in which my most personal and private affairs were being exposed.

"Your Honor," Prosecutor Marino said, "she is not his wife. They have never been married. It is obvious that this is just a maneuver. She has been instructed not to testify. She knows who conspired to murder Marlene Steele; we have a statement in her own words that says she does. This woman has substantial evidence material to this case. If she would rather go to jail than testify voluntarily, then she must be forcefully brought to the witness chair. Just bring the jury back. If she wants to deny her written statement, let her deny it before the jury. Let them decide as they witness her cross-examination."

The prosecution desperately needed me to talk about my statement to support their case. Prosecutor Albin Lipold blurted, "May I add one more thing, Your Honor? Whether or not she answers any questions, we should not be deprived the right to ask our questions. She can then deny, admit, or say whatever she wants. We feel we do have the right to ask our questions, and that's all we are challenging. We want her statement to be brought before the jury."

Despite all the witnesses called to validate our marriage, Shaughnessy and the defense team failed to influence the judge.

"Bring that woman right now to the witness stand," Judge Joseph J. Nahra demanded. I stood frozen in shock, listening to the judge. "Owen and you have no common-law marriage," he said.

Was the prosecution really winning the argument that Owen was a pimp and I was his prostitute?

"No way!" I roared in Shaughnessy's ear. "It's not true. I am his wife. I will not testify against this man, the father of this little boy!"

Shaughnessy, driven to my defense, exclaimed in a stern voice, "She can't and won't testify!"

My breast was filling up with milk; it was time for Ryan to nurse. I gave him a pacifier, hoping it would temporarily soothe him. Shaughnessy tried again. "Your Honor, Mrs. Kilbane needs some time with her son." Ryan began squirming, he was about to let out a holler. I was grateful when the judge called a recess so I could feed my son.

When we came back into the courtroom, Shaughnessy picked up where we had left off, "As you have heard, Your Honor, she has chosen not to testify, refuses to be sworn in, and will refuse to take the witness stand."

The battle raged on. I felt helpless as Shaughnessy, Judge Nahra, our defense attorneys, and the prosecutors quoted law back and forth. Both sides were desperate to win. Despite the uproar, I sensed I was on the winning team. We had always won.

My continued refusal to approach the witness stand infuriated the judge.

"Young lady," he said, glaring at me, "this court orders you to testify! This court has ruled you are not the wife of Owen Kilbane. There is no husband-wife privilege question here to argue. You are susceptible to be called like any other witness, and your lawyer should have told you that."

No! No, this can't be happening! Panic flooded through me. I will just run with Ryan. What about Owen? I stood paralyzed with my dilemma, my options dwindling. I looked at Shaughnessy and then turned to Owen, expecting one of them to do something to help me. All their power was stripped in the face of the judge's ruling.

"Your Honor, I can't testify! It would destroy my family, especially my relationship with my husband," I yelled. I was desperate to convince everyone that I was not a prostitute but a loyal wife who would not expose her husband. I certainly was not going to be labeled a snitch.

"Mr. Shaughnessy, I find you and your client's actions in this case completely reprehensible," the judge said sternly.

"Now, I want to say to this court today," Shaughnessy countered, "I have counseled and advised Mrs. Kilbane of all her rights, pursuant to the constitution of the laws of the State of Ohio. We have discussed the fact that a wife does not have to testify against her husband. I have been instructed, Your Honor, by my client, Mrs. Kilbane, to advise this court, claiming both the privilege and the immunity as a wife of the defendant, Owen Kilbane, that she refuses to testify, to be sworn in, along with refusing to approach the witness stand."

"Your Honor," Prosecutor Lipold said, "it is apparent, as I indicated before, she has been badgered not to talk, and now from her counsel's own lips, he says she is not going to testify. Your Honor, she is our significant material witness in this case."

"Have your client step forward, Mr. Shaughnessy," Judge Nahra ordered.

"Your Honor, my client will not step forward."

Judge Nahra was fed up. "Swear in the witness," he said.

"Your Honor, my client will not be sworn in," Shaughnessy repeated.

"I will ask you again, Mr. Shaughnessy, to have your client step forward to be sworn in."

I shook my head back and forth with refusal. Looking away from the judge I kept my eyes focused on Ryan.

"May I have a moment to consult with my client to determine her wishes?" Shaughnessy asked. Turning to me, he asked, "What do you want to do, Carol?"

"Miss Braun," the judge spoke furiously, "I want to caution you again. Failure to be sworn in to answer questions constitutes a contempt of court charge. If I find you in contempt, I will sentence you to jail. Do you understand that?"

"Your Honor," Shaughnessy interceded with one last attempt, "this young lady walks in here today, in absolute good faith, has in effect said to this court, 'I am the wife of Owen Kilbane.'"

Judge Nahra, looking fiercely at me, pounded his gavel. Darts of raging anger rushed from his eyes. "Mrs. Kilbane or Miss Braun, for failure to step forward, to be sworn in, and to testify in the case now on hearing I find you in contempt of this court. Is there anything you wish to say before sentence is imposed upon you?"

"Yes, Your Honor. I could never step forward to be sworn in. It would cause irreparable damage for my husband and my child," I said.

"Miss Braun, you are sentenced to six months in the county jail, or until such time as you purge yourself of contempt by testifying in the case now on hearing. What you are doing and what your lawyer is advising you to do are inexcusable. You have been called as a witness in this case. You must testify. Take her away! Make arrangements for her baby."

My stomach churned with nausea. "Your Honor, you can't separate us. I'm breastfeeding him. He won't take a bottle. I need to stay with him!"

"Make arrangements for that baby! Take Miss Braun into custody!" the judge ordered.

Shaughnessy leaned toward me, his hands open in a gesture of helplessness. "You have to listen to the judge. There is nothing I can do at this moment. You will have to go with the officers."

My heart shattered. I felt torn in so many directions. "Shaughnessy, you must help me. You said you would," I begged.

"I will appeal this decision immediately," he promised.

Reluctantly I walked over to the table where Owen was sitting. Looking down into his face with desperation, I pleaded quietly, "Please do something. You can stop this. You must stop this." I could see he was infuriated with the lack of power he had. He held his arms up in defeat.

Owen was a very powerful man who could do anything, yet he had no control over this situation. I reached across the table to put Ryan in Owen's arms. My mind was racing. Where am I going? How long will I be there? What is Ryan going to do for milk?

"Come this way," the guard said, grabbing my arm and forcing me out of the courtroom. Fear and helplessness gripped my body even more. I started screaming. My body became so heavy as my knees weakened. I sat on the floor in defiance.

"Please get up," the female guard said. "You have to come with us now. We know the separation from your family must be painful. We wish we did not have to do this."

"My baby needs me. He will need my breast," I shouted.

Reaching down for my arms, the guards lifted my frozen body forcefully down the hall into the small holding cell surrounded with metal bars. They slammed the iron door behind them and used the ring of keys to lock me in. I felt like a caged animal. The shuffling feet of the guards became faint as they moved farther away.

I clutched my hands to my breast, my sobs rising to a heart-wrenching scream. "Let me out of here. You have to get me back with my son," I screamed.

I lay my head back against the cold metal bed frame that was attached to the wall beside the iron toilet. Where were they going to take me and when? All I could do was close my eyes with hopes of escaping this terrifying moment. Anything was better than staring at the soundless walls that surrounded me. I remained in agony. The tighter I squeezed my eyes, the quicker the tears flowed down my cheeks as if a faucet had been turned on. A puddle formed on the cold, gray cement floor. What were Owen and Ryan doing and would I see them again? Surely the authorities wouldn't keep my baby from me, would they? Shaughnessy will get me out. But when?

Oh God, please help me. I just want to go home.

The truth is always painful, but your arguments prove nothing. Here I am desperate, and you consider my words as worthless as wind (Job 6:25-26 CEV).

CHAPTER ONE

Childhood Rebellion

I grew up in Shaker Heights, Ohio, a wealthy, predominantly Jewish suburb on the east side of Cleveland. Surrounded by the well-to-do, our family was among the poor of the neighborhood.

Mom stayed mostly to herself. Raising me and my siblings, Barb, Richard, and William, was a challenge for her. Her days were consumed with watching her daily soap operas, completely distracting her from motherly duties. Her house cleaning mirrored her lack of care for herself and her children. It was hard enough not having a nice house like the other kids; Mom's lack of pride in what little we did have made it worse. Screaming was our only way of communication.

Dad worked two jobs. During the day he was a janitor at the same high school my sister and I attended, and in the evenings he pumped gas at a local station. When he wasn't at work, which was very seldom, he kept himself busy at the Masonic Lodge. We really only saw him on Sundays when we attended church together, one of our only family connections.

With no discipline from my parents, I became totally unruly. I grew up fast on the streets, having no one tell me what was right or wrong.

I spent most of my time away from home with my best friend, Dar, who lived a few houses down the street. Her home was always in turmoil, and her relationship with her parents was dysfunctional, just like mine.

At sixteen I experienced my first arrest after thinking I could get away with stealing some cosmetics in my purse from our local drug store. I never made it out of the store. The police were called. Since I was a juvenile, my parents were called, and I was transported to the local Shaker Heights police station. I was more afraid of what the police were going to do to me than my own parents.

When any of us kids got in trouble, Dad always showed up. Mom had no clue what was going on.

"We'll release you to your dad so you can go home with him. Be in court in the morning," the officer said.

It was a quiet ride home. Walking in the door, I went straight to the phone to tell Dar the news.

The next day, Dad had to take off work so he could go to court with me. Standing before the judge for my first court appearance, I wasn't sure what was going to happen. I had issues with authority figures telling me what I could or couldn't do.

"I am going to give you a chance. I will place you on probation for six months. Do you think you can follow my rules?" the judge asked.

"I'll try," I said with a smirk on my face.

Dad dropped me off at the school office so he could return to work. Class had begun so I stayed in the office until the next class. When the bell rang, I darted out of the office and bumped right into Dar.

"What happened?" she asked.

"Oh, the judge just asked me if I could obey his rules. He placed me on probation for six months. I just laughed at him," I said.

"Carol, I hope you can listen so they don't send you away," Dar warned.

"My parents are pushovers. I'll be okay," I said.

The next few weeks I spent more time in the principal's office than I did in my classrooms. I was flunking all my subjects. Skipping classes became the norm for me. I would hide out in the woods across the street where meeting my friends was more exciting than school. We would sit around smoking and waiting for school to end so we could hop on the bus and pretend we had been at school the whole day. Eventually, the counselor called my parents to tell them I wasn't attending my classes.

I arrived home to Mom asking, "Why did you miss your classes?"

"It's none of your business," I snapped back at her and ran up the stairs to my room only to change my clothes and rush right back out the door.

Two weeks later I was expelled from school and headed right back to the judge.

"What do you have to say for yourself?" he asked.

"I couldn't keep your rules. I guess I got out of control."

My heart was becoming hard as my actions weren't getting me what I really desired from my parents. Attention from the courts was better than no attention at all.

My parents accepted the court's advice to send me to Scioto Village, an all-girls reform school several hundred miles away in southern Ohio. I would be there for one year. I said goodbye to Dad. I didn't even get a hug or "I will miss you" from him as I turned to climb into the police van, and on our way we went. I watched the countryside on the way there, wondering where in the world I was being transferred to. I was in the middle of nowhere, surrounded by cows and farmland. I so was far from the city, it would take hours to get to town.

We arrived at what looked like a large college campus. I didn't know how to express the emotions I was feeling. I cried on the inside but shed no tears.

When I entered the administration building to check in, I was assigned a picture badge and a few personal items. One of the CEOs handed me a set of rules and escorted me to my dorm.

The buildings, which were called cottages, were so old they looked like they were going to collapse anytime soon. I was assigned to Scioto Cottage in the middle of the campus.

We were given linens for our beds and it was our duty to make the bed. I wanted to make a good impression so I dropped my belongings and immediately made my bed to show them I could follow rules.

While I made my bed, I overheard a couple of the girls talking in the hall, telling wild stories of girls drowning while trying to escape by crossing the river that ran along the back of the grounds. It was that fear of drowning that would prevent me from trying to escape. I had never learned how to swim.

Joining them after I finished organizing my room, I got a whole new education on bank robbery, shoplifting, and cashing bad checks. Some of the girls talked about how they sold their bodies to make money. I had done some bad things but nothing compared to what I was hearing.

"Where are you from?" a girl named Sandra asked.

"Shaker Heights. My dad's a lawyer. We have a lot of money. He's going to get me out," I lied.

"I'm from the west side of Cleveland," Sandra replied.

"We'll have to see each other when we get out," I said.

The bell rang signaling lunch time. Sandra and I shared our stories as we walked together to the large dining hall a few buildings away.

After lunch I was sent to the social worker.

"Carol, we have classes that you can take while you're here. Take a look to see what catches your interest," she said.

Scanning down the list my eyes focused on cosmetology, and I told her I wanted to take those classes.

"Why did you decide on that?" she asked.

"I always liked working with hair. How long does it take to get your license?"

"Your classes last about nine months then you have to take a state board test in Columbus. We pay for all your supplies as well as the classes."

"Since I have to be here almost a year, I might as well take this since I enjoy working with hair," I responded.

"Great. I'll sign you up for the class. You can start on Monday."

The reform school staff tried their best to give us some hope for a future and get us on the right track in life. Most of the girls were just like me, coming from unstable homes where all they needed was some discipline.

When I wasn't studying we sat around talking about how we wouldn't get caught the next time we broke the law. Since the system did not rehabilitate, I received no guidance on how to change. My defiant lifestyle was all I knew. Five months had passed, and I was given an early release for good behavior so I was unable to finish my cosmetology classes.

I was put on probation but quickly returned to what I had always done, being hateful and more rebellious than ever. I didn't want to change. I was so angry inside and now I had become boy crazy.

———————————

Larry was my first teenage love. We spent a lot of time together driving around in his '65 Chevy. I craved his attention and did whatever he wanted, including giving him my virginity in the back of the Chevy. After a few weeks of nonstop sex with no birth control, the inevitable happened. I ended up a pregnant teen. Gathering my courage, I finally told my parents and my mom broke the news to Larry's parents. They didn't take it well. Larry's parents called me a whore, strongly suggesting I wasn't good enough for their son. My heart was ripped apart when Larry didn't love me enough to take a stand for us. I truly felt not good enough for Larry. I gave him something so special, yet he rejected me. I had thought for sure we would get married. Larry escaped his responsibility by joining the service.

When my probation officer was informed of my pregnancy, I was found in violation of probation and sentenced back to Scioto Village.

I wasn't the only pregnant girl at Scioto Village. A few of the pregnant girls and I would talk often about what was ahead for our babies. It was early 1965, and we were given two options: send the baby home to your family or give the baby to state foster care. Most of the girls' mothers or families said they would take their babies. I wrote my mother every week pleading with her to take the baby when it was born; however, she repeatedly refused. I was a disgrace to the family.

I enrolled again in cosmetology school, determined to make it work this time. I would have about a year after the baby's birth to finish my sentence and wanted to put the time to good use.

At seventeen, I didn't fully understand my monthly cycle or how this baby was being formed inside of me. All that I knew came from listening to the girls who already had babies talk about what would happen when my labor began.

During the evening of November 15, 1965, I was sitting in the TV room of the cottage. Dashing to the bathroom, I found water was gushing down both of my legs. Frightened, I lifted my legs, thinking the baby was going to fall into the toilet. The labor pains started to increase, and I screamed for the cottage officer.

"My baby is coming! It's coming!" I had never been so frightened.

I was escorted to the hospital in Delaware, Ohio, by way of cab. The cab driver appeared unemotional and unsympathetic to my situation. I didn't say a word to him. The ride took forever as we traveled down the dark bumpy country roads. I yearned for someone to be there to hold my hand.

"Please God, stop the pain," I pleaded.

Arriving at the hospital, I was placed in a room by myself. Within a few minutes, a nurse came in, turned me on my side and injected a large needle into my back.

"I am giving you a spinal block to lighten the pain," the nurse explained.

Terrified and on my own, a child myself, I was in a strange hospital about to become a mother. I felt like my insides were about to burst onto the bed as the labor grew stronger. I screamed at the top of my lungs, and one of the nurses scolded me to shut up.

"You got yourself into this mess, now be quiet," she blurted out. "You are disturbing others around you."

Humiliated and helpless, I felt unloved. There was no one there who cared for me. Was I really the disgrace my mom had accused me of being?

The labor intensified and as the baby's head crowned, I forced my final push.

"It's a girl," the doctor announced.

I tried to lift my tired body to get a glimpse of her, but the nurse instantly removed her from my sight. I wasn't even allowed to hold her. She was now a ward of the state.

For three days I wondered how she was. Was she still at the hospital? Did foster care take her? I yearned to hold my child, to be a mother to her.

Finally a nurse let me know what was happening.

"What name do you want placed on her certificate?" she asked.

"Antoinette Sharoni, Toni as a nickname. How is my baby doing?"

"She's doing fine," she replied.

"I want to see her."

"Carol, you know the rule. You're not allowed to be around her since she is a ward of the state at this time."

I smashed the pillow to my face and let out a loud scream.

The doctors released me to return to Scioto after four days. Walking past the nursery, my eyes focused on each baby laying there, trying to see which one of the babies was my daughter. I thought if I could read the name tags attached to the tiny beds, I could identify my daughter and get a glimpse of what she looked like. But the nurse pushed me out so quickly, I didn't even get a peek. The ache in my heart was unbearable. Tears gushed, falling down upon my feet. I was leaving her, and there was nothing I could do about it.

Arriving back at my cottage, I could hear the other girls calling their parents making arrangements for their babies to be picked up after their births. Who was I going to call? No one. I had no hope of my mother giving in. She just didn't care. A lady from the welfare department came to visit me, telling me I had only a few weeks to find a place for Toni with my family. In desperation, I wrote to my mom again, pleading with her to take my daughter. She refused me again.

The extreme dislike I felt toward my mom grew even stronger. How could she do this to me? All I wanted was love and acceptance in spite of what I did. A mother's love wouldn't treat me like this. What kind of mother was she, forcing me to sign papers to put my baby girl in a foster home? I wanted nothing to do with my mom ever again. These thoughts kept flooding my mind. Knowing I would have to fight for my baby on my own with no help from my family, I was determined to one day show I could take care of Toni by myself.

The social worker would not give me the foster parents' name or any other information about them, but she did say she would tell them to write and send me a picture of my daughter.

A few weeks after my visit with the social worker I received an envelope from an address I wasn't familiar with. I opened up the envelope and saw a picture of a smiling baby girl. "Dear Carol, I wanted you to have this picture of Toni. Hope you are doing well. Enjoy, I will send some more soon." No signature. Her name would remain a mystery to me. I was grinning ear-to-ear as I looked at the picture. I was so proud. I ran through the cottage, showing her off to all of the girls in my dorm.

"She is getting so big, look at her beautiful smile," I shouted with excitement.

Wondering what all the excitement was, the leaders came to look also. My heart was jumping inside, knowing the family who looked after her cared enough about me to send me a picture. I placed her picture on my dresser and every day I would talk to her.

"Mommy is coming home very soon. Get ready for me to get you."

I took my State Board exam and received my cosmetology license. My release date came the week before the Thanksgiving holiday. I was finally heading home. Saying goodbye to a few of the girls wasn't easy. My new friends felt like family. One girl named Jackie urged me to look up her friends when I got home.

"My friends, Hutch and Billie, will take you out to show you around town. You'll have a great time with them. They know how to party," Jackie said.

Maybe I could even go live with them, I thought. I was already scheming on how to get out of living with my mom.

———— ·•◆•· ————

I took a three-hour bus ride back home to Shaker Heights. Trying to prepare my emotions for seeing my parents, I rehearsed the scene that I thought would happen over and over in my head. I was tricking my mind into believing it would happen in a way I could envision. I was not about to accept my parents the way they were. They needed to accept they had a hurting daughter and try to help me. It was wishful thinking on my part. Mom and Dad met me at the bus station. The little girl in me wanted a hug from her dad. I never got it. It was silent in the car most of the way home, except for a short lecture on looking for a job. I knew they hadn't changed. There was no emotional tie.

Instead, I thought I would turn to my friends. I no longer wanted to see my parents, and I certainly didn't want to take orders from them.

I started work at a beauty shop and made a few friends there. But I still wanted to keep my promise to contact Jackie's friends. She told me they lived in Cleveland so I gave them a call. "Hello, Billie. This is Carol. Jackie told me to give you a call when I got home."

"Yeah, she wrote telling me you would be calling. Can you get a ride to Fifty-Fifth Street? We can meet you there," she said.

"I'll ask my brother. I'm sure he won't mind as long as you can get me home."

"Sure, we can do that. Meet us at seven."

"Okay, see you then."

My parents did not want me to go, which made me even more determined to do so. Richard dropped me off at the meeting spot. I waited on the corner of what looked like an all-black neighborhood. A tall black man with a dark suit and black hat approached me with a light-skinned girl.

"Carol is that you?" I was the only white girl around so they knew it had to be me.

"I'm Billie; this is Hutch. Jackie said you two became close," the girl said.

"Yes. There weren't too many that were cool the way she was," I said.

We drove to a well-known nightclub called Leo's Casino. The stage act for that night was a famous singer, James Brown. I was so excited to meet such an important star. I felt important as Hutch and Billie began to introduce me around to everyone. I was treated like a celebrity. James Brown brought excitement to the place, and his energy wore off on me. Feeling the alcohol starting to take effect, I was all over the dance floor.

Billie, Hutch, and I closed the place up and headed back to where they lived. There was a tug of war going on for me. Billie and Hutch each wanted to have me for themselves. I could sense the rivalry that was going on. I felt uneasy. I really didn't know what to do. I was in a very bad neighborhood, and they were the only people there I knew. I had to trust them, so I stuck close to them. We walked into their apartment, and the next thing I knew, they were rolling a joint. It was passed to me after they took a few puffs. I already had a few drinks in me and my eyes were so heavy I was at the point of passing out. A hand started running across me. I looked up; it was Hutch. He pulled me toward him. Fearing the results of not doing what he wanted, I gave in. Here I was again, doing something that I hated.

When he was done, he made his intentions clear. He explained to me that Billie prostituted for him, and how good she was at making him money. Realization hit me! He was a pimp, working his plan on me to set me up as the next girl to work for him. What was I doing? Why was I letting this man touch me like this? What if I got pregnant? I had to get away. Billie pulled me over to where she was laying.

"I work for Hutch making him money," she said. Billie was doing her best to convince me that it wasn't hard to do what she did. "I've been doing this for five years. You can do it too," she tried to reassure me.

What did I have myself involved in now? I didn't want to do it. I also didn't want to tell Hutch or Billie that I was at a place in my life where I was so rebellious that I would try anything. But they could sense it. Now here I was lying in a strange apartment with two strange people I had just met. We finally all drifted off to sleep.

Seconds later, it seemed, the dreaded morning came. Hutch drove Billie and me to a corner not far from the apartment and dropped us off. All four corners of the street were filled with girls of different ages and races. Every time a car came by, one of the girls quickly approached, sticking her head in the car window, then jumped in and off the car would go. They were competing to see who could get to the car the fastest. The job must not be that hard if all of them were there, I thought. Billie walked toward the curb, approaching a car that was slowing down in front us. She leaned into the passenger side window speaking to the white man.

"Twenty-five dollars for each of us," she said.

"Okay," they agreed.

Billie climbed into the front seat motioning me to get into the back. My heart was racing as the man began to touch my body. I could feel myself getting nauseated.

"I can't do this," I cried. "I want to go home!"

The man became furious pushing me against the door. "What kind of stuff is this?" he yelled. "Give me my money back and get the hell out of here."

"Hey Rocco," Billie called out to a dark-skinned man standing near the car. "Can you take this girl home?"

I got out of the car and went with Rocco. Billie was scared of Hutch, so she stayed, working on both tricks.

Rocco said he needed to stop by his apartment before we could leave. I had to go to the bathroom. I could feel myself getting sicker. I followed Rocco upstairs. He went down the hall a few doors and pointed to the door of the bathroom. I tried to shut the door behind me but felt it being pushed back. Someone kept pushing harder. A man entered, then another, and another. I screamed, thinking it would attract someone to my rescue. Instead one of the men slapped my face hard, dropping my body immediately to the hard tile floor. I was being raped and mauled; I was powerless to stop them. It seemed to never end. Eventually, each of them began to leave, walking into the apartment across the hall. My clothes were torn, and there were body fluids coming from every part of my body. I stood up, pulling my clothes together. Weakened from the experience, I kept trying to get dressed. I just have to get out of here, I thought. But my body was just plain numb.

"You were supposed to take me home," I yelled at Rocco.

"Get your own ride."

"Can I at least use your phone to call someone?" I asked.

Choking back the tears, I phoned my brother, Richard, acting like I was okay. It seemed like hours before he came. The ride home was silent. Richard had a temper and I knew because he loved me, he would have tried to avenge me. He probably would have gotten killed. It would be better to keep the rape to myself for now. I jumped out when we arrived home and ran up the stairs into the bathroom. The water in the tub could not get hot enough to wash away the filth I was feeling. I tried to clean myself and brush away what I had just experienced. If I scrubbed long enough, maybe the horror of what had happened would disappear from my mind. Lying safely in my bed, my mind repeated the scenes over and over and over as I cried silently into my pillow. I couldn't escape the memory. Oh God, why did this happen to me? I couldn't even tell my mom.

Early the next morning the phone rang. It was Hutch. "Carol, why did you leave? I need you to come back to work."

"I'll never come near you again. What kind of friends you have! I ask for a ride home and I get raped."

"I'll take care of them, just come back," he promised. I believed him, but my conscience still would not allow me to go back into that situation.

"Don't call this house again," I screamed and hung up.

--------◆•◆•◆--------

I tried to put the whole experience behind me and began to take steps on my own to get Toni back. I had already lost two years of her life. I needed to get us back together. I called to set up an appointment with the lady from human services. I wasn't allowed to know where she was living. I could, however, visit with her under supervision. I would go to a house on Chester Avenue, a place that was used for getting reacquainted with children separated from their biological parents. The staff prepared me for this moment, letting me know that it could be a shock for Toni to just be returned to me. We would have to establish a bond and that would require some adjustments for her and me. I would have to spend a few weeks visiting with her for both of us to adjust and bond.

I was excited about my first visit. The day finally came, and I waited patiently in a waiting room. I kept staring at the door, anxiously waiting for my little girl to come through. I wondered what she looked like. I only had the baby picture that was sent to me. I hoped she looked like me. She must be walking and talking. I hoped she could say Mama. The door opened wide. My heart was pounding so hard I thought it would jump out of my chest. My hands were sweating uncontrollably. There she stood with light brown hair clutching a small teddy bear in her arms. I wanted to run to her, but I was told to move slowly and let her come to me. She was as much a complete stranger to me as I was to her.

Making her way over to where I was seated, she stared directly at me, as if she knew who I was.

"Hello, Toni, you look so pretty in your yellow dress," I said as I reached out my hand to touch her. She pointed to the doll that was on the table in front of us.

"Baby," she said.

"Yes, honey, that is a baby. Want to hold her?"

She shook her head yes. I reached out to grab the doll and as I placed it in my arms, I reached for Toni, picking her up and placing her in my lap. I wanted to assure her that she was safe, that her mommy was here and I would take care of her. But she didn't know I was her mom. To her, I was a complete stranger and I had to earn her trust. Looking into her blue eyes, my mind went over all the words I wanted to say to her, but my lips couldn't move. I wanted to explain to her that I could not help giving her up and that I was her mother, I gave birth to her, and I just wanted to love her.

Although it was a very happy day for me, I knew Toni was confused.

My time was up as the social worker came in and took Toni's hand to lead her out of the room. "Mommy will be coming back soon and taking you home," I whispered in her little ear as I hugged her. "Bye, sweetie, I will be back soon to see you." I turned my head, not wanting her to see my tears. My heart was longing for her to come back as she disappeared around the doorway.

Weeks later, after several meetings of getting acquainted, I arrived at the home for my last visit under supervision. It was time for Toni to come home. She said her goodbyes, and clutching her little hand, I walked her toward the car.

"Mommy is going to take you for a ride in the car."

"Ride in car," she repeated back to me.

"Yes, Mommy is going to take you to her house so you can play."

"Bye-bye, bye-bye," she kept repeating.

"Yes, we are going bye-bye."

Mom was sitting in her usual place watching TV when we arrived home. Toni began exploring her new home, touching everything that was in her sight. Mom had saved our high chair from when I was little. I placed her in the kitchen in the chair so I could begin my motherly duties of taking care of her. It was her first meal at her new home. Her little hand could hardly hold onto her spoon as she ate her macaroni and cheese. By the time we were done, there was more on the floor than what she got in her mouth.

After lunch, we went to the backyard and played for a bit. It was now nap time. Up the stairs, in my room, I placed her crib right next to my bed. I wanted to be able to hear her if she stirred at all in the night.

"Time for nighty-night," I said, picking her up and placing her into the crib. I wrapped her blanket tightly around her so she could feel snug, and I tucked her teddy close to her. Her little face looked around at the strange surroundings. I lay down on my bed next to her to help her feel safe.

"Mommy will be right here. Let's go nighty-night."

My voice was soothing to her and within seconds her little blue eyes closed tightly, off to dream land. I lay there for a bit, looking at this little girl and hoping that she was feeling as secure as I was. I dozed off myself and woke up to two blue eyes staring directly at me. "You're up. Let's go potty, and then we can go out and play."

I had heard that Toni's father was stationed somewhere in the south and I decided to write Larry, telling him I was home. I placed a picture of Toni in with the letter and waited with anticipation, hoping he would say he wanted to see us both. Maybe he had grown up enough to ignore what his mother had said about me. He must want to take on his fatherly responsibilities by now.

The letter finally arrived. He began by saying that Toni was cute; however, he didn't want to recognize her as his daughter. His letter didn't even make sense to me. I thought maybe if I pursued him, he would give us the love we needed. I wasn't going to give up. I wrote him again, begging him to be with Toni and me. Not wanting the responsibility of supporting his own child or me, Larry never wrote again. I hurt for myself, but I also felt pain for my baby. It wasn't fair to her that she was brought into the world like this. Larry didn't see that. He didn't care how it would affect my life or our child's.

I was devastated again. Larry could have offered a new beginning for Toni and me. Instead, he added to my cycle of pain and rejection. I wondered if anyone was ever going to truly love me.

I was excited to finally talk with Dar after all I had been through. She was my best friend and it had been two years since we talked. We had a lot of catching up to do. She had been sent to a reform school in Cleveland while I was gone. I called her house and her mom said she was in the hospital having tests done.

"Hi Dar, I made it home. What are you doing in the hospital?" I asked when I caught up with her.

"My nerves are so bad that I keep getting headaches. I'm having some tests done," she said. "Hey, I have this guy named Owen Kilbane I want you to meet. He's here right now. Why don't you say 'hi'?"

"Why don't you come down to the hospital?" Owen asked when he got on the phone.

"I can't; I have to work in the morning."

"When can I see you?" he pursued.

"How about tomorrow after work?"

"Okay, I'll see you around six."

"Say goodnight to Dar for me," I said, hanging up the phone. I couldn't help but feel excited for what tomorrow would bring.

I am blameless, yet I do not know myself; I despise my life (Job 9:21 NKJV).

CHAPTER TWO

Meeting Owen

Anticipating Owen's arrival, I stared through the window at every automobile passing down our street. My eyes focused on the metallic blue car that stopped right in front of our yard.

"What kind of car is that?" I asked my brother in breathless anticipation.

"A Cadillac! Wow, his parents must be rich to let him drive their car," Richard answered. My brothers teased me mercilessly. A tall, slender man with brownish-red hair approached the front door.

"Hi! Won't you come inside? I want you to meet my daughter, Toni." Reaching down, I touched the top of her head.

"How cute you are," he said, giving me the impression he must like children. That was a good sign to me.

"These are my brothers, Richard and William," I introduced them and they all shook hands.

Toni wanted to jump into my lap so I sat down, asking Owen to join us.

"So do you boys play baseball?" he asked my brothers.

"Yes," Richard said, "I play on a team."

William was acting shy. The conversation seemed to be all about my brothers, and I was desperate to find out more about him.

"Would you like to go for a ride?" he finally asked me.

"Sure!"

As I turned to Richard, he was chuckling, teasing me more. Imagine! A guy was paying attention to his big sister.

"Richard, please put Toni to bed for me," I asked holding back my nervous laugh.

"You owe me!" he grinned.

I felt like a princess whose knight in shining armor had arrived in an elaborate car to sweep me away. This only happens in movies, I thought, as he drove me around. This was my chance to be the star. We arrived in Coventry, a small suburb in Cleveland Heights.

"I've never been here before," I said.

"You'll like this community. They have some very charming stores. The best deli in town is right across the street," he said.

Glancing in the store windows, I could see what he was talking about. "Old-fashioned places always fascinated me," I told him as we walked toward the deli.

"They have the best milkshakes in town," Owen assured me.

After the waiter seated us, Owen placed our order. I tried not to stare; I couldn't help but admire this man. Was he real? Where did he come from? I had to find out more about this charming guy. I was mesmerized by his physical appearance and attracted to the muscles on his freckled arms.

"How old are you?" I asked.

"I'm seventeen. I was born on August 23rd, 1947."

"I was born two days after Christmas, the 27th, of the same year. You're only six months older than I am." We smiled at each other.

"Do you have any brothers or sisters?" I asked.

"I have an older sister, Peggy. She's married with two children. And I have a younger brother, Martin."

"What do you do for a living?" I asked, trying so desperately for him not to see me staring.

"I own a barber shop," he responded.

"I work in a beauty shop in Severance Center in our local mall. I started working there a few months ago after I got home."

"Home from where?" he asked.

"I was in Scioto Village for the juvenile delinquents."

"I was in Mansfield Reformatory," he quickly replied.

"What's that?" I asked.

"It's a jail in Mansfield, Ohio." As questions bounced from him to me, I could sense we had a lot in common. We were from different sides of town, yet we were both juvenile delinquents. I was in reform school for truancy and incorrigibility. Owen, by time he was sixteen, had been involved in an assault with a deadly weapon and stealing a car. He had gone to reform school for robbing a grocery store.

Our personalities meshed as we talked for hours. He was beginning to really make an impression on me. Not only did he have his act together, but he was also wealthy. He appeared to like me too. Perhaps he would find me irresistible enough to take care of me and my daughter. He could be my hero who would rescue me from my home life. With his money, looks, and fancy car, he could get any woman he wanted. Could someone as impressive as he was really want to be with me? So many questions flashed through my mind. It was hard to convince myself that this was real.

"Would you like to take a ride?" he asked, paying the bill.

"Sure!" I wanted to spend as much time as I could with him. I knew Toni would be sleeping, and I hoped this night would last forever. After we drove for what seemed like hours, both of us talking nonstop, we ended up at the local park.

As he parked the car, I could not help but look around to see if I could recognize any other cars. Our bodies began to get closer as the night progressed. There were butterflies in my stomach. The physical attraction between us became clear, and we were drawn to more than just talking. Owen slipped his hand behind my neck, slowly pulling my face towards his. Our lips locked in place. His kiss felt magical. This time, I really didn't want to say no. I was afraid that if I refused, our relationship would end here. We slid down into the back seat and became one flesh.

After we were done, I couldn't help but get nervous. What was I thinking? I should've played hard to get. Silence surrounded us as we drove off. We pulled up to the front of my house and I opened the door to get out.

"Can I see you again?" he asked.

"Sure, give me a call."

"What are you doing tomorrow after work?" he asked.

"I have to go home to take care of Toni."

"Is it okay if I drop by?"

"Sure, I get off at 6 o'clock. Come by around 7."

———————•·•·•———————

We spent a lot of time at my house so I could watch Toni, and it never seemed to matter to him. Toni was getting both our attention. I had never experienced this type of interest from anyone. I was soaking it all in, never wanting the moments to end.

Owen started picking me up after work from the beauty shop practically every night. Like giggling teenagers, the girls I worked with rushed to the window, wanting to see what he looked like.

"Oh, he's cute. Does he have any friends?" they all asked.

Equipped with charisma, he knew just what to say and how to act. He was very secure in himself, giving the impression he knew what he was going to do with his life. He could be whatever he wanted. He had a way of gaining power and maintaining control. He bragged about how much more money he would have in the next few years—more than he already had. And I was becoming a part of this amazing man's life. I didn't want to be deprived anymore. I wanted him to take care of Toni and me.

"Owen, I want to tell you about Toni's father. His name's Larry. He wouldn't even recognize her as his daughter," I told him.

"He rejected his own daughter? What kind of man is that? If Larry doesn't want any part of her life I sure do," Owen said.

Yet, I still wanted Toni to be with her real father. My heart was breaking for her. In the depths of my heart I longed for the day Larry would call and want to see us both.

"You don't want that loser; you have me now," Owen said.

Here he was, someone who took an interest in my daughter and me, making us both feel so special. I was working many hours at the shop and spending any spare time I had with Owen. His focus was on me as well. I was so sure that having sex with him was different from the other guys. He seemed to really love me.

I liked feeling that I was accountable to someone. If I were going to be his, I had to live up to that honor. He said that if I didn't do what he expected, he would go somewhere else. Owen was beginning to manipulate me, but I was so in love I couldn't see what he was doing. The thought of losing him was terrible. Not only did he seem to care for me, but he had so much to offer. I gave in to whatever he asked, hoping to convince him that I was out of the ordinary and did merit his attention.

"Hey, do you want to go over to my house and see where I live?" Owen asked.

I was about to meet Grandma Kilbane for the first time. Getting out of the car, I stood looking up at the large white house. It looked like a mansion compared to what I lived in. The windows were enormous with black shutters, and there were two sun porches on the sides of the house.

As we entered the large red door, a tiny elderly lady came walking down the hall.

"Ownie, is that you?" she called. Her eyesight was not the best.

"Yes, Gram. I want you to meet my friend Carol."

"Hello young lady. Would you like a cup of tea?" she asked.

As we walked to the kitchen, I couldn't help but think that the house looked like something I had seen in a home magazine. As I sipped my tea, Owen's grandma stared at me.

"Are you Irish?" she asked.

"I have some Irish in me. I'm also German. My grandparents were born in Germany."

As I sipped my tea, I noticed the strange relationship she had with Owen. There was a distance that I had not seen in him before. It surprised me how cold he could be to a family member. He was very blunt with her, and there was no respect in his words. He seemed to brush her off, as though she was a nuisance instead of family.

"Come on, Carol, let me show you the rest of the house," Owen said, interrupting my thoughts. The winding staircase led to four large bedrooms. Grandma's was the first one at the top of the steps. She had her dresser neatly arranged with little knick-knacks that seemed to be very old. The poster bed reminded me of what I had seen in the movie *Gone with the Wind*. Owen took me to his room, and I stood for a moment amazed at how large it was. It was like a mini-house. He had a bathroom connected right to his room. Surrounded by shiny tile, the tub was so big that two people could fit in there at once.

"Come on, I'll take you downstairs," he said after we finished touring the upstairs.

The large living room had a sun porch surrounded by windows that reflected the sunlight. I was startled to see a half-dressed man sitting in the corner by himself, begging for some wine.

"Who is that?" I asked.

"That's my dad. Don't pay attention to him. He just wants to drink." I could see that his dad was helpless; here was another cold side of Owen I hadn't seen before.

"What's wrong with him?" I asked quietly.

"He's paralyzed, and he just feels sorry for himself. All he wants to do is drink. My growing up years have been dysfunctional at best," Owen replied.

A large-framed woman came into the room then and from her staring, I could tell she was not all there. What could be wrong with her, I thought?

"Hello," she called with a loud voice.

"Hello," I responded.

"Let's go," Owen shouted before I could talk to her further. He walked quickly out the door embarrassed.

"Who takes care of these people?" I asked.

"Don't worry about them, someone does," Owen snapped at me. I was surprised again at how he related to his family. Where was the warm, caring Owen that I thought I was getting to know?

A few months had gone by since Owen and I had started dating. We spent a lot of nights parked in my driveway, talking about the different things criminals did to make money. Our closeness grew enough for me to share openly about my experience with Billie and her pimp, Hutch.

"Owen, I wanna tell you about something that happened to me when I got home from Scioto Village."

"Sure, what do you want to tell me?" he responded

As I proceeded to share about my rape, Owen showed neither sympathy nor sorrow for me, only saying, "I will kill those niggers if I find them."

Weeks passed by, and I fell madly in love with Owen. The bitterness toward my mom never diminished. I became envious of his lifestyle. He had the material possessions I wanted.

He picked me up after work one day, and we drove for a bit talking about what we wanted in the future.

"Carol, you're not going to get anywhere by working in the beauty shop, standing on your own two feet. Let's move into an apartment. Let's start a call girl operation. It would be just for short while. We can get some money so we can buy what we want. You wouldn't have to work on the streets; I would take care of you."

I couldn't believe he was suggesting this. I was so torn. On the one hand, I was thrilled he wanted to move in together and take care of me and Toni. But how could he want me to sleep with other men for money? He made it sound like it would just be a job, not a big deal. I tried to convince him to just let me live with him and continue working at the beauty shop, but he was adamant that this was a good idea.

I was so desperate to get away from my family. I figured that once we lived together, I'd be able to convince him it was a bad idea. After all, he loved me. He was the first man to accept me, even with the responsibility of a baby. Nobody else had done that before and I doubted anyone else ever would. And now I wondered about his feelings for me. How could he care for me and suggest I work as a call girl? The more I thought about it though, the more I started to believe that Owen was right. Beauticians rarely became wealthy. I didn't want to live with the shame of being poor. And I was afraid if I didn't agree, I would be rejected by Owen for the rest of my life. I convinced myself that he must love me. I needed him. He would be my ticket out of my old life into a better one. And if I had to sell myself to win his love, I would do it.

But I am not surprised! Even Satan can disguise himself as an angel of light (2 Cor. 11:14 NLT).

CHAPTER THREE

Call Girl

After only a few months of discussing and planning, I left home to be with Owen. We moved into a single bedroom apartment on Page Avenue in Cleveland. My parents didn't want me to go, but I had not forgiven my mom for not initially taking Toni. Owen would give me more love than my mother ever had. As I walked out the door with my belongings, my mom told me that if I moved out, I could never live at home again. As much as I didn't want to ever move back home, I knew that I was now under Owen's control. I had no other choice.

I decided to quit my job. Owen would support me. He would give me the emotional and financial security I so badly needed. Who knows, I thought to myself, maybe he would one day be my husband. I wanted to be a part of his dream to make a lot of money. And yet I was still surprised when he kept pushing the call girl operation. I had hoped that once we lived together and he saw me as a mother with a child, he wouldn't want me to do that. He kept telling me ours would be a high-class operation, working out of an apartment. Call girls were high class compared to prostitutes who just pick up men on the streets. Most of the girls on the street were on drugs, and Owen hated drugs. I knew he wouldn't let that happen to me. He said it was just a business. Now that I had moved out of my parents' house, I had no other choice. It was too late. I was cornered.

I didn't want to face the way this business would scar and degrade me. I didn't want to face the hurt I would feel when men paid money to use me to their liking. But I was afraid to say anything negative or let Owen know that I dreaded it. I didn't want him to kick me out of our new home. I was terrified of him leaving me. So I hardened myself to all that, convincing myself that he was right and that it would only be temporary. I was going to do it for Owen—not for his love, but for the fear of being abandoned.

Toni and I were adjusting to our new place when Owen brought something home to show me.

"What's that?" I asked.

"It's a book I purchased off a pimp."

26

"What pimp?"

"You don't know him. His name is Arnie. He and his wife have their own operation going. They gave us some names of men that are interested in seeing girls. Just go through the book and make the calls and see what you get," he told me.

I had no idea what I was doing or how I was going to make those calls.

"What am I going to say?" I asked Owen.

"Tell the guy where you got his name and that you want to know if he wants to meet you."

My heart was pounding as I made my first call. I prayed the contact wouldn't answer or that he would turn me down.

"Hello, Jim? My name's Carol. Marty gave me your number. She said that I should call you because you'd like someone to party with."

He was interested. How was I going to back out now? Owen drove me to the hotel where I was to meet my first trick. I still couldn't believe this was really happening. I kept waiting for Owen to tell me that I didn't have to really go through with it, that he was just testing my love for him.

"What am I going to do? What does this guy want me to do?" I asked.

"Just pretend you like him and do what he likes. He'll tell you what he wants." Owen dropped me off and drove away. I had no choice. I had to go through with it.

When I went in the room, I could feel the trick's anticipation to get me in bed. I didn't want a strange guy touching me. As we both climbed into the bed, all I could do was block my emotions. I must not think; I must not feel. I am playing a part in a movie, I told myself. This really is not me here; it is someone else. As his hands touched my body, I became numb and the acting became more real. Thank God it was over quickly. It was a horrible experience. Finally, he handed me the money for my services, and I left. I climbed into a cab to take me home, feeling like I wanted to throw up. I felt soiled. All I wanted to do was get home to Owen and have his loving arms around me.

Owen was watching Toni and when I arrived home, there was a strange girl sitting at the dining room table, looking at me as if she had the right to be sitting at my table. Her eyes were fixed on me. I walked into the living room where Owen was standing with Toni.

"Who is she and what is she doing here?" I asked.

Glaring at us, she instantly stood up and ran out the back door, slamming it behind her. Owen dashed out after her, shouting back at me, "I'll be back soon. I'm going to take her home."

I picked up Toni, giving her a hug. "Mommy is home now. I missed you, honey." I tried not to get emotional, thinking of what I had just experienced. Owen was home within the hour.

"What is going on? Who was she and why was she sitting in our home while I was gone?" I immediately asked.

"She was just visiting and there's nothing to worry about. Stop worrying."

"Where does she live and how did she get here?"

"She lives in Cleveland Heights."

"What's her name?"

"Her name is Karol T."

I was not satisfied, but that was all Owen would tell me. I felt betrayed. While I was out making money for Owen, he had someone else in our house. I didn't know what was going on, and I didn't know what to believe. Was it all innocent or did I have something to worry about? I was furious at him for bringing her into our home, regardless of who she was and what they were doing, but I was afraid to show him my jealousy.

Bedtime had arrived for Toni. As I tucked her in bed for the night, I could see Owen sitting in the living room through the small crack in the door. What is going on? What am I doing? Who really was that girl? The thoughts kept coming. Hours went by and he finally came to bed, and all I could do was to sink into his strong arms and feel safe knowing he was here with me and not her.

Our good friend Sy called a few days later. I began asking him questions about this Karol T.

"She's a girl that Owen dated for a few years," Sy said.

I had heard about her, but since Owen and I had been spending so much time together, I thought she was a thing of the past. Owen had been lying. Now what was I going to do? Sy liked me, and he didn't want to see me get hurt. He began to tell me how Karol was furious when she saw me. Owen had told her that he was getting rid of me. I wanted to get rid of her. I was better than Karol. Owen really loved me, not her, I tried to convince myself. I had asked Owen about her before, and he always said he gave her up. He had done a good job of hiding Karol from me.

I was losing him. I felt so betrayed. She was taking Owen from me; she was taking his affection. I began to attach myself to Sy. We had a lot of fun together. I knew Owen was out with Karol, so what could he possibly say about me?

Sy said, "We have to be careful, because no one crosses Owen."

Somehow Owen heard about our secret time together, and Sy was cut off from Owen's friendship. And I was punished like a child. He walked out that night telling me that he was not going to stay with me for a few nights to punish me. I knew he probably was going to stay with Karol.

I never heard from Sy again.

Owen began to tell me he would leave me unless I did whatever he asked. Fear and loneliness returned. I wanted to be with Owen so much that it was easy for him to convince me to do things I never wanted to do. I was expected to do sexual favors for whomever he told me I had to. What could I do? I couldn't go home to my parents.

He refused to get rid of Karol. Instead, he tried to convince me to have her work with me as a call girl. He told me she would work more than I did, which would make it be easier for me. I would not have to work as much.

I believed him. Karol previously worked as a waitress, but Owen convinced her to work as a call girl with the promise of more money. Business was picking up, so Karol and I took turns doing tricks. I thought if I stuck it out long enough, I would finally get him all to myself. He repeatedly told me he really loved me.

I was living in such a strained situation. Karol practically moved in except to go home to her mom in the evenings. We worked in the same apartment, but never talked, except for business. Owen wanted Karol and I to feel like we were a threat to each other. He knew exactly how to keep us from communicating. He told us each something different, so we would agree to live together.

"I feel bad about kicking Karol out. I just can't get rid of her," he said, telling me she was nothing to him and that I was the one he wanted to be with. We both believed we were his special woman. I knew she hoped she would have him in the end.

One time, Karol and I got into a big fight. I became so angry I beat her by hitting her head against the bedroom dresser. I could have killed her. She ran to the phone and called Owen on his car phone to tell him what had happened. Owen punished me when he got home; I wasn't allowed to sleep with him for a week.

In many ways, Owen was a father figure to me. By punishing me, he showed me that he did love me. My father never stood up to me, but Owen did. The respect I should have had for my father, I had for Owen.

I began to feel guilty about Toni living in this situation. Soon she would be old enough to know what was happening, and I certainly didn't want her to know what I was doing.

One night, I came home and Toni had a cast on her arm. Owen told me she ran and fell, and that was how she hurt her arm. He took her to the hospital where the doctors put her arm in a cast. I wondered if Owen or one of his friends had hit or slapped her. I didn't want to believe that he would hurt her, but I was afraid to ask.

Owen and I began to talk about what would be best for Toni. The finality in his voice convinced me it would be better to give her up. I loved them both, but one of them had to go. I had to choose between the baby I had fought so hard to get back and the man with whom I thought I was building a life. His love and attention were worth more to me than caring for my child, and I agreed to send Toni back to the foster home. My heart sank because I didn't want her to go, but I felt I had to give her up or I would lose Owen. It was hard enough losing Larry; I didn't want to lose Owen too. I made the call.

"Hello, Mrs. Jones? This is Carol Braun, and I need someone to come and pick up Toni. You told me I was to call if I felt I couldn't take care of my daughter. Well, I'm at that place."

"Did she do something wrong?"

"No, I'm living with my boyfriend, and she is not getting along with him or any men. I think something must've happened to her. We just can't deal with her, and I am not able to take proper care of her needs." My voice choked as I asked, "Do you think you can find her a good home or can she return to where she was? Please come and get her."

"We can get her tomorrow if you like. We'll be there in the morning, around 9 o'clock."

I felt like I was stuck in a bad dream. I couldn't believe what I was doing and yet I felt powerless to stop. Was I really giving my baby away?

"Did you make the call?" Owen asked me.

"Yes, they're coming first thing in the morning." I choked back the pain. I had to win his love. I didn't want him turning to Karol. I really wanted him all for myself. I was so confused. I cried my heart out the rest of that day, knowing every hour was closer to the time they would come to get her. I had no one to turn to and share how my heart ached. I certainly couldn't talk to Karol.

Owen left, and it was just Toni and I, alone. I pulled myself together. I held her close to me. I began to tell her that I loved her and that I needed to do what was best for her. She had no idea of what I was about to do. She was just beginning to say her first words. Mommy was one of them. Mommy was about to give her away. What kind of mother was I? Owen's power over me was stronger than the love I had for my own daughter.

Night came and I placed her in the crib as I always did. This time would be the last. I sank into Owen's protective hug that night and stuffed in the emotions as I tried to drift off to sleep. Maybe the morning would not come.

Morning did come, and only silence filled the room as Owen went to shower. I was afraid to stand up to him. I wanted to yell, "No way will I get rid of her for you." But my silence continued.

I packed Toni's belongings. She stood in her crib watching me as she did every morning. I picked her up and held her tightly, knowing it would be my last hug. The horrible moment came with the knock at the door. I opened the door to see the tall, slender woman. I kept telling Toni she was going bye-bye. The big brown door closed behind her as she walked out with her teddy bear, saying goodbye to me in her little girl voice. My tears flowed. Gone was the child I had fought so hard to get back and whom I needed to love. I was letting her go because I couldn't stand the thought of being without Owen. I wanted to run and grab her and say I changed my mind. I was young and knew there was nowhere to go with her. I stood in the kitchen, feeling the pain well up inside of me. I held my head as if I could contain the explosion happening within. I burst into tears. The trembling in my body got stronger with each rip of my heart.

Owen walked in and saw me sobbing. "Stop your crying," he said with no sympathy. "She's better off. What life do you have to offer her?"

———•◆•———

The call girl operation continued to grow. Money was starting to come in quickly. We moved into a new apartment, a taller high rise on the east side of town. As a call girl, I met all kinds of businessmen, including Robert Steele, a criminal lawyer and the prosecuting attorney for the City of Euclid, a suburb east of Cleveland. He was trying to become a judge for the city. By this time, I had been in the business for well over a year. He came to our apartment giving me his business card, telling me I could contact him for help if I ever had any trouble with the police.

That evening I handed Owen the card. He was thrilled. Not only did we have a steady customer, Owen and I began to talk about what an asset he would be for us as an attorney with some political clout. He was married, but his wife didn't know that he frequently had sexual relations with the girls he represented.

I was trying desperately to get Owen's attention. A few months earlier we had a big argument. I was so frustrated at him for calling me a "nigger lover." I loved to listen to Johnny Mathis. In the heat of our argument he took my albums and broke them into pieces. I couldn't hit a six-foot man. I grabbed a high heel shoe, wanting to smash in his head, but instead I headed over to the large window in the bedroom. As I banged the shoe into the window, I yelled, "I can't stand when you say that to me."

"Carol, you need to calm down," he said.

I continued smashing the shoe against the glass as hard as I could, causing the window to shatter. Pieces of glass went flying in to the air. A small sharp corner flew into my right upper chest. I dropped the shoe, grabbing my chest as the blood splattered everywhere. He took me into the bathroom to put pressure on the cut to stop it from bleeding. Just then there was a knock at the door. Karol answered it.

"The custodian's here. They heard the glass land beneath the apartment on the pavement," Karol said.

"Tell him I was hanging drapes in the bedroom and the ladder slipped and as I fell into the window the glass shattered," I said.

"Is she okay? I need to come in," the custodian called.

Owen shut the bathroom door as Karol let him into the apartment.

"I think I need to go and get some stitches," I told Owen.

"I'll keep putting pressure on it, and hopefully it'll be okay," he said.

"The custodian's going to come back in a minute to board up the window for the night. He'll come back first thing in the morning to replace the glass," Karol told us.

Owen and I remained in the bathroom until he was done. He took me to the hospital since I needed some stitches. Then that night I wanted to lay in his arms and I lucked out. Karol had to sleep in the other bedroom that night. My acting out had at least won me him for the night.

We ended up needing Robert Steele's services sooner than we thought. During the spring of 1968, the Cleveland police arrested Karol and I. We were in a downtown hotel walking to the room of one of our customers when motel security stopped us. It was obvious to them what we were there for. After questioning us they called the police, and we were busted. It was the first time we would use Robert's services. He negotiated our case with the judge, getting our charges reduced to loitering and sleeping on a bench. Although we did escape a jail sentence, the charges were added to our records. Robert was really good at reducing sentences, as we later learned. Within months the relationship between Owen and Robert grew.

Owen kept adding more girls to our operation. Karol and I were the only ones who lived with him. I still competed for his attention, and it made me miserable. I decided that if I took my life no one would miss me. I could escape the pain I was now living. I took aspirin from the medicine cabinet, placing a handful in my mouth, swallowing them down with a large glass of water. I stayed in the bathroom for a while, waiting for the pills to take effect. Eventually, I opened the door to walk out to the living room and collapsed onto the hall floor. Owen was getting dressed to go out. Karol walked by me. As she entered the bathroom she could see the pills spilled onto the floor, and the bottle open on the sink.

"I think she took an overdose of pills," Karol shouted to Owen.

"Carol, what did you do?" she yelled, shaking me. I could barely hear her. I felt like I was sinking into a sleep. I felt like someone dumped a bucket of cold water onto my head. I kept fading in and out. I could see Owen standing over me. He looked down.

"Just let her be," he said.

"You can't leave here like this. She could die," Karol said.

I could see him placing one foot in front of each other as he walked right over me. He turned around to look at Karol.

"Call the rescue squad if she doesn't get up in a short while," he said, then walked out the door and slammed it behind him. I lay there in disbelief. It was the second time he acted like it didn't matter to him if I lived or died. He was off making his money. I survived my overdose but was sick to my stomach for a few days. I knew taking my life wasn't going to get his attention. He just didn't care. Karol and I continued to share his affection. I was trapped in a web of disaster.

———⋅•◈•⋅———

We moved to a place on the west side of town called the Gold Coast. The high-rise apartment would be better for the customers. We bought some fancy furniture and were attracting more businessmen, lawyers, and doctors. I thought I had won Owen because we signed the lease as Mr. and Mrs. Kilbane. I was now Mrs. Kilbane, not Karol. We even got a brand new 1969 Camero, but Karol drove it more than I did.

The call girl operation grew even more. Owen added a variety of new girls. It was a perfect set-up. Owen provided girls in exchange for Robert's legal assistance. He had a lot of people who would do him favors, and he used the girls for payment.

It was the Fourth of July. Owen was out on a boat that he purchased with the money we were making. He and his friends used the boat often. The weather was bad as the waves from Lake Erie were coming up to the first and second floors of the apartments. I began to get frantic and I kept calling the car phone. The line would not go through. The winds kept picking up. I finally called the coast guard to report that I could not get through to Owen. Finally he made it home.

"Come outside and look at this," he said. Trees and debris were everywhere. As we approached the car, I could see there were large limbs sticking through the broken windows of the car. With no insurance for our new car, all we could do was look on in with disgust.

It seemed like that storm started an unlucky string of events for us. A girl named Bonnie would work with Karol and I once in a while when we needed her. Once Karol was out visiting her mom and Bonnie took a call for some guys who wanted to come over.

"Four guys are coming and they want us, so get ready," she said. When they knocked, she went to the door. There stood four well-dressed men.

"Come in. Would you like a drink?" she opened the door for them.

"No thanks. We need to get back to work," one answered.

"Who wants to go first?" Bonnie asked.

"Let Pete and Jeff go first, and we'll wait," another one said.

"Okay," I said, "Who wants Bonnie?"

"I do," Pete said.

"Okay, Jeff, come with me," I said.

When I shut the door, I asked for the money up front, like I always did. The man reached into his pocket. Thinking he was getting out his money, I turned around to get undressed. As I looked back again, there it was—a shiny police badge. Something we had always feared had finally happened.

"You are under arrest," he said. "Let's go."

I walked into the living room, all the other men all stood with their badges showing. How did these guys get past the screening we always did? Who had they used as their reference? I turned to look at Bonnie. She was the one who took the call.

"We are taking you to Cleveland. You have to come with us."

More policemen arrived and began to search the place. We were taken to jail. Robert was called again. I used my maiden name Braun for the police records, and we pleaded guilty to misdemeanor charges. Our sentences were suspended, and we escaped without serving any time. Owen was charged with keeping a house for immoral purposes. The City of Lakewood would not put up with our behavior and asked us to leave and never to return. If we would leave Lakewood, they would drop the charges. The deal was made. We moved back to the east side of Cleveland.

Robert had come to our rescue again, getting our charges reduced. It was amazing how well Robert kept his relationship with us a secret. He had a wife and two small boys and was having an affair with his secretary. I could not imagine what he needed us for. It was Owen who needed him more.

Among My people are wicked men who lie in wait for victims like a hunter hiding in a blind. They are continually setting traps for other people (Jer. 5:26 NLT).

CHAPTER FOUR

Folk Singer Slain

The year 1968 was a difficult time for everyone. I don't remember much about the turbulent 60s, but while we were doing our thing, the war in Vietnam was going on and there was a great deal of racial unrest in most major cities. Cleveland was no exception. In late July of that year racial riots erupted in an old neighborhood in Cleveland. Black nationalists killed three white policemen and, as a result, there was a lot of racial bitterness between blacks and whites.

The apartments were in full operation for the working girls. Owen, Karol, and I moved into Owen's grandma's house and only went to the apartments to work tricks. I spent most of my evenings at home where Owen was conducting weekly card games in the attic. His office was located on the sun porch through the doors of his bedroom. Business associates would come in and out, and no one but Owen's younger brother Martin was aware of what was going on. I often overheard proposals between Owen and his shady associates, but I was afraid to mention to anyone what I knew.

Martin had a close friend, Rick Robbins, who would come to the house a lot. Rick held a lot of racial hostility and bitterness. He had a rough childhood. Rick's father, a police officer in Cleveland Heights, was often abusive toward him, beating his small frame at the slightest provocation. Rick acted out, committing outrageous acts to gain attention.

By age fourteen Rick had become a serious disciplinary problem in junior high school. He stole two microphones from the school assembly room, and on another occasion he smashed a display of model airplanes and railroad trains in his science class. In 1965, while in the ninth grade, Rick shot himself in the leg with his father's 38 police special following an argument with a girlfriend. He was involved in a series of fire bombings in the spring of 1966 in the Edge Hill Road area. The ineffective devices were placed at the homes of residents who had complained about his gang, Rat Pack. That same spring Robbins was arrested in the Heights after he and a friend tortured a young boy with cigarette lighters. One month later he and another friend stole a car in Cleveland and were arrested in Key Largo, Florida. When he tried to escape, the police shot him in the foot. He was sent to Boys Industrial School in Lancaster, Ohio.

According to the word on the street, Rick wanted racial revenge. He was prepared to take all of his anger out on the blacks. The night after the Glenville riots, Rick was at a party where he bragged that he was going to kill the first one that he came into contact with. Pulling out a bullet from his hip pocket, his friends watched as he carved an "N" in it. One of his friends said that he was just amusing himself and wasn't serious.

Wandering away from the party, Rick went on his mission, the gun loaded with the bullet. He stopped at Cedar Hill, a large intersection at the top of a giant curved hill. Rick raised his gun in anticipation of shooting the next black man that came into his sight. The light switched to red, and a station wagon approached. Rick bent down to look in the window, and he could see the man had dark skin. He had his target. As the gentleman turned to see who was at his car door, Rick aimed and pulled the trigger.

Not looking back, Rick ran as fast as his feet would take him. A few of his buddies who had left the party and were on their way home saw him running.

"Need a ride? Jump in," they yelled. "Why are you running?"

"Hurry, get out of here!" Rick yelled with a laugh in his voice. Rick blurted out what he had just done, bragging about killing a man.

"I just shot a guy," he said.

"You're kidding, aren't you?"

"No, I'm not."

His friends couldn't believe he had done such a dreadful thing, so Rick asked them to drive back to the scene. He was going to prove it to them. Police were everywhere. Yellow tape blocked anyone from getting too close. The police directed people away from the scene as the investigation took place.

News hit the airways fast. Radio and TV stations interrupted their programs with the breaking story. Ted Browne, a well-known and loved folk singer, was found slumped over the wheel of his station wagon. He had been shot at close range early in the morning. The stations urged us to stay tuned for more details.

Ted and his wife had left a party where they renewed their marriage vows. Ted kissed his wife goodbye as they got into separate cars to head home. However, Ted needed to stop by his lawyer's home for a meeting before going home. Ted left the lawyer's at about 3 a.m. and headed home down Cedar Hill where he met his tragic death.

Cleveland Heights police worked around the clock for weeks but were stymied from the start. They checked houses in the immediate area and learned there had been many parties that night. They never heard about the one Rick had attended. During the next few months the police began to listen to the talk on the streets. Informants were saying Rick Robbins shot Browne.

When Rick turned eighteen he was arrested for pouring gasoline on the shrubs and threatening to burn down the house located adjacent to a friend's house. Police arrested Robbins, and the judge allowed him to join the Marines in lieu of going to jail. Detectives did not see Robbins again until the following spring when rumors about his role in the Browne murder became more widespread. He had gone AWOL from the Marines and returned to Cleveland. After being questioned by the police, Rick returned to the Marines, thinking it was the end of it. The case became an ongoing investigation and was never closed.

But don't be afraid of those who threaten you. For the time is coming when everything will be revealed; all that is secret will be made public (Matt. 10:26 NLT).

CHAPTER FIVE

Pimp Killed

Owen and Andrew Prunella Jr., our competing pimp, had many disagreements over the years. Arnie had a serious gambling problem. He bragged to Owen that he had watched the black jack dealers in Vegas for months and could outwit them. Mentioning money to Owen got his attention, especially if it involved quick cash. Arnie convinced Owen he could beat the system, so Owen gave Arnie a few thousand dollars and he went to Vegas to triple their money. Unfortunately Arnie came back too soon. The system beat him, and he had lost it all.

No one ripped off Owen and got away with it. The arguments between them escalated. Owen was not about to forget, and Arnie was going to pay one way or another for what he had done.

Owen and his brother Martin met with their sister's ex-boyfriend Phil Christopher at the Redwood, a local bar where some of their shady business was conducted.

"Hey Phil, I need someone to take care of a guy I am having trouble with. Do you think you can help me out?" Owen asked.

"You mean get him bruised up a bit?" Phil asked.

"No, I mean get rid of him, like take him on my 26-foot cabin cruiser for his last boat ride," Owen said.

"Does it have an anchor?" Phil asked.

"No," Owen replied.

"I can take care of that," Phil said. "How much money do you have on you?"

"Here, we have $1,000 between the both of us," Owen responded.

"Good, I need a throwaway." Taking the money, Phil left to meet his contact and pick up a gun that would have no serial numbers so it couldn't be traced to anyone. Handing the man the money for the gun, he took it and traveled to a local factory. When he got to the end of the street, he jumped out quickly and pulled up a large sewer cover from the street and tossed it in the back of his car. That would be plenty to keep a body down in the lake, he thought. Next he went to a fence company in Cleveland and bought a ten-by-ten section of fence with some heavy-duty wire. The fence was going to be used to wrap around the body. The wire would be wrapped through the ends of the fence to keep the body in one piece so that it wouldn't float to the surface after the fish started eating it. The other end of the wire would be tied to the sewer cover.

Owen and Phil began to talk about their plan.

"Arnie knows who I am," Phil said. "Owen, can you get him to Culp's Bend at the bar by Lake Erie?"

"I am sure I can. That is close to where the boat is docked so that should be easy," Owen answered.

"I will wait at the bar and then when you come in you can ask me to go and see your new boat that you just bought. Then I will ask you if we can go for a ride," Phil replied.

The next evening Phil sat at the bar at Culp's Bend. He ordered a J&B on the rocks. Behind the bar was a large aquarium with piranhas. Phil watched the bartender feeding the fish. Soon, something else would be fish food, he thought.

"Damn, they are late," Phil, thought to himself. He looked at the door, watching and waiting. Arnie entered. Phil turned back to the bartender and ordered another drink. Pressing his elbow to his side he felt the reassuring pressure of the throwaway gun. Turning away from the bar, Phil continued to sip his drink as Martin walked in and pointed in his direction.

"Phil! How are you?" Martin called out.

"Hey Martin, nice meeting you here. Haven't seen you here for a while. What brings you out this way?" Phil went along with the charade.

"Oh, we are showing a friend of ours Owen's new boat," Martin said.

Owen and Arnie walked up to Martin and Phil as they were talking. Phil said hello to Owen, then turned to Arnie.

"Hi, Arnie. Haven't seen you around for a while," Phil said.

"Yeah, well, I've been kind of busy lately," Arnie, said.

"How've you been?"

"Good, good," Phil said. They talked for a little while longer.

"Why don't you join us out on my new twenty-six foot cabin cruiser?" Owen invited Phil.

"That sounds like a good idea. I haven't been out on a boat for a while. You sure you have the room?" Phil asked.

"Come on," Arnie pitched in. "There's always room for one more."

The group left the bar and when they reached where the boat was docked, they climbed aboard. Owen started the motor to begin their journey. The lake was clear and calm as glass. The small ripples in the water had a tranquil effect. The only manmade sound was the constant hum of the boat motor. They had been out for almost forty-five minutes and hadn't seen any lights from other boats for thirty minutes. Phil figured they were far enough away from everything. It was time for Arnie to go swimming.

Phil had thought through exactly what he was going to do. Owen was below in the cabin talking to Arnie. Phil reached back taking the .38 gun from his waistband. He felt the smooth, well-oiled barrel of the gun, cocked the hammer back and held his hand steady behind his back as he waited for Arnie to come to the top. Arnie came out of the cabin and walked over to Phil.

"Here is your drink, Phil. Beautiful night, isn't it?" Arnie said taking a sip of his own drink.

"Yeah it is," Phil commented. He was thinking about the best place to put the bullet and decided behind the ear would be perfect. It shouldn't take more than one shot.

"Yeah," Phil repeated. "Look at those stars."

Arnie lifted his head to look up. Phil pulled the gun out from behind him, placed it against Arnie's head behind his left ear and pulled the trigger. Phil felt the power of the gun go through his arm as it extinguished Arnie's life. Arnie fell hard to the deck of the boat, and Phil felt something wet and cold hit his stomach. He didn't have time to think about what it was. He turned the body over to make sure Arnie was dead. If not, he'd have to shoot him again. Not something he wanted to do. The body didn't move.

There he was, thirty-one-years old with his life taken from him by people he thought were his friends taking him on a casual boat ride—a ride that resulted in the end of his life.

Owen heard the shot and came up from the cabin. He looked down at Arnie lying on the floor of the boat.

"You piece of crap! No one messes with me and gets away with it." Owen kicked the body, yelling obscenities as if Arnie could hear him. He finally gained control of himself and reached down to touch Arnie's stomach. A clear liquid came off of his hand. Arnie's last drink was all over him. Owen finally looked over at Phil.

"Go get the fence up front in the storage compartment," Phil ordered.

Owen went to the tarp and grabbed the manhole cover and brought it over to the body. He took over, telling Martin to get the section of fence and cable-wire for Phil. Martin laid the fence down and panicked as he looked at the body. He became nauseous at the sight of the blood and holding his stomach, he bent over to throw up. He wiped off his face and looked out at the silent water. Owen continued giving orders, not wanting to get his own hands dirty.

"I think there's a boat over there," Martin said, feeling paranoid that someone would see what they had done.

Phil looked in the direction that Martin pointed.

"There's nothing out there. Come on, let's get this over with. Help me out with this fencing. We've got to get him on top of it," Phil said.

Reaching down to grab Arnie's legs, Martin began to throw up again.

"We've got to get this done," Phil said.

Phil tried to put Arnie up on the fence by himself, but with no help from Martin it was impossible. He grabbed the cable-wire and wrapped Arnie's legs, arms, and neck with it. After tying it off, he put the wire through the manhole cover making sure that it was tied tightly. They threw Arnie over the side of the boat and watched as his body floated. Then Phil reached down to grab the manhole cover and throw it into the water. Arnie's body sank like a rock. Phil watched the small bubbles until the boat got far enough away.

That summer of 1968 set off a chain of events that affected my life for many years to come. Owen came home, bragging about how they had killed Arnie. He said Arnie wasn't going to bother anyone ever again. Owen was very explicit in his description of the killing. I couldn't believe what he had done, and all the bragging scared me. It was as if he had no conscience, telling me that it was going to be all right.

"You're going to get caught," I said.

"No one will find the body, so no I won't," was his response. "The only ones who will see him are the fish, and they can't talk."

Is this real? I thought to myself. I mean, he's telling me he did this, but did he really do it? I was more afraid of him committing this murder. At that moment, I didn't think of Arnie as a person whose life had just been ended. He was just a story that Owen was telling me. I didn't think of Arnie's family that would never see him again, and I didn't think about how Owen was capable of murder. All I could worry about was Owen getting caught and going to prison. I didn't want to lose him.

"How can you be so sure the body won't come to the top? You're going to get caught. Just watch and see," I said.

"I will not! I know what I'm doing. Haven't I always been right?"

Disgusted at what I was hearing, I walked away. "We'll see," I mumbled under my breath.

You want what you don't have, so you scheme and kill to get it (Jas. 4:2a NLT).

Chapter Six

Judge's Wife Murdered

Months had passed since Arnie disappeared. Owen purchased a lot of properties with the illegal money we were raking in. One lucrative property was a motel in Euclid. It became a very popular spot after it was featured in *Playboy Magazine* for being the first motel to show X-rated movies in every room. Rooms were filled daily. Money was coming in so fast. Owen was quickly becoming known as a young entrepreneur rising quickly in the Irish community. He was given the opportunity to purchase a limousine from previous owner Tom Jones, a popular singer from California. Seldom did I have a chance to be chauffeured to parties in the limo. He kept me busy collecting money around town for him.

Bishop Apartments were running full force with all the new girls being brought into Owen's business. My job was to introduce them to the regular customers. They always liked new girls, especially Judge Robert Steele. Owen and Robert were spending a lot of time together. Owen mentioned to me that Robert was having an affair with his secretary Barbara.

"I can't believe he needs to come up to the apartments if he already has a woman. How many women does he need?" I said.

"He wants to be with Barbara," Owen said. "He mentioned to me lately that he wishes he could get rid of his wife Marlene."

"You can't get involved. Let him deal with it on his own."

"Don't worry. I can handle this," Owen said.

At first, I thought Owen was joking when he talked about killing Marlene. But the more he talked about it, the more I realized he was serious. From all the conversations I heard, it became apparent they were going to hire a hit man. Rick Robbins was still in the Marines and coming home on leave often. When he was home, Owen picked Rick up at the Cleveland Hopkins Airport and shared with him the plot that he, Martin, and Robert were putting together.

"I really don't want any part in this," was Rick's response.

"You already killed Ted Browne and got away with it, so you should have no problem with this one," Martin explained, hinting that if Rick didn't cooperate, he'd talk to the police about the Browne murder. Rick was smart enough to catch the veiled threat.

"We need your help. When we get back to my office, I'll show you our plan," Owen insisted.

When they got home, Owen pulled out a map of the first floor of the Steele house and pointed to Marlene's bedroom.

"We can do a dry run and you'll see how perfect of a plan this is," Martin insisted. After their dry run, Owen insisted they throw Rick's uniform, shoes, and service records in the furnace of one of the apartment rental properties he owned. They wanted to make him vanish from the system altogether, as though he had never been around.

After many days of discussions and trial runs, it was time for the real thing. Leaving Owen's office, the men shot a game of pool in the attic while waiting for their orders to begin. They had all the plans in order. Martin would drive Rick to the scene of the crime, dropping him off close to Steele's home. He would wear dark green pants, a dark sweatshirt, a dark blue jacket, and a black ski hat. Owen gave him shoes that were intentionally too large so the footprints in the snow would trick the police. Rick was to put the ski mask over his face with the rubber gloves. Owen handed the gun to Rick, wiping his fingerprints off the handle. Rick was nervous and the firing pin fell out as he removed a .38 caliber short bullet from the chamber.

As he replaced the bullet and firing pin, Owen asked him, "Do you think you can do it?"

"I don't know," he said.

"You can do it, Rick," Martin urged.

"Yeah," said Owen, "You killed the other guy."

It was a cold January night, and this run was for real. Owen handed Rick four pills to calm his nerves as they left the house, heading in different directions. Martin was the main driver, and he dropped Rick off close to the Steele house. Owen called Robert to say they were on their way. As Robert went into his office, he left the front door ajar so Rick could go right into the house. Marlene would be already in bed, with no knowledge of her fate. Her two boys would be sleeping in their rooms down the hall as the clock struck midnight. Trembling as he approached the Steele house, Rick was torn between the fear of killing an innocent person and the fear of what the Kilbanes would do to him if he didn't go through with the plan. Rick looked to the house and could see the lights on upstairs—the signal he could come in. Opening the door, Rick followed the map he was given and made his way to the bedroom where Marlene lay asleep. His heart pounded so loudly that he was afraid it would wake her. As he reached the frame of her body, he could see the covers were pulled up around her head. She had on what looked like a hairnet. Approaching the right side of the bed he pointed the gun and fired two shots. The body did not move.

Immediately he ran back to the door he left open and tripped over a telephone cord, knocking the phone off the table and across the floor. He ran out the door past the front of the garage and along the side of the house into the ravine. He came to Green Road and pulling off his mask and gloves, Rick could see car lights approaching. He hoped it was his getaway ride. When he saw it was Martin, he jumped into the car.

"Did you do it?" Martin asked.

"Yes, just drive. Get away from here," Rick screamed, out of breath as his adrenaline began to fade.

Owen's alibi was his friend Larry whom he drove around with at the time of the murder. He didn't want anyone to be able to pin it on him.

Karol and I waited in Owen's room and watched TV. I couldn't believe this was all really happening. I felt like I was a witness in my life and not really a participant. It was as though I were watching a movie. My heart was hardened to all that was going on around me. After all, none of this was really real. Karol and I didn't say a word to each other, but we were both battling our emotions about what was taking place. Neither of us had the courage to call anyone for help. Instead, we struggled with our fears, keeping silent as we waited for Owen to return. I was afraid that they would actually go through with it, and I was also afraid that Owen would get caught. Finally, he arrived home. The phone broke the silence as Robert called, according to plan.

"It's done. I'm going to call the police now," Robert told Owen.

Owen hung the phone up and just stared at me and Karol. It was 2:10 a.m.

"There has been a break-in. Something has happened to Marlene. Get over here right away," Robert screamed into the phone to the Euclid police dispatcher.

"We will be right there."

Robert also called his father, "Get over here, something has... Someone has broken into the house and shot Marlene."

The ambulance sped down Euclid Avenue and reached the Steele residence in minutes. Robert was distraught and sobbing profusely. He shouted aloud, "Why would anyone want to kill Marlene?"

"I don't know," the officer replied. "Where is she?" Robert pointed down the hall.

"I can't look at her," he yelled as the officer headed to the bedroom.

The officer lifted Marlene's lifeless wrist. It was cool to the touch. "She's dead," he said.

We waited for the next call, to see what the police were going to say to Robert.

It was a long night, and we refused to talk about what was going on. It was Karol's turn to sleep with Owen so I went into the room across from Grandma's at the back of the house. I tip-toed so I wouldn't wake her up.

The top story on the morning news was the death of Marlene Steele, murdered in her home. Owen anxiously watched the news to see what Robert had to say to the reporters.

After a few days, it was clear that Robert had become a suspect. Investigators said his story was shaky and requested that he come into the station for questioning. They grilled him over and over about his story of what happened that night. The facts didn't add up.

"I just turned off the TV and went upstairs to check on the boys. I heard a sound standing by the boy's door. I heard a pop-pop sound. I flew downstairs. I heard a noise of running footsteps, then the door banged. I ran into Marlene's room. I could sense something was wrong. I flicked on the light by her bed and I kneeled down, leaning over the bed to check on her. I pushed her, I shook her, then I grabbed her hand, shaking it to talk to her. There was no movement. Looking at her head, I could see blood running down the side of her face. I could then see that she had been shot. That is when I phoned you guys.

"I paced back and forth. While waiting for you to arrive, my dad got there. I told him that Marlene had been shot and he asked me who could do such a thing. I didn't know, but I was sure that whoever killed my wife would be caught."

––––––•◦•––––––

The investigation of Robert Steele lasted for weeks. Owen received a call from the police department, asking us to come in for questioning. After talking with Robert, Owen told us that all we had to do was to be calm. He assured us that they were just fishing and had no proof.

We were ordered to take a lie detector test. Owen gave us Valium to help us remain calm. We were placed in different rooms to be questioned separately. As I sat by the machine and all the wires, I wondered if they would be able to tell if I lied. The officer attached the wires to my arm and began to ask his questions.

"What is your name?" he asked.

"Carol Braun," I answered.

"Where do you live?"

"In Cleveland Heights."

The questions felt like an interrogation. There was no way that I could tell what I knew. I had to be the loyal person for everyone. As long as I listened to what Owen and Robert said, it would be okay. I told myself that they had this all planned, and we were not going to get caught. As a judge, Robert knew the system, and he was working it. We didn't hear from the police after we left, and they never let me know if I passed the lie detector test or not. None of us brought up the subject again, and we went on with life, despite the murder. Robert continued to represent us in legal issues.

As all of this was going on, Grandma Blodgett became very ill. She was one of the few people who had showed me any attention when I was a child. I was so busy trying to win Owen that I never got the chance to be with her on her dying bed. I didn't get the chance to say goodbye and tell her how much I really loved her. It weighed heavy on my spirit along with the murders plaguing the back of my mind.

I tried to erase the memories of the murders from my mind, but they wouldn't go away. I finally started to see a counselor, but it didn't really help. Owen grilled me repeatedly, asking me if I was telling them anything. I just wanted to talk. But who could I tell? I finally signed myself into the psych ward of a hospital. I felt like I wanted to die. I would go to group sessions and listen to others pour out their souls. But I felt like a mute. I couldn't open up my soul. After a few days of taking the medication they gave me, I felt numb and the doctors released me. But I still couldn't escape the turmoil. I was trapped in my own mind.

Time past and we were still haunted by the murders. One day, Owen was relaxing in the bathtub when we heard commotion out on the front lawn. I went down the steps and opened the front door. A young man whose eyes were glazed from drugs staggered toward me, forcing himself into the house while he drunkenly screamed at the top of his lungs.

"Repent! Repent!" he yelled.

"Get away," I told him.

"Repent!" he yelled again.

The man drew his fist back and punched me directly in the face. I fell back, covering my face with my hands as blood began to pour down. Grandma came down to see the ruckus, and she immediately rang for the police. I needed their help this time.

"You better get over here right away. We have an intruder who has forced himself into our house," Grandma yelled into the phone.

Owen ran down the stairs in his underwear, grabbed the young intruder by his neck and threw him out the door. The fighting continued on the front steps as he continued to scream at Owen to "Repent."

"I am God, and I want you to repent," he growled loudly in Owen's face.

I stood there holding my nose as the blood filled my hand. Grandma gave me a cloth with ice and told me to put my head back. As I heard the sirens get closer, I ran outside and taking a lit cigarette, I smashed it into his hand.

"Take that you bastard! How does that feel?" I yelled as my blood dripped down on him.

The sirens stopped as the police reached our house. They watched as Owen continued to try to shut the intruder's mouth before they finally grabbed him and took him into custody.

"You better go to the hospital and have your nose checked. It looks like it might be broken," the police said to me.

I arrived at the hospital where a series of x-rays confirmed that my nose was broken. The doctors had to stuff cotton up my nose to straighten out the bone. I screamed as they used the huge clamps within my nostrils and moved the broken bone back into place.

Owen wanted to go to the jail to see who the creep was that had done that to me. The young man had been booked, and the police wanted to know if we were pressing charges. He was convinced that Owen had a hand in Marlene Steele's murder. He had been hanging around in bars where there was talk among friends of Marlene's murder. Someone had told him that Owen had been involved. The police dismissed the incident as the simple ravings of a drug-crazed hippie but tucked the information away in a file.

He frustrates the plans of the crafty, so their efforts will not succeed. He catches those who think they are wise in their own cleverness, so that their cunning schemes are thwarted (Job 5:12-13 NLT).

CHAPTER SEVEN

FBI Raid

We moved out of Grandma Kilbane's house and into a Swiss chalet type A-frame home with a horse barn and five acres of land. I was excited to be listed as Owen's wife on the loan for the house. There were large windows in the front of the house that gave us a view of the local ski resort, Alpine. We were now living in the Ohio Snowbelt, where winter was the prettiest season of the year. The snow made the design of the house all the more beautiful.

Owen decided he wanted a horse so he brought home a white appaloosa that we named Trojan. He was a large horse but was gentle to ride, and he loved to walk the yard with me. He acted more like a dog than a horse. Walking with Trojan was an escape for me, allowing me to be alone with my thoughts and away from the endless drama of my life.

Owen rented out Grandma's house to bring in extra cash so he moved Grandma Kilbane and his parents into one of the rooms in the motel. We were working out of the Indian Hills apartments so I traveled back and forth from the apartments to the house.

Karol moved into the house with us. My anger toward her continued to grow. I argued often with Owen about getting rid of Karol, but he refused. I wanted out of the call girl operation so badly, but every time I would talk about quitting, Owen would give me some story about how we need to just hang on for a little while longer. I began to see behind his exterior as his lies were exposed. My competition was still there, the web of deception was growing, and the fear of never getting out was magnified more than ever. With all that we had going on, the memory of the murders faded into the background

I became close friends with one of the working girls, Sonja. Owen had brought Sonja to meet me a few months back, telling me she lost her sister from an overdose of drugs. She wanted Owen to find out who had been involved in her sister's death. He used that to convince her to become one of his girls. She needed money so she moved into the apartments. I began to spend a lot of time with her, and we shared our dreams for the future.

Owen never allowed me to have close friends; he screened everyone that came into my life. He always told me the girls would want him, using my jealousy to keep me from having friends.

As my friendship with Sonja grew, I began to confide in her. I decided to spend the night at the apartment with Sonja.

"Do you really love Owen?" she asked.

"Yes, I do. One day I'll settle down with him and start a family."

"It's very hard for me to hear you talk like this because Owen told me the same thing," she replied. She told me how he convinced her to get into the business.

"Remember the night you came to the motel? He jumped out of the window so you wouldn't catch him there. He came to the apartment at night to sleep with me."

I knew she was telling the truth; he stayed out many nights. I had always wondered where he was; now I knew. Sonja and I began to plot how we would run away from him. We planned to move to another state, somewhere he couldn't find us.

The next day some of our regular johns come to see us. They were from Atlanta, Georgia, and would come visit when they were in town. I told Sonja that we needed to convince them to help us move to Georgia with them. I talked with Jeff and told him that my pimp wouldn't let me go. I told him I never received any money I made, and it was time to get away.

Jeff asked me, "If I give you a job at my company and pay for your ticket to Georgia, will you come back with us?"

"I would have to talk to Sonja to see what she says."

They left us alone in the apartment, telling me they would call us in a few hours to find out what we wanted to do.

"Owen will never let us quit; he would kill us first," I told Sonja. She didn't want to believe me. I told her about the murders.

Scared for her life, she finally agreed, "Let's get out of here."

I called Owen. "Sonja and I are spending the night with a couple guys, and they are going to pay us $150 for the night. I'll call you in the morning." I tried to remain calm as I told him the lie, hoping he would focus on the money.

Karol was at her mom's so I planned to sneak back to the house to grab some of my personal belongings to take with me. My heart raced as I drove home and rushed quickly into the house. I knew that I was leaving that house, probably never to return again. I grabbed what I could and got back to the apartment just as the phone rang. "Oh, please be Jeff," I thought.

"What did you decide?" Jeff asked.

"We'll go with you."

"I'll get you and Sonja's tickets and pick you up early in the morning." The plan was set.

"Okay."

"Are you sure you want to do this?" he asked.

"Yes, definitely," I answered. I was sick of this life.

The more I thought about Owen lying to me about Sonja and their relationship, the madder I got. "How dare he tell me he loves me while he's sleeping with you and who knows who else?" I screamed. My anger led me to destroy the apartment. I wrote on the walls, "You murderer! You killer!" I took a hammer to the TV, shattering the glass. I grabbed whatever I could to smash whatever was in my sight.

We had trouble sleeping that night, thinking Owen was too smart. He was going to know we had lied to him. He was going to catch onto us before we left. What would we do then?

"What would we do?" Sonja asked me.

"We have to stop him from coming after us. Let's take his trick book. We can blackmail him. We'll tell him that if he comes after us, we'll turn it over to the officials," I said, cramming the book into my bag.

Morning finally came and the apartment buzzer went off.

"Carol, it's Jeff. Are you ready?"

"Yes, come on up."

We opened the door for him. Jeff eyed the damage in the apartment. "You really do hate him, don't you?"

"Yes, let's get out of here," I said. I was done with this place. We headed to the parking lot to get a cab to take us to the airport. Sonja and I hoped no one would see us go

The drive to the airport seemed to take hours. We finally got there and checked-in for our flight.

"We made it!" I said. We were finally escaping.

I was so nervous, and it didn't help that I could see Sonja was having second thoughts.

"We can't go back, he'll kill us for sure, especially with what we did to the apartment," I told her.

I kept reassuring myself that we were doing the right thing, the only thing. It was finally time to get on the plane. I had never flown first class before, and it made me feel important. Once we landed in Atlanta, we went directly to the hotel.

"Are you hungry?" Jeff asked us. "Get ready and we'll take you to dinner."

As he shut the door, Sonja began to worry. "We really did leave Cleveland and here we are in Georgia! What if he finds us?" she asked.

"Come on, stop worrying. We're going to dinner. Let's just go and have a nice evening," I told her.

As we sat at the dinner table in one of the most exclusive places I had ever been, Jeff told us about his company and what jobs he had available. He was offering us a legit job, no more working tricks for money. It felt like a better way of life, and I was so glad he was helping us. Hoping to calm my nerves, I ordered a glass of red wine with my steak and lobster.

After dinner, Jeff drove us back to the hotel.

"I'll see you both in the morning. Have a good night's sleep," he said as he left.

With Jeff gone, the fear bubbled up. "What did we do?" Sonja asked and we began to argue about calling Owen.

"I want to call Owen to see what he knows," I insisted.

"I don't want you to call. I'm afraid that he'll send someone to get us," she yelled. Since I had told her about the murders, Sonja was really scared that Owen would kill us. But I was determined and I won the argument. I was making the call.

I dialed the phone. Owen answered. "Where are you, Carol?"

"What do you care?" I screamed at him.

"I do care. I need you to come home."

"I won't come home. You lied to me. You've been sleeping with Sonja."

"It was for business," he said, making excuses as always.

"She is right here! You told her that you wanted to be with her," I said, annoyed that he was playing me.

"Well, what do you think I would've told her?"

"I don't care," I said. "I'm not coming home."

"Carol, you know how I've been going to the clinic?"

"Yeah."

"I'm sick and I didn't want to have to tell you."

"Sick with what?"

"You know the open sores that I had?"

"Yeah."

"I have a disease. I need you home. I love you," he said.

My emotions began to melt. He got me again.

"What am I going to do with Sonja?" I asked him.

"I don't care what she does. I only want you to come home."

"I'm not gonna leave her here. I need you to get us both a ticket to come home or I'm not coming," I insisted.

"Can you get to the airport?" he asked.

"Yes, I'll call a cab."

"I'll get you tickets for the next flight out. Just get to the airport," Owen said.

"Okay, bye," I agreed. I was going home to him.

I told Sonja I had to go back home. "He needs me," I said to her. She was still afraid and we argued about it.

"He's not going to want me there. What are we going to do?" she asked.

"I don't know. Let's just get to the airport."

The cab came and we rushed out the door, afraid that Jeff might catch us leaving.

"We made it!" I said to Sonja as we approached the ticket counter.

When we arrived at the Cleveland airport, we were greeted by Owen. Standing on his right side was his brother Martin. On his left side stood his friend John. John's expression of anger made me really wonder what Owen was going to do. I was afraid we had made a mistake in coming home. The ride home was hushed and as we reached the motel, Owen began to question us.

"Why did you go to Atlanta?" he asked.

"I wanted to get away," I said.

"What did those guys do to you?"

"Nothing."

"John, I want you and Martin to fly to Atlanta and tell those guys they messed with my women. Put a scare in them and maybe we can get some money out of them. Take Sonja back to the apartment," he ordered.

Owen and I left for home. I wanted to bring up the subject of him being sick. Even though I was afraid to ask, I blurted out my questions.

"What's wrong with you?"

"I'm okay. Don't worry, the doctors have it under control."

"What do you mean?"

"I just have to take some pills and use a cream. Then, I should be okay."

I wanted to believe that he was going to be okay, so I stopped asking questions. He wouldn't give me any details anyway. I knew he had tricked me into coming home, and my worry for him turned into a feeling of betrayal.

"I want you to get rid of Karol," I told him.

"She moved home with her mom," he said. "We'll be in the home by ourselves. I want you to be the head girl and run the business for me."

Finally, I thought, Karol was going to be out of our lives. I had won. Owen finally realized I was serious, and he was showing me he cared. I was glad I had come home to him.

I called Sonja the next day and she was almost in tears as she told me what happened the night before.

"John stayed at the apartment for a while, just sitting with his gun in his hand, twirling it around his fingers. I finally yelled at him that I couldn't take it anymore and he should just kill me already, just pull the darn trigger already! I screamed in his face. After about an hour of tormenting me, he finally stopped. He left and I just collapsed onto the bed, crying myself to sleep," she said.

"Owen won't let me come around you anymore," I told her. "He said we are bad for each other so he won't let us be in the same apartment again."

A few days later I returned from a trip to the grocery store and was headed for the elevator when a man approached me.

"Do you need any help with those?" he asked me, motioning to the bags of groceries I held.

"No thanks. I can handle them," I smiled at him. He stayed on after I got off at my floor.

———— • ◆ • ————

After a few weeks, I started to sneak calls to Sonja.

"What are you doing?" I asked.

"Carol, I'm still scared that Owen is going to hurt me."

"No, he doesn't care about you," I told her. "He just cares about making money."

"What if I told you that Owen is seeing another woman?" she asked me.

"How do you know that?" I asked, my heart racing with fear.

"I talked to someone."

"Who?"

"I can take you to her apartment, and you can ask her for yourself."

"Okay, I'll be right over."

Jealousy motivated me to act impulsively. Sonja knew that saying Owen was cheating on me would trigger a reaction from me. Many times, I told her that the worst thing I could find out would be that Owen had another woman on the side, one who was not involved in the call girl operation. I convinced myself that if a woman were working for us I could justify it as a job, not as a personal affair between Owen and her, thinking Owen had no real feelings for her. It was my way of shutting out the jealousy and believing I was his main woman. I convinced myself that I was the one who would be with him in the end.

I got to the apartment building and met Sonja. She walked to apartment 102. I knocked, the door opened, and a tall blond looked down at me.

"What do you want?" she asked angrily.

"I am Owen Kilbane's main lady," I said to her. "I want to know what the hell you are doing with him. Are you having an affair with him?" I asked as she began to shut the door in my face. I pushed back, shouting even louder.

"I want to know what you are doing with Owen!" I yelled.

"I don't know who you are talking about," she said and convinced me that there was nothing going on. I left and drove Sonja back to the apartment. She insisted that the woman was lying. I kept asking Sonja where she got her information from, but she refused to tell me. She must have gotten a bad tip, I finally concluded.

After dropping Sonja off, I drove to the motel. Owen was sitting behind his desk and looked up when I walked in.

"Why did you go to the apartment?" He knew. How did he know, I wondered?

"What apartment?" I started to lie.

Owen gave me a stern look and asked again, "Why did you go to the apartment? Joyce called me and said you showed up at her place demanding to know about her and me."

"Sonja told me about her," I responded.

"Did she say how she knew about her?" he asked.

"No."

"Get over to her apartment right now. She is talking to the Feds," he ordered.

"How do you know that?"

"Because no one knows Joyce's real name. She must have gotten it from the cops," he said. "Get over there and find out what's going on."

I called Sonja to tell her I was on my way over and that I wanted to talk to her. Opening the door, I saw her suitcases in the middle of living room floor.

"Sonja, what are you doing?" I asked. "Where the hell are you going?"

"I met a guy," she said. "I'm getting away from here."

"What guy? When did you meet this guy? Why don't I know about this?"

"Carol, please come with me."

"You know I can't," I told her. "I love Owen, and I'm never leaving him again."

"Please Carol," she pleaded. "You can come and get a new start."

"I can't go," I said. "Where are you going anyway?"

"I can't tell you, but I'll call you when I get there," she said.

I knew she was lying to me. She wasn't acting like herself. She was too nervous. I felt like there was nothing I could do, so I left Sonja's. Getting in my car, I waited to see what would happen. After a few minutes, I saw a car pull up to the front of the apartment complex. Two men got out and waited until the lobby door opened and Sonja came out with two other men, one on each side of her. It's the Feds all right, I thought to myself. Owen was right. They drove away and I wanted to follow, but I needed to get back to Owen to tell him he was right about the Feds.

When I told Owen, he said, "Go back to the apartment and see if the trick book is there." I felt uneasy going into the apartment when I knew she had just left with the police. What if they are still there? I thought. Opening the door, I flicked on the light and walked to the desk. I opened the drawer where the book was kept. I reached and nothing was there. I reached again, still nothing. Owen was right again. It was gone. I looked around to see what else was gone, but only the book and a few papers were missing. I closed the door behind me and went home to report to Owen.

We lay in bed that night and tried to figure out what Sonja was doing. We came to the conclusion that the Feds had been trying to question her for some time. We told her constantly not to talk to them, but she must have finally given in. I wondered if she told them what I had told her about the murders.

• • ◆ • •

Weeks passed since Sonja had left. I talked to the guy on the elevator often, thinking he must be a tenant in the building. He always had groceries or laundry in his arms when we would meet. I was sitting in the apartment with Barbie, a new girl, making calls when there was an unexpected knock at the front door. I peeked out the peephole and could see the janitor of the building standing there.

"What do you want?" I yelled, not opening the door.

"I need to come in to check the heat pipe in there," he said.

"This isn't a good time for me," I said. "Can you come back later?"

"I have to come in now or we'll have a serious water leak problem."

I didn't want him to see the way we were dressed, so I yelled, "Hold on one moment." I threw on some sweats and motioned to Barbie to go in the back room and get dressed. I opened the door to let him in, and it was shoved forward quickly. A shiny badge was held to my face.

"Carol, this is the FBI," a man said. "Get back."

"You can't do this," I panicked. "Where's your warrant?"

"Right here!" He flashed a paper in my face. "My name is Robert Ressler," the man said. I was shocked as I realized it was the man who rode the elevator with me.

"I want to call my attorney."

"Sit down! You can call later," Ressler said.

The door opened again, and a group of men came in. They started to ransack the apartment, beginning in the kitchen and moving to the dresser drawers in the bedrooms. They brought everything they found and placed it in a pile in the middle of the living room floor. The pile grew as they confiscated the trick book and records I kept of men's visits, the dates, times, and charges.

"What are you going to do with those things?" I asked. They refused to answer me. I was finally allowed to make my call, and I reached Robert Steele at his office.

"The FBI is here," I told him. "They're raiding the apartment."

"They're at the motel too," he answered.

"Why are they doing this?" I asked him.

"I don't know, just be quiet," he said. "We'll figure it out later."

"Did you talk to Owen?" I asked him.

"Yes, he knows. Martin just called and said they're out at the house too."

I hung up the phone as the Feds finished rummaging through everything they could. They carried out large garbage bags full of contents they had confiscated.

"How can you just come in here and take my things and get away with it?" I asked angrily.

"We have the authority to do so. You can make your call to Owen now," Ressler said as he was the last to leave. I grabbed the phone and hastily dialed the motel.

"Let me talk to Owen," I said. "Did they leave? What did they do there?" I asked when he got on the phone.

"They went through my desk here and took a lot of my papers. Martin said they took a lot of papers out of my desk from the house also."

"What are they doing? And what are they going to do with the papers they took?"

"I'm not sure; meet me home" he said.

I left the apartment promptly to go home, feeling like my privacy had been invaded.

Owen had arrived home to find the Feds taking more bags of our belongings. The remainder of the team left as I was pulling in.

Martin was furious as he told us what happened to him. "I was sound asleep when the dogs began to bark. I got up to look, and there were police everywhere in the yard. One was standing by the patio door, staring straight at me. He yelled at me to open the door. I could hardly get the door open all the way when a rush of cops pushed their way into the house, scattering in every room."

We rushed upstairs to see what they had taken. All the records that Owen kept of what the girls made were gone as were phone books and checking account information. The list went on and on. Rick Robbins had given Owen a sawed-off shotgun for his birthday, and we had it hanging on the wall. The Feds took it.

There were no arrests made that night. Robert called a few days later to inform us that the FBI learned about us from talking to Sonja, who was now under protective custody. We were getting charged for going over the state line for the purposes of prostitution.

Robert had papers from the FBI that charged Owen, Martin, John, and I with violation of section 1952, Title 18, United States Code from approximately January 1973 to July 17, 1973. They said we used and caused others to use an interstate facility, namely, the telephone, in interstate commerce as well as traveled and caused others to travel in interstate commerce between the Northern District of Ohio and the Northern District of Georgia, with intent to promote, manage, establish, and carry on a business enterprise involving a prostitution business, which was in violation of the laws of the State of Ohio.

"That is not correct," I yelled to Robert. "I was running away. I wasn't running to do prostitution. I wanted out of this lifestyle."

"They have a few charges here, and the big one is the gun that was on the wall. It's illegal, and they really can get you ten years for that. So they want you to plead with the interstate prostitution," Robert said.

Again, Robert was called upon to come to our rescue. Since the gun was illegal, it held a ten-year sentence minimum. I wanted Owen to plead away the gun charge so he wouldn't go to prison for ten years. Owen was able to get the charges against John and Martin dropped but not the charges against me. I was charged separately from him. We went to the Federal Court Building to plead our case. I was going to plead guilty so that Owen could avoid the gun charges. We were both sentenced to six months in the federal prison system plus fined $5,000, to be paid off before our six-month sentence was up. I expected Owen to pay the fines. We weren't allowed to sell any of our property to pay the fines.

In addition to our sentences, the FBI turned over the bookkeeping records from the raid at our house to the IRS. They placed tax liens of over $90,000 against all the property we owned. Based on the bookkeeping, the IRS claimed that we made that much income from the prostitution and even though it was from illegal activities, the government still wanted tax money. Our property would be held until we found a way to pay the taxes. This left us feeling like the government was just as crooked as we were.

I am everywhere—both near and far, in heaven and on earth. There are no secret places where you can hide from Me (Jer. 23:23-24 CEV).

CHAPTER EIGHT

Federal Prison

After we pled guilty, the police handcuffed us and placed us in different squad cars to take us away. Separation anxiety hit me as I looked at Owen in the other car. We were headed in different directions. Both Owen and I were going to be held at a local jail to await our transfer to federal prison. I was headed to the Federal Penitentiary in Alderson, West Virginia, and Owen was going to be transferred to Safford, Arizona. For security reasons we weren't told the day we would be moved.

Karol escaped any charges. She would be Owen's contact with the outside world and would look over the affairs at the motel.

After settling in at the local prison for a few days, I heard the guard approach my cell early one morning before everyone rose. I knew it was the day of my transfer. Handcuffs were placed tightly around my wrists, and I was escorted to an unidentified vehicle parked behind the jail.

"How long of a ride is this?" I asked.

"A few hours, just sit back and relax," the officer growled.

Arriving at the front entrance of Alderson, I looked at what appeared to be an enormous, secluded village in the middle of a corn field. It didn't look like a prison. All the buildings were dark brick with large framed windows on all sides. I was taken to the administration office to fill out forms and check into my home for the next six months. A woman named with a name tag that read, "Cheri, Trustee" assigned me prison clothing.

"Come with me so I can assign you to your building," said Cheri.

"What does trustee mean?" I asked her.

"I have special work privileges," she replied. "I can roam the campus freely without a guard. I'm leaving to go home soon."

"Oh, boy. My time is just beginning. I need to make my stay as easy as possible," I said. "Any advice you want to give me?"

"Yes, just do the time and stay out of the gangs," she responded. "This is yours," she pointed to a building in the middle of the campus. Cheri handed me off to the CEO, the head of the shift, who checked me in to my building.

"Are all these items yours?" the CEO asked and I nodded, as she made a list of my personal belongings and shoved them into a locker. Another one of the inmates escorted me down the hall to my room. The large doors to our rooms were old-fashioned, with big, glass windows at the top where you could open or close the hinge to get fresh air. There were no jail bars. How strange, I thought to myself, anyone could get out of here.

A large-framed black girl walked in and introduced herself. "Hi, my name's Kathy. I'm your roommate."

"Glad to meet you. I'm Carol."

"I'm from Toledo," she told me.

"I live near Cleveland."

I looked at the empty bed and assumed that was mine. Her bed was covered with stuffed animals. Each of us had a dresser to place our belongings in. Her dresser was filled with pictures of smiling faces that I imagined were her family. I didn't have any pictures for my dresser. I was able to put the few things I was given in my dresser before the dinner bell rang.

"Follow me. I'll show you the way," Kathy said.

We walked to the dining hall, which was located in the middle of the campus. This place is so clean you probably could eat off the floor, I thought to myself.

"Most girls get assigned here first for their duties," Kathy told me.

"I hope I don't have to cook," I said.

"It's not that bad," Kathy said.

The food was prepared by the inmates. My first meal wasn't that bad— beef stew. After dinner, Kathy and I walked back to the dorm. I was introduced to Patti, whose room was directly across from ours. Lights had to be out by eleven o'clock. There were no excuses allowed; you had to be in your room. I tossed and turned my first night, unable to shut out the sounds of my new surroundings.

Six a.m. came too early. I was taken to the counselor's office where I would get my duty assignment.

"Carol, all girls start with the cafeteria. I'm going to assign you to cleaning the tables and mopping the floors. Your job will need to be done every morning and evening after each meal," the counselor said. I walked back to the dorm, disappointed with my assignment. But I had no choice; I had to do it.

I kept my distance from most of the girls and stayed close to Patti and Kathy. Time was passing faster than I thought it would. One month had gone by when a letter arrived from Owen telling me that Grandma Kilbane had passed away. He was allowed to attend the funeral. My heart filled with disappointment as I wasn't able to say goodbye to the woman I had grown so fond of. I was the only one who had taken care of her, often going into her room to make sure she was still alive. I knew I was going to miss having tea with her.

That night I sat in bed and wrote a letter to Owen, telling him how I was feeling. I heard a scream at the other end of the hallway and ran to the door to see what was going on. I could see fire coming out of one of the windows above the doorway. As the screams got louder, I realized it was a girl named Becky. Her room was on fire! I ran quickly to help her as she darted out of the doorway, trying to escape getting burnt.

"You did this! You threw this in my room," she yelled to Belinda, whose room was next to mine.

"No, I didn't!" Belinda shouted back.

The shouting got louder and louder, the closer they got to each other. Another girl came running toward them with a broom handle and tried to jab Becky in the stomach. I grabbed the handle to stop it from ramming into her. The guards rushed up the stairs to break up the commotion. The girls were taken downstairs to the office and I was left in the hall, outside my room where Patti and I discussed the incident.

Belinda finally came back to her room. She was being sent to a separate cell away from the rest of the population. Called the hole, it was a place where girls were sent to be punished. Prisoners were stripped of all privileges, including smoking, and there was only a metal bed, no pillow or covers.

As she left her room, Belinda pointed her finger into my face and screamed, "Bitch! You better not be here when I get back."

I could feel rage rise up inside of me and jumping to my feet, I grabbed her by the back of her neck. She tried turning her face away as I threw my fist as hard as I could into her cheek bone. She fought back and we twirled around and around in the hall, falling back against the large heat radiator. I grabbed her hair and holding on tightly, I hammered her head as hard as I could against the radiator. Madness had taken over; I was totally out of control. A few of the guards struggled to break the firm lock my hands had on her. Loosening my hold, they were finally able to move me away from Belinda. After all this, I was being sent to the hole with her for one week.

Time passed very slowly; sleeping was the only way to make it go faster. For entertainment, we shouted through the metal doors at each other. Belinda and I became friends and promised that we would not fight again. I was desperate to smoke. It was the hardest part of being confined. I craved a cigarette so bad.

When the door finally opened for our release, we darted out and ran back to our dorm as fast as our legs could take us. I had earned respect from many of the girls. They now knew I was not going to back down from a fight. Many of them said they were glad to have me back. Not having cigarettes for a week often made me so dizzy I felt like I was going to pass out. But that didn't stop me from lighting up.

During my stay, I was concerned about the $5,000 fine that was part of my sentence. I called Robert Steele's office on a regular basis. I wanted to know what Owen was saying to him, but Robert never took any of my calls. His secretary always said he was not in or at a meeting. A month before my release, I called again and demanded to speak to him. He finally came to the phone.

"Why haven't you taken my calls? What's going on Bob?"

"I've been busy," was all he would say.

"You know I am in here! I only get phone privileges at certain times," I yelled to him.

"What do you want, Carol?"

"What is happening with my fine?"

"You need to find a way to pay it."

"What do you mean? Isn't Owen going to pay my fine?"

"Owen doesn't talk about it to me," he said.

"He must be telling you something," I insisted. "He needs to pay my fine."

"That is between you and him," he said. "I will tell him. Bye," he said, slamming down the phone.

I went back to my friend Patti and told her what had just happened. She was a madam and had reminded me all along that Owen was strictly a pimp, looking out for himself, and he wasn't going to help me.

"You need to think real hard about him," she told me. "If you ever need me, I will be there for you."

I was worried when it came time for my release that they would hold me because of the unpaid fine. I had earned a month off my sentence for good behavior so I was able to be released in five months instead of having to serve the full six. Two weeks remained on my shortened sentence, and my fine still was not paid. I was summoned to the warden's office. I was trembling inside as I made my way to his office, thinking I was going to be told I couldn't leave when my time was up. As I walked to his office, I rehearsed the conversation in my head so I could have my answers ready. I knocked at his door.

"Who is it?"

"It's Carol Braun. You sent for me."

"Oh yes, come on in."

I entered the room and saw a man with his back to me standing by the warden's desk. As he turned around, I saw it was Robert Ressler, the FBI agent who was responsible for my prison stay and also the man whom I often encountered in the elevator of the apartment. At the opposite side of the room stood another gentleman, Lt. Martin McCann Jr. I turned around to walk out of the room, but the warden stopped me, "You better stay, Carol, and listen." Turning to Ressler, he said, "I'll be out in the other room if you need me."

My voice shook as I said, "I don't want to stay in here with these guys."

"You must talk to them, Carol," the warden said.

I was afraid that if I refused, I would be denied my early release.

"How are you, Carol?" Ressler began.

"What do you care? And why are you here?"

"Carol, we hope that your time spent here has given you some time to reflect about what you are going to do when you are released from here. Hopefully you are not going back to Owen."

I giggled nervously at him. Owen had warned me often never to talk to the Feds. They will take your words and twist them to say what they want them to say, he told me. They were known for using your words against you. Cops always go after the weakest link, he would tell me. I didn't want to be that weak link, I thought.

"Carol, we have some questions we want to ask you," Ressler said.

I chuckled again, looking toward the window to avoid eye contact with Ressler. Feds always worked with a nice guy and a mean guy. Ressler was playing the part of the nice guy. His partner raised his voice at me, getting frustrated with my lack of cooperation.

"Carol, we know that Owen had something to do with the Steele murder."

Smiling at him, I said, "You don't know what you are talking about."

"Do you know Rick Robbins?"

"No."

"Do you know an Arnie Prunella?"

"No."

"Have you ever heard Owen talking to Robert Steele about killing his wife?"

"Leave me alone," I said. "I don't know what you are talking about."

"Carol, we are going to get to the bottom of the murders. Do you want to go down with those guys?"

I thought to myself that they must know something, but I sure wasn't going to be the leak and give them the ammunition they were looking for. "Just let me go back to my cottage," I yelled.

"Before you go, Carol, take a look at this."

Drawing my attention to the round table in front of me, Ressler dropped some pictures. I couldn't help but glance out of the corner of my eye. The picture was of a bloody women lying in a bed. I could only stare for a second. It still didn't seem real to me and subconsciously, I knew if I looked at those pictures for too long, it would be a real person.

"Carol this is Marlene Steele. You know who she is. You know how she was murdered. You know who did this!" Ressler spoke in a firm voice.

"No, I don't!" I hollered.

"You better tell us what you know. One day you will end up just like her—dead! We want to protect you. Owen doesn't care about you. He will end up getting rid of you one day, maybe the same way."

I reflected on the fine Owen hadn't paid. Maybe he was right. I might get killed. Owen wasn't even worried about paying my fine. It had been four months since I had heard from him. All of my letters had gone unanswered. But I wasn't going to break. They had to see some concern on my face, even though I tried to hide my emotional turmoil.

"I want to go. Let me out of here."

"Here, Carol, this is my card. Take it just in case you might need it someday," Ressler said. As he placed the card in my hand, I couldn't help but take another glance toward the table to see the woman who had been shot in the head. The image of blood was stamped in my mind as I left the room. I walked away wondering if I could be next.

"Don't forget; Carol. Call me if you need me," Ressler called out.

I ran back to my cottage, straight to Patti's room to tell her what had happened. Even though I was scared, I spoke to her for the first time about the murders. I better shut up, I said to myself. What if she is a cop; and they placed her in here for me to confide in? I had watched movies where a person got caught when they talked to an inmate about details of their crime. I better not tell her anymore. I stopped before I gave away more details.

"Carol, you need to take care of yourself. A pimp is a pimp. They have no feelings. Look what he did to that woman who was sleeping in her bed. You really think he cares about you? He would kill you in a heartbeat," Patti said.

"What am I going to do? I'm leaving in two weeks. I need to go home. Where else can I go?"

"I'll be out in a few months. You can always come to see me," Patti responded.

The two weeks went by slowly. I packed my belongings, giving away a lot of my things to some of the less fortunate girls. I said my goodbyes and headed to the car that would take me to the airport for my trip home. I refused to turn around. I was determined only to face forward to what was in front of me. Girls told stories about how if you looked back you would jinx yourself and would come back. There was no way I would come back and do time, I thought. As I walked through the prison gates, I knew I was finally free, yet I still felt imprisoned by what I knew.

It is better to trust the Lord than to put confidence in people (Ps. 118:8 NLT).

CHAPTER NINE

Protecting Myself

My brother Richard came to get me at the airport. I was so excited to see him and could barely contain my excitement as we hugged. It was weird to see all the familiar places after I had been gone so long. When I arrived at the motel, I immediately began to look around. Seeing things after five months seemed strange. I was glad to get away from the call girl operation for those five months, and I thought we would be done with it.

Karol was still running the motel, and she was standing by the large back switchboard in the office. I knew that Owen would be calling soon; it was a daily routine for him to call and check up on the activities at the motel. I was tense as I waited for the line to light up with an incoming call. I could hardly wait to hear his voice. The outside call light finally lit up in red. I was so out of practice with answering the phone, it took me a few tries to plug in the right cords. I hope it's him, I thought to myself.

"Hello. Carol, is that you?"

"Hello, Owen," I said with a giggle in my voice. I felt like a little school girl. "How are you doing?"

"I'm fine. When did you get out?" he asked. "I got here just a few hours ago."

"I can't wait to see you!" I said, waiting for him to say the same. But he didn't.

"I'll be home tomorrow around 2 p.m.," he said. "I'll see you then."

"Bye," I said, my voice dropping to a disappointed whisper.

Being with Karol was very odd. I was uncomfortable with all her questions. I really didn't want to talk to her at all.

"How are you doing?" she asked.

"Okay," I answered in a soft tone. "I'm so glad to be back." After an awkward pause, I said, "I'm anxious to get home, so I'm going to go. I'll see you later." I rushed out the door quickly so she couldn't ask me another question.

Richard drove me to the house. As I got out of the car, our dogs, Leo and Tippy, leaped up at me in their excitement. I was happy they hadn't forgot me. They followed me around, licking my hands and nudging me to pet them.

My brother stayed the night to help me adjust to my new freedom. I could come and go as I pleased without asking anyone permission. I hardly slept that first night. The sounds of the country were so different than the sounds at the prison.

Having Richard there helped, but he had to get back to work. I was now on my own, for the first time in five months. I got into my car to drive to the motel. The familiar route made me feel like I hadn't been gone a day. I imagined Owen sitting next to me. I was so excited to see him after such a long time.

Arriving at the motel, I said hello to everyone and walked into the office at the back of the motel. I was planning to relax and prepare myself for Owen's arrival. It was hard to concentrate on anything besides the fact that he was going to be there soon. With my heart racing from anxiety, I walked outside for a breath of fresh air. A familiar car approached the motel and I did a double take. It's him … it's HIM! My mind was racing as the car stopped and the door opened. Owen got out of the car. I wanted to fall into his arms, and hug him as hard as I could. I composed myself and held back the emotion as he walked to the motel door.

"Hello, Carol," he said. That's it? That's all I get after five months? I thought to myself.

Karol was standing by the check-in desk, and he walked toward her. "How are things going?" he asked.

No hug for her either, I couldn't help but notice. He turned to walk down the hall to his office, nodding to some of the employees to say hello. Owen went to his large desk, sat down, and began going through some of his mail. He glanced through the records, catching up on what had taken place for the last five months. His bookkeeping system would show him if something wasn't right. I never wanted to make a mistake because I was sure to hear about it and so would everyone else. He was tight with his money. He finally reached down to get his briefcase and glanced up at me.

"Let's go," he said.

We walked outside and got in my car. Finally, we were alone. I wanted to reach over and kiss him. It felt so wonderful to be with him again. As we drove away from the motel, he let down his guard a bit and began to relax with me. I felt comfortable with sharing what I had been going through emotionally.

"Owen, I really missed you," I said, grabbing his hand.

"I missed you too," he said, not letting go. "How does the house look?"

"It looks big and the dogs really missed us." I paused for a second. "Owen, I have something to tell you. Remember that FBI agent, Ressler, who busted us?"

"Yeah. What about him?"

"A few weeks before my release, he came to visit me. They locked me in the warden's office with him and Lt. Martin McCann Jr. from Euclid."

"What did they want?"

"They asked me all kinds of questions, wanting to know if I knew certain people. Rick and Arnie were just a few they mentioned."

"What did you say?"

"Nothing. I just laughed at them. I was nervous that I was going to be detained from my release so I just sat there. They said they're going to get to the bottom of the murders."

"Don't worry. They're just fishing," Owen said.

It was the first time since I had mentioned the murders to him since they happened. I had been afraid to say it aloud.

Opening the garage door, Owen was greeted by the dogs with the same enthusiasm they had greeted me with.

"Hi Tippy and Leo," he said to them, climbing out of the car to play with them.

We walked through the garage door to the family room. It was a freedom I had not felt in months, and I was thrilled to be enjoying it with him. I knew Owen was feeling the same freedom as I was. He walked through the house, making comments in each room. "This feels so good to be home. I really missed the dogs, and I can't wait to get into our own bed."

"I know," I said to him. "When I slept last night, I tossed some, but it was so good to be here. I'm going to the kitchen to pour us a rum and coke. I'll let you enjoy looking around."

"The rooms look so big," he said as I handed him his drink, and we walked over to the couch and sat facing each other. We spent hours just talking, catching up.

"I really have missed this place," I said. "I missed our time alone and I missed our intimacy. Do you want to take a shower?"

"Yes," he answered. We made love until the sun came up, trying to make up for the time we had spent apart.

I spent the next few months adjusting to being at home and running the motel. I tried to stay at the house as much as I could. Karol was still in our lives, but she was living at home with her mom after only a few months of our freedom. Owen began falling back into his old pattern of spending nights out, not coming home until morning. It scared me; I knew he had to be with someone. No one does business in the middle of the night, I thought to myself. He must either be with Karol or someone else. When he finally did come home, I would question him.

"Where have you been?" I asked.

"The less you know, the better off you are," he would say. "Don't question me. I don't want to tell you everything."

"I'm worried that you're seeing Karol or someone else."

"I love you! You should know that by now. I'm trying to get things going well, so soon we'll be able to start our family. Just trust me."

"Why didn't you pay my fine?" I asked him.

"I didn't have the money," he said. "I had to raise it. I'll have it together soon. That's what I've been working on."

"Who could you possibly be meeting in the middle of the night?"

"Don't worry about it. Let me take care of it. I will have our fines paid off soon."

I began occasionally working at the motel on the night shift, midnight to eight a.m. It gave Owen the chance to do what he wanted at night, since I was the clerk on duty. He knew I couldn't check up on him since I was unable to leave the hotel unattended.

We hired a new clerk, Martha, to relieve me of some of the hours I was stuck behind the desk. Her boyfriend, Bobby, was a friend of Martin's. It gave me the chance to remodel some of the rooms in the motel that needed repairs.

Owen kept purchasing more property. He moved his dad to a nursing home up the street, and his mom moved into the house with us.

Owen's video business began to grow. He would go to the nightclubs to record the local bands and charge them a fee for a video of their live performance. It was becoming popular for groups to want their acts on video.

Our relationship became very shaky. I wanted to get away from Owen to think about what I really wanted. I thought some space from him would help me decide if I wanted to stay with him or leave for good. I convinced him I needed to make a short trip to see Patti in St. Louis. He agreed to let me go. I never told him she was a madam, only that I met her in Alderson. I knew he wouldn't let me go if he knew what she did.

The night before I left, I couldn't sleep. I tossed and turned most of the night, unable to stop myself from rehearsing what I was going to say to Owen as he dropped me off at the airport. Daybreak came and I questioned whether or not I really wanted to leave. As I watched Owen sleeping in bed, he looked so innocent, which made it even harder for me. I really didn't want to leave him, but I needed to go. I could get another perspective on our relationship.

I grabbed a cup of coffee to wake up, while Owen packed my luggage in the car and drove me to the airport. I hoped I didn't look nervous.

"Just drop me off at the ticket gate. I can go in by myself," I said to him. "I'll be okay."

"Are you sure?" Owen asked.

I wasn't even sure if I would be coming back, but I certainly wasn't going to let him know what I was thinking. I swore he could read my mind.

"I'll call you when I get to Saint Louis," I said and he drove away.

The flight went quickly and when I arrived in St. Louis, Patti met me by the baggage check.

"It's so good to see you," I said.

"Did you have a good flight?" she asked.

I had seen the great big archway in magazines before, but now I was seeing it in person as we drove by. It looked enormous. I felt like I had stepped into another world, free from Owen's hold. He wasn't there to tell me what I could or couldn't do. It felt like being released from prison all over again.

Patti and I stayed up late that night, catching up on what we had been doing for the past few months.

"I'm going to have you meet some of my friends tomorrow," Patti said.

"Great," I said. "I'll pour us a drink."

My nights with Patti were spent partying. I was drinking heavily and hanging out with her friends at the local bars. I felt like I was going backward in my life instead of forward. One night when we were out, a young man approached me. We flirted and I ended up back at his place, in bed with him. I found out he was a pimp and had his woman in the other room. I was drawn to the same situation I was trying to escape.

"She won't bother us," he said, trying to convince me not to care about the other woman.

What am I doing? I thought to myself. I might as well go back home. "I need you to take me home," I said.

"Okay," he agreed. "But you'll be sorry."

"No, I won't," I said.

Patti was a madam, and she wanted me to work for her. I told her I wanted to get my own place to start my life all over again. She was offering me fifty percent of the money I made. Back home, I had to give everything I made to Owen. In addition to working for Patti, I started a couple nights a week working at the local bar, making good tips.

Coming home late one night, I told Patti that I was concerned that Owen was going to find me and bring me home. I wanted to get a place where he couldn't find me.

"Carol, I think you need to get some protection," she said.

"What do you mean?"

"You know how you told me about those murders. You should tell that FBI guy what you know, so if anything happens to you, they would know who to go after. They would have the details to solve the case. They can protect you."

"I have his card," I said, thinking about her suggestion. "I think I'll give him a call." The phone seemed to weigh a hundred pounds.

"Hello, Mr. Ressler. This is Carol Braun. Do you remember me?"

"Yes, Carol. What can I do for you?"

"I ran from Owen, and I'm afraid that he might come to hurt me," I blurted out to him. "I'm not going back to him. I am tired of being used. I'm staying with a friend in St. Louis. Do you think you can protect me?"

"Yes, Carol. Can I come and see you?"

"I think so. When?"

"How about tomorrow morning? Are you thinking about getting out of the scene with Owen altogether?"

"Yes, but I'm so tired my head hurts. He had me brainwashed for so long. I go to bed at night fighting my mind—maybe I should go back, then I say no, I can't go back. I know what it will turn into if I go back."

"Okay, where can we meet?" he asked.

"There is a Hotel Ramada on Grant Avenue. Meet me in the parking lot. I'll connect with you there," I said. "I'm so nervous. Last night, I couldn't sleep. I woke up three or four times, feeling like he was calling for me. I had to fight myself not to call him. I don't want to go into depression. See you tomorrow."

As I hung up the phone, I began to feel guilty.

"You need to meet with them," Patti reassured me. "Don't worry about Owen. He doesn't care about you. He's probably with another woman right now."

It felt like I jumped out of my skin when the phone rang. Maybe Ressler forgot something, I thought.

"Hello, is Carol there?"

"Hold on," Patti said. Whispering to me, "Carol, I think Owen's on the phone."

I took the phone from her. "Hello, Carol. Are you relaxing?"

"Yes. I've been going out on different appointments. Patti's giving me some customers so I can make a few spending dollars."

"When are you coming home?" he asked.

"I'm not."

"What do you mean?"

"Owen, I'm tired of what we have, and I'm not coming home to you and Karol."

"I love you. I need you to come home," he pleaded.

"I'm not coming home ever. What took you so long to call me?" I couldn't help but ask.

"I've been working here at the motel training a new guy to replace Karol," he said. "I can't see how this is helping our relationship thinking about you going up there. You're listening to people who are giving you negative input about me."

"Owen for the past ten years I have done everything for you. I've been taken advantage of. Listen to me. I needed to get away from you. I've lived your life, your ways, your thinking, your dreams. It's going to take me a hell of a long time to figure out who I am and what I want out of life. I feel like a junky going through withdrawal. I'm going to hang up now. Bye."

As I hung up the phone, I wondered if he could read my mind, knowing that I had just talked the FBI. It was scary that he had called just when I had hung up with Ressler. He always had a way of finding out things. What if he hears about this? I will be dead for sure, I thought.

I could hardly sleep, even after Patti had given me a sleeping pill. As I got dressed the next morning, I smoked one cigarette after another, trying to calm my nerves.

Ressler arrived in St. Louis. Patti drove around the streets as she took me to our meeting place, avoiding anyone that could possibly be following us.

"Meet me back here in an hour," I told Patti as she dropped me off. I watched Ressler walk toward the car.

"You think we are being followed?" Ressler asked.

"I hope not because we will all be dead," I answered.

"I don't trust Owen at all," Ressler said.

"Neither do I. Let's get out of here."

We walked in the back door of the hotel, trying not to look obvious. I followed him as he led me down the hall to the elevator and onto the second floor. He opened the door to a room and a man stepped back to let me in.

"Carol, do you remember Lt. Martin McCann Jr. from Euclid, Ohio?" Ressler asked me. "He's been working on the case for a few years."

"Wasn't he the guy in the warden's office you had with you?'

"Yes," he said. "You don't think Owen knows you called me?"

"I hope not. He'll kill me," I said.

"So Carol what are you doing?"

"I'm making my break from Owen. I want to let you know what I know about the murders in turn for my protection."

"Okay, we can do that."

"What do you want me to say?" I asked.

"Before you begin I want to advise you of your rights on this form entitled, 'Interrogation, Advice of Rights.' Read it and let us know if you agree." My eyes scanned it quickly, and I wrote my initials where they wanted me to sign.

"We are going to record this statement. Is that okay with you?" Ressler asked.

"I agree."

He started the recorder and I began my statement.

"I, Carol Jean Braun, currently living in St. Louis, Missouri, I do hereby make the following statement to Special Agents of the Federal Bureau of Investigation. My employment for the past ten years has been that of a prostitute and during this time I lived with and worked for Owen James Kilbane who resides in Chardon, Ohio. The majority of the money I earned as a prostitute was given to Owen James Kilbane.

"I have known Owen since I was eighteen years of age; I have a great deal of knowledge concerning his activities and his associations with people in the Cleveland, Ohio area. I first met Robert Steele in 1968 when I was involved in prostitution at the Indian Hills apartment located on Euclid Avenue. Bob Steele came to my apartment as a customer, and at that time he had given me his business card which identified him as a prosecutor for the city of Euclid, Ohio. He told me, at this time, that if I ever had any trouble with the police that I could contact him. I have heard a number of conversations indicating that Owen James Kilbane was to arrange the killing of Marlene Steele for her husband, Robert Steele. Conversations between Owen and his brother Martin Kilbane were that concerning the murder of Marlene Steele. Owen had arranged for an alibi for himself on the evening of the murder, and to the best of my knowledge Martin Kilbane and Rick Robbins were actually directly involved in the murder. It was Owen's idea that Rick Robbins wear shoes several sizes too large to confuse the police should any footprints be left on the grounds of the residence of Judge Steele. Rick Robbins was to enter the Steele residence and kill Marlene Steele upon a pre-arranged signal from Judge Robert Steele who would be in the house at the time.

"I wish to state that all information provided is the best of my recollection. However, I have lived under extremely trying circumstances over the past ten years and some of my recollections concerning the sequence of events that occurred in the killing of Marlene Steele are hazy. In my own mind I know that I heard the murder plans being put together prior to the killing which did take place. I also heard the murder discussed after the killing by Owen and others whose names I can't recall at this time.

"I also have overheard conversations of the killing of Arnie Prunella where Owen took him out onto his boat and Arnie was killed and dropped into the lake."

My body was so tense as I gave them what details I could remember. "That's all I can remember right now," I said as we finished. "I want to get out of here."

"Carol, I suggest you find yourself a place here and stay, never telling Owen that you made this statement. Do you think you can get him to talk on the phone about the murders?" Ressler asked.

"I can try." Ressler handed me a recorder with an adapter.

"Keep in touch, Carol. We don't care what you do here but just stay away from Owen. Call me when you get the recording."

"Okay, bye." Terrified, I walked out first. As I got into Patti's car, I looked across the parking lot and saw Ressler racing to his car, jumping in faster than I could blink my eye.

I was shaking as I called Owen that night after connecting the adapter to the phone. The Feds assumed I was safe and didn't need protection from Owen in St. Louis, but I don't think they knew the effect he had on me, even over the phone.

"Hello, what are you up to?"

"I'm watching the news," Owen replied.

"I need to talk to you about something. Owen, one of the reasons I left you was that you had murdered Arnie. I have always been afraid that you would kill me."

"What reason would I do that for? I love you and I won't harm you."

"You get rid of people that have crossed you," I said.

"You haven't crossed me, so what do you have to worry about?"

"Marlene did not cross you so why was she killed?"

"That's between her and Bob. I don't want to talk about this over the phone," he shouted. I was frightened that he was catching on to the recording.

"Owen, I am going. I will talk to you later." I hung up quickly.

I continued working in St. Louis, getting involved deeper in my despair. I was still not feeling secure with my life. I found myself being drawn to a life I hated, the same one I had run from. The only difference was that I was working with a madam instead of a pimp. It was the same, except Owen had been taking the money I made and using it for investments. Was I wrong for leaving him? The guilt wore on me. I had Patti and a few new friends, but I was beginning to miss Owen a great deal. I decided to call him.

"Hi, Owen. What are you up to?"

"Working as usual," he said. "What are you doing?"

"Just sitting in my apartment. Why haven't you called me?"

"You haven't called me either," he said. "You didn't go to St. Louis knowing you were going to call me up and tell me that you weren't coming back. You're being persuaded by someone."

"Are you saying I'm being influenced? Owen, you know I've struggled with Karol for a long time and yet she's still around. I'm asking you to wake up to realize why I have left."

"Carol, I told you how I feel about you," he said.

"Owen, do you know that I fear you?"

"Fear me from what?"

"Come on, Owen. You know the things you've done."

"Those things have nothing to do with you."

"No, but you could very easily do something to me."

"For what?" he asked.

"I don't know."

"Carol, just come home and we'll work it out, just like we have in the past."

"No way. I can't. I've done something that you will never forgive me for," I admitted to him.

"Come on, Carol. Nothing you do will change my feelings for you," Owen said.

"Oh, yes there is. I crossed you like no one has ever done," I said. I had to tell him. I had to know if he would still love me, even after all I had done.

"What is that?"

"I talked to Ressler, the FBI agent. I was never planning on coming back to you. I needed to protect myself on what I know so I made a statement to him with another agent from Euclid."

There was silence on the other end of the line. It seemed to go on forever. I was afraid of what he was thinking. He must hate me, I thought. Finally, he spoke. "That's okay," he said. "Come home and it will be okay. We'll work through it."

"I need to get a flight," I said, giving in. I couldn't believe he was forgiving me for turning him in to the Feds. He must really love me, I thought. Not only did he still love me, but he wanted me to come home to him. "I'll call the airport. I need the card info to pay for my ticket."

"Okay, call me back when you have all the plans."

My emotions were bouncing back and forth. I called to book my flight before I could change my mind. I was excited to see Owen again but afraid of what he was going to do to me.

I called Owen to let him know when I would arrive home. "Owen, my flight arrives at 10 p.m. Meet me at the airport."

"You sure you're going to make the flight?"

"Yes, I will be back. Bye, see you soon."

My heart raced as I packed my things. The cab arrived and took me to the airport. Looking around, I imagined everyone was staring at me, knowing what I was up to. Maybe Ressler had someone follow me, I thought. I boarded the plane and tilted my head back to rest my eyes.

The flight ended quicker than I really wanted it to. I couldn't change my mind now. I was here. I waited for almost everyone to get off the plane before I picked up my bag and exited.

Owen had a half smile on his face as I slowly approached him. I looked into his eyes. Taking my hand, he led me to the car. Thoughts raced violently back and forth in my head. I didn't know what to think on the drive home.

What's he really thinking? He must really love me. Maybe he is going to take me somewhere to kill me. He'll just stop the car while someone else does it.

My mind was full of fear, but home looked so good to me. We walked into the dining room. Owen sat me down at the table with a pad of paper.

"I want you to write down all that you remember from your statement."

My hand was shaking uncontrollably as I wrote what I could remember. I looked up at Owen.

"Here is what I can remember."

Looking back at me, he turned and walked toward the door. "I'll be back soon," he said. "I have to go to a meeting I had planned."

I began to shake violently. He's going to kill me. I know he is. He's out making his plans. Why did I come back? Why did I tell him I made the statement?

The night passed slowly. I tried to calm my mind and distract myself by watching the TV. Eventually I was able to go to sleep.

The dogs barking roused me, and I heard the garage door open. He was home.

Part of me felt secure that he was home, but then the thoughts I had pushed back began racing across my mind. I'll have a drink, I thought. That will relax me.

"Do you want a drink?" I asked him.

"Yes, I'll have a small one," he said as he rolled a joint.

I felt uneasy next to him. The rum and coke helped to numb my thoughts. I took a puff of the marijuana, escaping all emotions outside of my love for him. We went to bed and I slipped into his arms, trying to forget this day had even happened. Owen slept peacefully, but I couldn't stop my mind. What if? What if?

Exhaustion finally overcame me.

Owen left for the motel in the morning as usual. The phone rang as I was cleaning the house.

"Hello," I answered.

"Carol, why did you leave St. Louis?" the familiar voice of Ressler asked.

"I just wanted to come home."

"I hope you were smart enough not to tell Owen about your statement. He'll kill you if you did."

"No, he won't." I slammed the phone down.

What did I do? Maybe Ressler is right.

Paranoia overtook my life. I spent many nights alone in bed, jumping at every sound, gripping Owen's loaded gun. The dogs slept at the foot of the bed. I wondered when or if someone was going to come and get me. I kept imagining someone coming up the steps. Every little sound was magnified. Terror had become an everyday feeling for me.

> *Those who live in the shelter of the Most High will find rest in the shadow of the Almighty. This I declare of the Lord: He alone is my refuge, my place of safety; He is my God, and I am trusting Him. For He will rescue you from every trap and protect you from the fatal plague. He will shield you with His wings, and shelter you with His feathers, His faithful promises are your armor and protection* (Ps.91:1-4 NLT).

CHAPTER TEN

Triggerman's Arrest

Time seemed to ease my fears over what could happen to me. A year passed by; Karol and her mom moved to California to be near her sister. She still was involved in our lives, but now there was distance between us. Owen's video business was expanding. He was flying from Ohio to California. He would stay one week with me, then two weeks in California with Karol. When Owen was gone, I kept myself busy working long hours at the motel. I hated being alone. Martha and I spent a lot of time at the motel, taking turns checking in the customers. She confided in me about her boyfriend's abusive behavior.

After two months of missing my cycle, I started having morning sickness. I just knew I was pregnant. I made an appointment to see my gynecologist.

"Congratulations, Carol," the doctor said. "You're going to be a mother."

I hoped he couldn't tell by the look on my face all the questions that flashed in my head. Was Owen ready for a family? What is he going to say? We certainly hadn't planned this.

I left the office wondering how I was going to break the news to Owen. I didn't want to tell him over the phone. He was coming in over the weekend so I decided I might as well wait to tell him in person. The weekend could not get here fast enough. Picking him up at the airport, I was quiet.

"Are you okay?" Owen asked.

"Yes." I didn't want to break the news until we were at home. We stopped at the motel for a short time, then headed home. I made us a steak dinner; and we sat as usual talking about things that went on during the weeks we hadn't been together. Getting up the nerve to tell him the news, I started to shake.

"Owen, I have something I have to tell you. I went to the doctor because I wasn't feeling well."

"What did you find out?" he asked.

"Well... I hope you'll be okay with this."

"What?"

"I'm pregnant." I held my breath waiting for his reaction. I wasn't sure if he would let me keep the baby.

"That's okay," he responded. "We talked about having children. I'm ready to start a family."

"I'm so relieved to hear you say that," I said. "I was so worried that you would tell me to have an abortion."

"I am happy," he said, taking my hand as we moved to the couch. I snuggled in his arms. I felt such relief. I was finally getting him all to myself. I was going to have his baby. Not Karol.

"When are you due to have the baby?" he asked.

"Sometime in the first couple weeks of February."

"Maybe he'll be a St. Patrick's Day baby," Owen smiled.

"I don't think so. That's in March."

"We'll have to give him or her a good Irish name, maybe Patrick if it's a boy," he said.

"We have time to see what we want to name the baby," I said, smiling at his enthusiasm. I was finally going to have the life I had always wanted.

The weekend went too fast and before I knew it, I was taking Owen back to the airport so he could go back to California. But this time, I had hope that my dreams were going to start to come true. Was he going to tell Karol that I was going to have his baby, or was he going to let it be a surprise? What if she tries to get pregnant and wants to have his baby? I thought for a second but quickly dismissed it. My dreams were finally going to be reality.

Five years after the drifter had struck my nose, he was standing in the office of Cleveland Heights Prosecutor Paul Greenberger. He went in to report his abusive father, but ended up telling Greenberger about Rick Robbins' involvement in the murder of Ted Browne. It set off an investigation that led to the arrest of Robbins. Martin was concerned about what his friend was going to say and do. He knew that Robbins would probably tell officers about his involvement in Marlene Steele's murder. He was right to be worried.

Martin called me to say that Robbins had been arrested, and the police had been asking him questions about the Steele case.

"I told him they were just fishing," Martin said.

"Okay. I'll give Owen a call," I said. Panic took over as I dialed. Was this it? Was he finally going to be caught?

"Owen, Marty just called. Robbins has been arrested. He's being questioned," I rambled.

"I'll be home over the weekend and we'll talk some more," Owen said, calm as usual.

My nerves were getting the best of me and I wasn't getting enough sleep. All the talk about Robbins' arrest had me very worried.

The trial began for Robbins and lasted for only a few days. Rick was found guilty of murder and sentenced on August 31, 1976. Prosecutors won their case with the testimony of one of Rick's friends as well as a fingerprint that was found on Browne's car.

The racial pressure was on Robbins. He was being harassed by inmates who knew he had shot a black man. He feared for his life and was ready to get protection. One night, sitting in his cell, Robbins recalled a conversation he had three months earlier with John T. Corrigan, a Cuyahoga County Prosecutor. "If you ever want to talk about the Steele case," Corrigan had told Robbins, "get in touch with me. My door is always open." Robbins was ready to walk through that door.

The law enforcement in Euclid, as well as the FBI, were continually working to solve the murders. Lt. John Walsh, an 18-year veteran of the Euclid police department, looked like one of those distinguished, late-night television private eyes. He was selected to study at the FBI's National Academy in Quantico, Virginia, where his instructor turned out to be Robert Ressler. They struck up a rapport and began talking about the Steele case. One of the things they found eight years later was Robbins' name scrawled in handwriting inside one of the many manila folders Steele kept in his files.

Walsh returned to the Euclid force, determined to reopen the Steele case after discussing it with Ressler. He was ready to pounce when the moment was right, and it seemed like the time was now. Knowing Robbins would be stewing in prison, Walsh waited two weeks and then he visited Robbins at the Ohio Penitentiary.

"I was in the service when it happened," Robbins said when questioned about the Steele murder.

"That's bull!" roared Walsh. "You decide which side of the table you'll be on in the next trial."

Robbins softened. Walsh was encouraged by Robbins' new, amenable attitude. On a second visit, Robbins said he was concerned about his family's protection, but he still would not reveal anything.

"How do I know I can trust you?" he asked Walsh.

"You make the choice," replied Walsh. "Trust us, the Kilbanes, or your-self."

Meanwhile, as Walsh went back to Cleveland to discuss Robbins with Cuyahoga County Prosecutor John T. Corrigan, Robbins was confronted by a situation that further softened his attitude.

"You're the guy who said you will kill the first n___ you see!" a black inmate screamed at Rick in the prisoner's dining hall. Robbins didn't reply, but when lunch was finished, several black prisoners moved toward him menacingly. He was protected by white inmates.

After the incident in the dining hall, Rick checked himself into protec-tive custody, with guards around him 24 hours.

"No way am I going to survive," he told Lt. Walsh during their third visit. Still not admitting anything, he asked what deals might be forth-coming for his cooperation. Walsh indicated immunity in the Steele case and a possible reduction of sentence in the Browne murder. Robbins' wife Sandra joined Walsh on the fourth visit and urged her husband to coop-erate. He was still not convinced that his family would be safe. Walsh told him that he had the word of the Justice Department.

On the fifth visit Walsh asked Robbins if he were ready to make a statement. Robbins hesitated. He wanted to know if Walsh understood ex-actly the role that he had played in the murder.

"Rick, you shot her," Walsh said softly.

"Yeah," he finally confessed.

On December 2, 1976, the day after his wife and sons were relocated, Robbins testified to the Cuyahoga County Grand Jury about his activities during the early morning of January 9, 1969. He could not get the image of Robert Steele out of his mind.

At the same time, my pregnancy was starting to show, and I grew out of my clothes. I was still working hard at the motel to get the rooms remod-eled when the unimaginable happened.

Whatever you have said in the dark will be heard in the light, and what you have whispered behind closed doors will be shouted from the rooftops for all to hear! (Lk. 12:3 NLT)

CHAPTER ELEVEN

Arrest Warrants

Martin called to tell me that Robbins had talked, and they had a warrant for his arrest for the Steele murder.

"Call Owen," he said, hanging the phone up quickly.

My fingers trembled as I dialed. "Owen, Marty just called. They picked him up on a warrant for the Steele murder. They're probably on their way to get you. You need to get out of there. Where are you going to go?"

"I have to go," he said. "I'll call you later. I'm going to Vegas."

The night seemed to drag forever as I waited for the call. I tried to get some rest, but I couldn't take my eyes off the clock. Nine o'clock, ten o'clock, eleven o'clock. He finally called.

"Karol and I are in Vegas," Owen told me. "I'll stay here for the night and call you in the morning."

I had a hard time falling asleep so I laid on the couch, watching TV. I furiously switched through the channels, trying to find something that would keep my mind off the dilemma that he was in. The next thing I knew, I woke up on the couch with the sun pouring in the windows. The phone rang and startled me.

"Hello." Martin was on the other end. "My bond is set at a hundred thousand."

"We have to wait for Owen to get back," I said. "I don't know what to do; he does. Call me back later. I'll tell you what he says."

Afternoon came, and I headed for the motel when Owen finally called.

"Carol, they busted into my hotel room last night, and I'm heading back to Cleveland. I have to turn myself in. Come and pick me up at the airport," he said.

"Okay," I said. "Martin called. He has a bond."

"How much?"

"One hundred thousand. You'll probably get the same," I said.

"I'll take care of it. Tell Martin when he calls back."

"Okay. I'll see you at the airport."

Here I was pregnant and due to have a baby in a few months, and I had to make bond for Owen and Martin, who were being accused of murder. After I picked up Owen, we drove downtown to the Justice Center where he was to be booked. I had everything ready to post his bond right away so Owen would not have to be in jail any longer than necessary, just long enough for them to take his picture and get his fingerprints. I called the bondsman as soon as I dropped Owen off at the door, and he was over there in moments. I was afraid the press would get wind he was there. The murder had already been in the papers over the past few days, with the arrests of Robert Steele, Martin, and Owen making headlines. I was sure they would try to get Owen's statement. After he was released, Owen and I ran to the car to avoid media as we dashed for home.

It was the first time we had a chance to talk about the indictment. What was Rick Robbins was doing? Had he made a deal? What was next?

———————

It was December, and winter had started. We went through Christmas, not knowing what the next year had in store for us. Owen kept reassuring me that everything was going to be okay and they couldn't prove anything based on what Rick Robbins was saying. They were not going to take his word, he told me. Owen hired a top criminal lawyer, Ralph Sperli, who began to plan out a strategy to defend him.

As my pregnancy progressed, I was spending many nights alone. Owen told me he was out working on his case. I was wondering whom could he be with in the middle of the night, but I didn't want to stir things up. I thought he had enough to deal with, and I didn't want to add to his worry. The trial was scheduled for the end of February, and I was worried it would conflict with the birth of my child. I was lucky, and they postponed the trial date to March.

On February 10, I woke up with strong pains in my groin area. I looked out the front window of the living room and watched the lights from the ski resort as the pains began to get stronger and closer together. I finally went in and woke Owen up.

"It's time to go," I said. "My pains are getting closer and closer together." Owen took his time getting dressed, going to the kitchen to make coffee as I sat on the couch.

"I gotta go!" I screamed to him. "The pains are getting stronger!"

We drove to Hillcrest Hospital where my doctor was to meet us. I could hardly stand the pain; it began to get so intense. I was screaming with pain as I walked in the door of the hospital. They put me in a wheelchair and took me to a room where I changed into a hospital gown. Owen had already told me he was not coming in the room with me. He would rather sit in the waiting room since he didn't want to see me in pain. So I was by myself. It crossed my mind that he didn't have a problem murdering someone, but he couldn't stand to watch the birth of his child. I knew he was conducting business in the waiting room.

I couldn't help but think of the birth of my daughter. At least this time, I wasn't alone, even if Owen was out in the waiting room. I was excited to be having a baby this time. I knew that I would get to hold my baby and take him or her home with me.

The nurses helped me to breathe as the pain was gaining control over me. Finally, it was time to push, and my child was about to be born. The doctor came in and with my last push, my baby emerged.

"It's a boy," the doctor announced. I was thrilled. I knew Owen wanted a boy to carry on the Kilbane name. I was delighted I gave him a boy.

"That's great," I said. "Go tell his father."

The nurse asked me if I had decided on a name. "Ryan Patrick," I told her.

"That's an Irish name," the nurse responded.

"I know. He's Irish."

Owen came in with a big smile on his face as he saw his son for the first time. He held the tiny baby in his large hands, where Ryan fit so snugly. We were finally a family, and I was so content that for a few moments we forgot about the upcoming trial. After half an hour, Owen left for work, and reality set back in. I had no idea what the future would hold for my little boy. Would his father be a part of his life or would he be in prison?

I left the hospital after two days and took Ryan to his new home. I had placed the bassinet in our room, close to my bed. Ryan's room was decorated in red, white, and blue. His crib had a clown on the front. I had all kinds of neat gifts that we received at my baby shower, so Ryan was set with what he needed when he entered into the world. I was so happy. I felt like Owen and I were finally starting to become closer. I wanted the world to see me as Carol Kilbane, Owen's wife and the mother of his child. I hoped the image of being his prostitute had faded.

Owen was consumed with getting ready for the trial that was about to begin in March. He spent a lot of hours away from home, staying at the office often. When he was home he spent his time holding his son he was so proud of.

We reject all shameful and underhanded methods. We do not try to trick anyone, and we do not distort the Word of God. We tell the truth before God, and all who are honest know that (2 Cor. 4:2 NLT)

Chapter Twelve

Protective Custody

In March of 1977, the trial began after the attorneys had finished picking a jury. I was snuggled with Ryan on the couch sleeping in my arms, watching the noon news. I was disgusted, listening to them smear my baby's father. I began to pray, thinking only of myself and what I wanted. I bargained with God not to let this trial go on. I had waited so long to have Owen's love all to myself, and I was sure Ryan would draw us together and we would finally become a family. As I pleaded with God while nursing my sweet, little son, I had no idea what awaited me.

Tippy and Leo began barking wildly, and I knew something had roused them. The barks got louder and louder. I doubted this was the answer to my prayer. I jumped to my feet and rushed to the window, hoping the disturbance would not startle Ryan. He needed his nap time.

It didn't take long to realize that something serious was happening as the driveway began filling up with police cars. Uniformed officers were everywhere. The forceful knock at the door didn't help my nerves any.

"Carol," one of the officers hollered through the front door, "We have a warrant for you."

"A warrant for what?" I shouted back. I couldn't imagine what I had done this time.

"We have a subpoena for you to appear in court. You have to come with us. Open the door."

"I'm not going anywhere with you." My fingers trembled as I hurriedly dialed the phone to contact Owen's attorney, Ralph Sperli. He needed to know what was going on.

"Hello, this is Carol Kilbane, Owen Kilbane's wife," I screamed in a panic to the woman who answered the phone. "There are police all in my yard; they want me to go with them. They say they have a warrant. What do I do? Owen is in court. Is there any way you can get to him? I need to talk to him or to someone."

"Hold on, Carol, let me see what I can do," she said.

My heart was racing with every second that the clock ticked; each moment seemed like an hour. She finally came back on the line. "Carol, the attorneys said you have to go with the police. You must cooperate with a warrant. You must obey the law. I will tell them as soon as they get back in the office what happened to you," the secretary said.

Terror gripped me as I very reluctantly opened the large wooden front door still holding Ryan in my arms.

"We're taking you into protective custody," the officer said.

"What about my baby?" I asked, trying desperately to hold back my tears.

"Do you have somebody who can keep him?"

"He needs to stay with me," I said. "I'm nursing him, and he doesn't take a bottle."

"You can't take him with you. We'll have to call child services to take him." No way was I giving my son to some strangers, I thought, holding him tightly. My mind instantly flashed back twelve years to the time I had given up my young daughter, Toni. I was not going to give up another child.

"I'm calling my sister-in-law," I wailed as I frantically dialed her number. "Peg, they want to take Ryan. They want to take him away," I yelled into the phone when she answered.

"Who's taking him?" she asked.

"The police."

"What's going on?"

"Just come get my son. I'll explain later." She arrived within minutes.

"What's going on here? Where are you taking her?" Peg asked, shooting daggers from her eyes toward the officers. No one answered her. I gave Ryan a hug, and kissing him on his downy soft head, I handed him to Peg.

"Let's go, Carol," an officer said, grabbing my arm and leading me outside to the squad car parked with an officer already inside ready to drive us away. Within fifteen minutes, I could see that we were headed toward downtown Cleveland.

"Where are we going? Where are you taking me?" I pleaded for answers.

"We're going to the police station," the officer replied.

"For what?"

"We just need to go there. You'll be all right."

As we pulled into the station, I could feel my breast filling up with milk. It was time for Ryan's feeding. He must be screaming. I hoped Peg was able to get him to take a bottle. She had children of her own, I reminded myself. She had experience; she could probably get him to take one. But, I couldn't stop the worry.

"Come on, Carol, let's go inside," the officer led me down a long hall. "Just sit in here. I'll be right back." The room across the hall was full of officers. I could clearly hear what they were saying.

"Where is her baby?" one of them asked.

"You better get him back to her, or we'll be in big trouble," another one said. "Get the phone number where he is. Let her call to make a meeting point and let's get them back together."

"Carol, what's the number for your sister-in-law?" an officer asked me.

"Why?"

"We need to get your son."

"You better!" I yelled.

"Peg, the police need me to get Ryan," I said when we got her on the line. "So where can we meet you to get him?"

"What is going on?" Peg shouted.

"I'll have to explain later," I said. "We'll meet you on the corner of Route 306 and Mayfield Road, in the parking lot of the car dealer."

I was handcuffed with my arms in front as they placed me back in the police cruiser. We headed toward our meeting point. When we arrived, the officer in the front seat got out of the car.

"Just stay in the car, Carol. I'll get your son," he said.

I could see Peg's car in the distance. I watched as the officer walked toward her, and she placed Ryan in his arms. They spoke briefly, then Peg got back into her car and drove off. As the officer began to walk toward me I could see Ryan was all bundled up. Just knowing that my baby was in that bundle of blanket made my breasts swell even more in anticipation. He reached down and placed Ryan in my arms. I drew him as close to me as I possibly could, trying not to cry. I took a deep breath to calm down. I wanted him to nurse and sense the comfort of my arms, not the turmoil that was going on inside me.

As we drove away, I realized we were heading in a different direction from the police station. We pulled into the driveway of a local hotel, the Charter House, which was a few blocks away from our motel.

"Why are we stopping here?" I angrily asked the officer.

"Just come with me," he responded. "And don't ask so many questions." As he opened the back door to the car, he grabbed my arm again, this time leading me to a room that was adjoined to another containing several policemen. Entering the room I caught a glimpse of several men standing on each side of the door talking.

"What the heck is going on?" I shouted out, about to lose the little patience I had left.

"Just relax and take care of your son," the only female cop said.

"I want to call my husband," I said. "I want to go home. Get me out of here."

I paced back and forth in the room for hours, wondering if Owen was doing anything to get me back home. Was he going to come and get me? Was he looking for us? Maybe he had no idea where we were. How was he going to find Ryan and me?

The police were trying to keep me comfortable and distracted, suggesting that I watch TV and relax. How could I relax? I didn't even know why I was being held against my wishes. At 7 p.m. an elderly gentleman arrived. Holding out his hand, with a smile on his face, he offered me his business card.

"Hello Carol," the man said. "Owen sent me. My name is Tom Shaughnessy. Owen has hired me to represent you."

"Represent me for what?" I asked, quite curious.

"You are being held in protective custody."

"Protected from what?"

"They are saying you need protection," he said.

"Protection from who and what?" I asked.

"Until we figure out what is going on, Owen does not want you to say anything to anyone. Just hold onto to your son and try to sleep. We will see you in the morning."

"What do you mean, 'morning'?'" I screamed.

"I'm sorry Carol, the court is closed. There is nothing we can do at this hour of the night. Don't worry, we'll have you out in the morning." He stood up to leave, instructing me once again, "Just be quiet. Don't say a word to anyone who might try to talk to you."

"Don't worry, I have nothing to say to these idiots," I stated indignantly, my last ounce of patience fleeing. "How can they just take me like this, out of my house, and get away with it?"

"They won't get away with it!" Shaughnessy answered. "Owen just wants to make sure you are okay and let you know he is working on this. They won't let him come up to see you, so he sent me to let you know that he is doing what he needs to do. He will see you in the morning. I have to go now. I will see you in the morning. The police will be bringing you down to the courthouse."

"This is insane!" I snarled at the attorney as though he were my abductor. Shaughnessy backed away, suddenly speeding up his departure.

"Bye Carol," he said. "Don't forget, lips closed."

I waved as he left, trying to behave a little more demurely. It was already late in the evening. I knew Ryan would sleep as long as he was dry and close to his mother. So, I laid back onto the bed, trying to turn my mind to what was on the TV. I wanted to get my mind on something other than the long night ahead. In my state, with tunnel vision, I could only see the officers as very unjust. I wanted to get away from them as soon as possible.

The female officer came into the room. "Do you need anything Carol?" she asked.

"Yeah. Let me call my husband," I demanded.

"We can't let you do that. Do you feel like talking?" she asked, too politely for my taste.

"No, get away from me. Just leave me alone," I demanded, knowing it was the right thing to do. But I wished I could talk to someone. I'd never felt so alone.

I tossed and turned in the midst of a forever night. When my eyes finally opened, I realized I was not in a dream. It was morning, and the drama was still going on. The cops' undercover mode continued as they snuck me out the back door of the hotel to the police car. We were on our way to the courthouse. I couldn't help but wonder if the drivers in the cars alongside the cruiser were wondering what they had me in the car for? I stared straight ahead, hoping they wouldn't recognize my face.

I was so anxious to see Owen. He had to have been up all night working on a way to get me out of the demented situation that I felt the police had created. As we approached the Justice Center, I could tell nothing changed. We pulled into the parking garage at the rear entrance. Once more, a strong arm of the law escorted me into the building and placed me in a room outside the courtroom. Placing Ryan in his little seat on the table in front of me, I could feel my anxiety churning to a boil. It was hard for me to sit still. The door opened suddenly, and I was confronted with the source of my anxiety. There stood Robert Ressler, the FBI agent. Being a man of action, Ressler got right to the point.

"I hope you didn't tell Owen about the statement you gave me?" Ressler questioned.

I remembered Shaughnessy's instructions not to answer any questions. This seemed like a good place to begin, so I didn't answer.

Ressler continued, "He is a very sick man; he needs to be locked up. You need to cooperate, or you will be joining him."

"Get away from me," I screamed. "You caused me enough grief."

He reached out his hand to touch Ryan, "What a cute baby."

"Get your hands off of my child," I yelled, shoving his hand away. "I know you're trying to scare me into thinking that I could lose Ryan and go to jail. I know that Owen has more power than you do. He'll have me out of here soon." I laughed at him. Shaking his head, he left the room.

I was eventually summoned to the courtroom. Looking around for Owen, I found him sitting over by a table next to his attorney. I walked over to him. Weary from all that had gone on the day and night before, I couldn't hold in my emotions anymore. It was like a dam broke, tears suddenly let loose and I began to weep uncontrollably.

"It'll be okay Carol," Owen assured me. "Our defense is already working on their strategy to get you back home. Just trust us," he whispered.

Martin and Robert Steele were also in the courtroom. They both looked at me, puzzled as to why I was there.

The prosecutors appeared, and I sat down in the swivel chair positioned in front of the defense table. Shaughnessy was talking to Owen, and I could tell what he was thinking from his facial expressions. It was obvious that my common law husband was feeling helpless; there was nothing he could do. He was angry that his wife and son had been kidnapped by the police.

Shaughnessy leaned over to me, speaking softly so no one could hear us, "Don't answer the prosecutors when they ask whether or not you were a prostitute."

Oh my God, I thought, flustered at even the thought that they were going to ask me that.

"That can't come out!" I furiously whispered back.

The court proceedings started as Carmino Marino, the lead prosecutor stood up. "We want Carol Braun to be kept in protective custody. She should be held under police guard as a material witness in this case," he said. "We're afraid for her life."

I couldn't think of who they were trying to protect me from, after all Owen would hurt anyone who would try to harm me or his newborn son. The attorneys chatted back and forth for several minutes.

"She has evidence that we need and they will harm her to keep her quiet," Marino insisted.

"Bring her to my chambers," the judge commanded. The bailiff ordered me to follow him as we walked behind the judge's bench into the private chambers of Judge Nahra. I stood, terrified, with Ryan in my arms.

"Take a seat," Judge Nahra said and he began to question me. "Are you afraid for your life, young lady?"

"No," I replied. "Who am I supposed to be afraid of?"

"Are you afraid of Owen?" he asked.

Looking down at Ryan, I said, "No way! He is the father of this little boy. I can't see him hurting either one of us. We are his family." I tried desperately to reassure the judge.

"We just want to make sure you are safe and not in harm's way," he explained to me. What did this judge know that I didn't, I wondered?

"Take her back into the courtroom. I'll be right in," the judge said.

We walked back into the courtroom, full of total silence. All eyes were focused on me, wondering what had taken place with the judge. They were waiting for me to speak. I looked at Owen and smiled.

"Arise. Your Honorable Judge Nahra," the bailiff commanded. Everyone stood as the judge entered.

"This young lady is being released and will be able to come back and forth to this courtroom on her own word," the judge ruled.

The defense was furious. Already the case was not going the way they wanted it to.

But soon, too soon, my turn was coming. I was about to be asked to take the stand to argue whether I was married to Owen or not. We were now having a trial within a trial before the actual murder trial could begin. I had to take the stand to prove I was Owen's common law wife, so that I wouldn't have to take the stand in the actual murder trial.

"Your Honor, may we have her take the stand so we can ask her a few questions?" Marino requested.

"Yes, she may," answered the judge. "Carol, take the stand," the judge ordered.

I had still had Ryan in my arms. I walked to the stand and placed my hand on the Bible. "I swear to tell the truth and nothing but the truth, so help me God."

My heart pounded loudly in my ears as I seated myself, turning to face a courtroom full of curious eyes. Marino began to hammer me with his questions about the prostitution charge. He focused on that one issue, hammering at it until he got what he wanted. I refused to admit my guilt.

"I don't remember!" I answered trying to remain calm.

"What was the charge?" he continued.

"I don't remember," I said again, realizing that I had just perjured myself.

"Wasn't the charge prostitution?" he reminded me.

"I don't know what you call it." It was apparent that I was not going to help them, especially not by admitting to everyone that I had been a prostitute. I wanted to slide under the judge's bench and disappear.

By this time our witnesses were being called forward. Their purpose was to try and convince the judge that I was Mrs. Kilbane, not Miss Braun.

"Will Martin Kilbane please take the stand?" Shaughnessy called out.

"Raise your right hand. Do you swear to tell the truth, the whole truth and nothing but the truth so help you God?"

"I do," Martin said.

"Is your brother married?" Shaughnessy asked.

"Yes, he is."

"Who is he married to?"

"Carol Kilbane."

"Will you point to her?"

"She is sitting right there," Martin said.

"Thank you. The defense rests," Shaughnessy said.

Marino stood up to cross examine. "Hasn't your brother lived with a number of women? Isn't there another woman living with him in Chardon right now?"

"Not to my knowledge," Martin said. One lie was being told to cover up the other.

"Is your brother married to Miss Braun?"

"Yes, he is."

"As a matter of fact, doesn't he have a lot of women?" Marino asked.

"I don't know what you mean," Martin responded.

"That's all."

Shaughnessy called our next witness. "I call J. Dubin to the stand." Dubin was Owen's brother-in-law, married to his sister, Peg.

"Do you do the taxes for Owen Kilbane?" Shaughnessy asked him.

"Yes I do."

"Does he file single or married?"

"Married," Dubin answered.

"Did he file married in 1969?"

"Yes, he did."

"Did you take a trip to Las Vegas back in 1967 with Carol and Owen?"

"Yes, I did," Dubin answered.

"You can step down now."

The defense's strategy was to bring to the stand anyone that could prove there was a marriage. They were trying to prove that we had exchanged vows in Vegas.

I finally realized that the defense was trying to hide the fact that I had met with Ressler in St. Louis when I made a statement. They desperately needed to keep me off the stand in the murder trial.

Don't tremble with fear! Didn't I tell you long ago? Didn't you hear Me? I alone am God—no one else is a mighty Rock (Is. 44:8 CEV).

CHAPTER THIRTEEN

Life Sentence

Now back to the beginning of my story when I had just been sentenced to six months in jail for contempt of court after refusing to take the stand against Owen in the Steele trial. . .

They had taken my six-week-old baby from me, and I had no idea when I would see him again. I could hear the keys clanging as an officer approached the door of my holding cell, outside the courtroom.

"Carol, let's go. We're moving you to the county jail," the officer explained.

Relax, I told myself as they transferred me to the new location; it will only be for the night. The pain in my breasts was becoming unbearable; milk was seeping through my clothes. All I could do was to hold on to them, hoping the pain would decrease. Ryan must be getting hungry, I thought, my heart breaking because I couldn't feed him.

A guard approached me, distracting me. "You should get some pills from the nurse so you can dry up your milk," she said.

"No thanks. I'll deal with the pain."

I stayed focused on the thought that Owen and Shaughnessy were working hard to get me home safely with Ryan. They were able to get Ryan to me before; of course, they could do it again. Shaughnessy was appealing my case. So how could they keep me?

I was restless, unable to get my mind off my son. One of the inmates noticed the discomfort I was experiencing with my breasts and approached me.

"You can release your breasts yourself," she said. "Just pump them and let the milk be released so there'll be less pressure."

"Thanks," I said. I stepped into the bathroom where I slowly began drawing some of the milk out. I could feel an instant relief.

What could be taking so long? I wondered. Why was I still here? I tried calling, but I couldn't find Owen anywhere. I finally resorted to calling our attorney.

"Sorry, Carol," the secretary said. "Shaughnessy isn't here. He said he will try to get you out in the morning. He couldn't make your bond tonight."

"I have to spend the night in jail?" I shouted. I was shocked. What a blow; my emotions went into a tailspin. The fears flooded my mind, and the questions came faster than I could express them: Where was my son? Who was he with? Who was taking my place with Owen tonight? My heart was breaking. I wanted to feel my child in my arms. I knew his heart had to be breaking like mine. He had to want his mother's touch, to be held and fed. I needed his touch too. My baby needed and trusted me, and I needed him. I could not stop incessantly worrying about him.

One of the women turned on the evening news. There we were, blasted across the airwaves as the feature story of the evening news. The camera showed me walking into the courtroom with my son all bundled up. They reported a prostitute of Owen Kilbane was arrested today for contempt of court. She refused to get on the witness stand. "Prostitute makes statement to FBI."

I was dying inside, but I had to remain strong in front of the other inmates. The secret life I had kept hidden so well from family and friends had just been emblazoned across the sky like a banner on the tail of a plane. Oh God, I want to go home, I thought. But no one knew, and no one heard my silent cry.

I had heard many times that while you are in prison you can't even give an appearance of weakness or the others will take advantage of that weakness. So, I just did what so many do. I stuffed my emotions deep inside. Playing it cool, I pretended that I wasn't hurting. After all, I was going to be out tomorrow. I was confident that I had a man who could do anything. He had enough money to buy anything, including my freedom. I was the talk of the dorm that night. The other inmates seemed to be impressed with me. I just wished the judge would see things their way.

Winter was ending, and cold air blew in where the windows were broken out. The plastic covering them didn't help. The place should've been condemned. Instead it was used as a holding place. A new facility was in the process of being built, and they weren't going to throw money into new windows here. All the inmates, including myself began yelling. "It's cold in here; we're freezing!" It didn't do any good.

"We're not carpenters," the staff yelled back.

My bed was a small, foam mattress on a metal frame on the top bunk. It was terribly uncomfortable. I was distracted from my self-pity when I heard a young girl in the corner of the room getting violently ill. She startled me to my feet when she started screaming uncontrollably.

"Leave her alone," the girls yelled. "She's going through withdrawal from drugs."

I wanted to do something for her, but there really wasn't anything I could do. "She has to go through it cold turkey," one of the other girls yelled. At that moment she collapsed onto the floor into an unrestrained seizure and passed out.

"Is she okay?" I called out. "She's not dead, is she?"

"No, she'll be okay. Just cover her with a blanket. She'll sleep through the night."

"She'll freeze to death," I said. "I'll have to get her another blanket. Guard, can I get another blanket?" I yelled out.

"There is only one blanket per person," the guard yelled back.

It was out of my hands; there was nothing I could do. I wrapped the blanket as tightly as I could to cover her completely and climbed back into bed. I thanked God that drugs were one thing that I'd never wanted to try.

I wanted to cry, for the girl, for myself, my baby, and for Owen, but I didn't dare. So I closed my eyes, shutting out the pain and eventually dozing off to sleep.

Breakfast came very early, and it was often the best meal of the day, generally consisting of boxed cereal with toast. As I glanced around the room, my eyes focused on the morning paper. I was unable to hide my shock. The headlines read *Prostitute Not Wife*. My picture with Ryan was plastered across the front page. I couldn't help but wonder who was going to see this. Everyone, I thought.

Shame covered me like a thick blanket, and I became anxious with this new development. How was this all going to play out? My sense was that there would be no fairy tale ending to this chapter in my life. I kept my eyes glued to the TV, watching the news every night. Ted Henry, the news caster, and I would probably never meet, yet each night he was the one who explained a little more to me about my life and just how my world was collapsing around me.

It was a very hard pill to swallow, realizing that Owen couldn't do a thing for me. He couldn't even help himself. So I remained in jail, waiting to see what was going to happen next. Such a short time ago my dream of us coming together as a family was within reach. Now that dream was as shattered as a broken window. Waiting in jail was probably the hardest thing I've ever done in my life. As I longed for my child, my milk was drying up. I wondered how Owen, Martin, and Robert Steele were doing as they waited to learn their fate. I hadn't heard from Shaughnessy since he had said he would be filing papers to win my appeal.

The final day of the trial came. The closing arguments were given with prosecutors demanding a guilty verdict and the defense doing their best to persuade the jury to ignore my statement to the FBI. The defense lawyers said there was no case, that a man already sentenced to jail was trying to save his own hide. The jury received the case on April 7th, 1977, Holy Thursday.

The deliberations went quickly. They didn't want to be away from their families for the Easter holiday. The jury had reached its verdict. Everyone was called back to the courtroom. Judge Robert Steele, dressed in a green plaid suit and chain smoking as he had done at every recess throughout the whole trial, approached the courtroom. He talked with the reporters as he moved along; they wished him luck. The Kilbane brothers were silent. It was reported that at 8:07 p.m. on April 11th, the jury foreman handed Judge Nahra the ballots. After reading them, the judge instructed the defendants to rise.

Then he spoke, "The jury finds all three defendants guilty of first degree murder."

Judge Nahra then sentenced them each to fifteen years to life. The local news interrupted the scheduled program to announce the verdict.

Life. Life. Life. The word pulsated in my brain. It was all I could hear. What was I going to do? Where was my son? Now that his father was going to be locked up for so long, my baby seemed like an orphan. I didn't know who had him. I began to panic. I ran to the phone to call my lawyer, but it was late at night. I wasn't able to reach him until the next morning. Many of our friends had been taking turns watching over Ryan. I discovered that our dear friends, Susan and Chief, were taking care of him that day.

Owen was given a month to get all his business affairs in order. He would be transported to Lucasville Prison in southern Ohio, a four-hour drive from Cleveland.

I burned up the phone lines calling Shaughnessy to find out what was happening with my appeal. Finally, after thirty days, I was allowed out on bond. I was getting released while the courts battled out my case. My thoughts were on Owen and our baby. I wanted so badly to be with them, even if just for a few moments by ourselves, to be a family before Owen was whisked away to prison. This became my obsession. I asked the courts if I could have a special visit upon my release and was pleased when they granted my request.

Chief and Susan were bringing Ryan to me for the first time. I was going to see my sweet baby soon! But I was also going to be saying goodbye to Owen. It was bittersweet. I didn't know if I was saying goodbye to Owen for a while or forever. Neither of us knew.

Part of me was jumping for joy at the thought of seeing Ryan, of being able to hold him once again. But the jury's decision drew a dark cloud over our future.

A guard placed me in a room to wait for Ryan and Owen. I knew that soon I'd be going home with Ryan. All these concerns were flying through my head as Susan and Chief walked in the room with Ryan sleeping contently in her arms. I wanted to wake him so I could see his eyes, so he would know that I was there, but I decided that it was best for him to sleep. I held him close, enjoying snuggling with my sweet baby boy. As I looked up, Owen came into the room, dressed in his jail coveralls. I could tell by the look in his eyes that he wanted to hold Ryan, so I handed him over. Susan and Chief left the room to give us the privacy we so desperately needed.

I turned to Owen, "I miss you. I'm so relieved that Ryan and I are going home, but, honey, I'm scared for you. The judge gave you fifteen years to life."

"Don't worry," Owen said with a bit of bravado. "We're already working on the appeals. Just as you won your bond, we'll win our appeal. What they did, they won't get away with it. I'll be home before you know it. Just hang in there and take care of Ryan. I'll write and call you as soon as I can."

I wrapped my arms around him tightly to say goodbye, letting his coveralls soak up my bitter tears.

"It will be okay. Trust me," Owen said. "Haven't I always been right? When I say I will do something, don't I do it?" he asked.

"Yes," I answered.

Our time ended. I turned to my freedom, walking past the guard toward the exit of the jail. Owen went through his door to confinement. We walked away from each other, not knowing what our future held. I felt like I was on a roller coaster ride of emotions.

I know all the things you do—your love, your faith, your service, and your patient endurance. And I can see your constant improvement in all these things (Rev. 3:19 NLT).

CHAPTER FOURTEEN

Visiting Owen

I was going to see Owen for the first time since he had been sent to prison, and I could barely contain my excitement. He was being held at a prison in Mansfield, Ohio, a two-hour drive away from home, for six weeks of observation. After that, he would be transferred to the top security prison in Lucasville, near the Kentucky border. It would take four hours to travel there, a trip I was dreading to make.

Ryan had started walking, and it was hard keeping him confined. I knew it was going to be tough keeping him at the visiting table. It took a bit of time to pass through the check-in station as all my bottles and my diaper bag were checked thoroughly before we were allowed to enter the prison. I tried to keep myself calm. I didn't want to draw any attention to myself. There was so much pent up anxiety, knowing I was going to be able to see and touch Owen. I handed the guard my pass, and he directed me to the table sitting against a gray brick wall. I sat myself down and took out some of Ryan's toys, placing them on the table in front of him. I needed to keep him busy.

"Daddy will be out soon," I told my little boy while we waited for him to come through the door. I glanced at everyone coming through. Owen finally appeared with a large smile on his face.

"I am so glad to see you both," he said as he hugged us. "I miss you."

"We miss you too," I said. "Oh God, I wish I could take you home."

Sitting next to him made me feel secure even though he was locked up. I felt complete when we were together. And it was amazing to watch him play with Ryan. They laughed together as if they had no cares in the world.

"Are you okay?" he asked me.

"No, I don't like our family being separated."

"I don't either, but it won't be for long. They're working on the appeal, and we are going to be home soon. Just take care of Ryan and run the business. I'll be home before you know it." The bell rang, and our two-hour visit was over.

"Tell Daddy goodbye," I told Ryan. "I don't want to leave you. This is too hard," I said to Owen.

"Carol, you have to be strong for us," he said. "I'll call you tonight. Have a safe trip home."

We could only hold each other for a moment. "I love you," he said.

"I love you too. I'll write soon." Watching him walk away broke my heart, I knew it would be a few weeks before we would see each other again.

Ryan and I headed home. He slept most of the way. I was glad he didn't see his mom crying. The songs I heard on the radio made me even sadder as they reminded me of our times together. How was I going to make it for fifteen years? I thought. What if he doesn't get his appeal?

Owen called that night to make sure we made it home safely.

"Carol, I know you're worried," he said. "I want you to stop that and keep taking care of our affairs. We need the money to pay the attorney. The appeals are going to cost us a lot. So your job is to make things run smooth. Can you do that for me?"

"Yes, I just want this nightmare to be over. I still have my appeal to worry about too."

"It's all going to be okay. Remember, the family that prays together, stays together," he said.

"Say goodnight to Ryan," I said. I handed Ryan the phone and helped him to hold it to his tiny ear. I could hear Owen saying, "Daddy loves you. Be good for Mommy."

"Da da," he squeaked, handing the phone back to me.

"I have to go, Carol. I'll call in a few days."

"Bye, I love you."

I didn't want Ryan to see me cry, so I wiped my tears, picking him up and tossing him into the air. He loved to fly in the air like an airplane. When he became exhausted, I gave him his bath and put him to bed.

I poured myself a drink. I needed to forget the pain, and I was coping the best way I knew how. I took the dogs out before bed and then climbed up the stairs. My room was at the top of the A-frame. It was very hard sleeping there without Owen. I decided I wanted to be closer to Ryan so I moved into the bedroom next to his and slept in the waterbed. I rolled a joint, knowing it would calm me down so I could go to sleep.

I spent the next two weeks trying to keep busy, traveling to the motel and back. I took Ryan some of the days and left him home with a sitter the rest of the time.

The rooms needed some major improvements. I was quite the handy woman. There wasn't too much I wouldn't tackle. I set my mind to replacing the roof, a real challenge. I was all about saving us money. Owen liked that quality about me.

Martha watched the desk often. Her boyfriend, Bobby, was acting more and more abusive towards her. He finally got busted and was sent to jail again. It was the only time she got a break from him beating her. I would watch her son, Bobby Jr., on occasions.

Owen called to update me, "Marty and I got transferred yesterday. You and Jenny can come down this weekend to visit," he said. Jenny was Marty's girlfriend. They had dated for years. He never did tell her the truth about his part in the murders. I wasn't about to tell her, even if she did ask.

"Great, I'll give Jenny a call when we hang up," I said. "How is the place?"

"It's rough. This is maximum security; these guys don't care. They'll kill you and not think twice about it. I really have to watch my back."

"Please be careful," I said.

"I will. Got to go," he said. "I'll see you Saturday. Bye, I love you."

"Bye, I love you too."

Before I knew it, it was 4:00 on Friday, and Jenny and I headed down south. The ride wouldn't seem so bad because we would share the driving. We decided going the night before and staying in a local motel close by would be better for all of us. Ryan could get his bath, and Jenny and I could freshen up in the morning. We had to arrive early to the prison to stand in line so we wouldn't miss out on the visit. If too many people showed up, we would be turned away. They only allowed so many in the visiting room.

The maximum security prison had strict rules we had to follow to go in. Getting through the security was harder at this place. We took a number, and when our number was called, we walked through a detector. All our belongings were completely searched. We had to take off our shoes and jewelry. Sometimes they searched visitors with a large paddle that was used to scan the entire body. They were making sure no weapons were going to be smuggled in.

Nothing came into the prison that was already open. We had to throw away anything that was already open. We could purchase food and drink throughout the visit from vending machines that lined one wall. I came with plenty of change. These visits were all day long.

I approached the guard sitting at the desk and handed him my pass. I was assigned to a table facing where the inmates would enter. All inmates were asked to face the same way. There was no body contact allowed except for a quick hug when the prisoner arrived. The visit could be terminated if they caught us touching. All hands must be above the table at all times. Ryan was very active, and it was going to be a challenge to get him to sit at the table.

Jenny sat at the table next to me as we both anticipated their arrival. Martin came first, then Owen behind him. Ryan ran up to Owen, a sight I loved to see. They both were grinning from ear to ear. He walked over and put his arm around me for a family hug.

The visits graduated from once a month, then twice a month, and finally, we could go every weekend. The first two years seemed to go by so slowly. I was very lonely. I craved attention. One of my brother Richard's friends, Bob, came around a lot when Richard would visit me. We would smoke pot and then have a few drinks together. One night my brother had crashed on the couch. Ryan was sleeping. Bob and I were sitting on the couch. Smoking pot caused me to laugh a lot. We were enjoying our time so much. My emotional needs were being met, and Bob and I ended up getting physically involved. This made me question whether I wanted to stay with Owen. Fifteen years was starting to wear on my mind. Maybe Bob and I could start a new life, I thought, even though he was younger than I was.

We spent a lot of time together, and our relationship grew. I was still going on my weekend visits to Owen, but I finally started to make excuses to avoid going to visit. Owen knew something was wrong. He fired questions at me, and I responded with lies. I finally got enough nerve to go on a visit. This time I was going to be open and tell him I had found someone else, and I wasn't going to come visit anymore. I also had to break the news that I had become pregnant. I wasn't looking forward to the difficult visit.

"Owen, I have something to tell you," my voice choked. "I don't think I can wait for you for fifteen years, and I've met someone else."

Silence. "I am in here," he finally said. "How can I fight for you?"

"I don't know, but I have feelings for Bob. We're spending a lot of time together," I paused. "I didn't want to tell you this, but I'm going to have his baby."

Owen lowered his head. I could see tears running down his cheeks. I had only seen Owen cry a couple of times since we had been together—once when a friend's wife was killed coming home from New York on a plane that crashed into the water. The same family lost their little boy on a vacation. When I looked at the tears coming down his cheeks, I knew he was hurting and it was real to him.

"Owen, it's so hard being away from you."

"I know," he said. "I'm trying to work on the appeal. Hopefully it will be in our favor soon."

"I am so confused," I said. "I believe you love me, yet something in me wants to run. I don't know what it is."

"Carol, I know our life hasn't been easy. You have to know that I care. Look at this little boy," he pointed to Ryan. "That should be proof that I care. You are the only one who has my son."

By the end of the visit, I was convinced I had to break off the relationship with Bob, and I was going to end this little life that was growing inside of me. I hugged Owen goodbye, reassuring him I would be back.

The ride home seemed longer than normal. I knew what I had to do, but I knew it was not going to be easy. I tucked Ryan into his bed, went down to the kitchen and poured myself a drink, preparing to call Bob.

"Hello Bob," I said.

"You're back. How did Owen take the news about us?" he asked.

"Not really good. I have some sad news for you."

"What do you mean?"

"Bob, I'm sorry that I've misled you. I really enjoyed our time together, but I won't be seeing you anymore."

"Are you serious?" he asked.

"Bob, I'm staying with Owen."

"You said that he'll be gone too long and that you won't be able to wait."

"I know what I said. I've changed my mind," I told him. "He'll be getting out soon. He's going to win his appeal."

Bob pleaded with me not to end our relationship. It was hard to let go, yet I knew what would be best for us both.

"Goodbye Bob, I must hang up."

I took another drink to drown out the emotional turmoil I was feeling inside.

I never told him about the pregnancy. I made an appointment the next week to have a D&C. The doctor made it sound like a normal procedure. It would be real quick, in and out in a few hours. After all, it wasn't a baby yet. It was just a blob, I was told. This way I wouldn't have any guilt. The doctor didn't say it, but he knew what I was really doing was covering up my mistake.

———————◆———————

I wrapped my life around taking care of the property, raising Ryan, and fighting to get Owen out on his appeal. I needed to keep myself out on appeal too. I still had five months hanging over me for contempt of court. Martha and I were becoming very close. Her boyfriend Bobby ended up going to jail again. I asked her to move in the house with her son, Bobby Jr., who was the same age as Ryan. Bobby and Ryan spent a lot of play time together. They attended birthdays and holidays together, since both of them had fathers who were incarcerated.

On my visits with Owen we discussed the tax liens that we had on our property and how someday we would have to deal with the IRS to straighten things out. We needed someone we could trust, and Martha's name kept coming up in the conversation.

Then, I got a call from my lawyer. "Hello Carol, it's Thomas Shaughnessy. I have some bad news for you," he said.

"What?" I felt panicked. "Owen's not getting his appeal?"

"No, that's not it," he said. "Carol, the courts have ruled against yours, and they're asking that you turn yourself in to do the remainder of your time."

"Can't you take it to a higher court?" I asked.

"No, there is only one more court we can go to," he answered.

"When would I have to go in?" I asked.

"You have to be down to the Justice Center by next week."

I decided to talk it over with Owen, to get his opinion on whether or not we should appeal again, or if I should do the time. It was Wednesday and I figured if I was going to turn myself in, at least I could go see Owen that weekend.

"I'll call you when I get back from seeing Owen," I told Shaughnessy. "I'll let you know what we decide then."

I went to see Owen on my own, leaving Ryan home with Martha. It was a lonely drive by myself, especially knowing I probably wouldn't be doing it for the next five months.

When I got there, I held onto Owen's arm tightly, discussing the ordeal I was about to go through. "Carol, I know you think we should keep fighting the appeal," he said. "But we've spent enough on appeal funds to

Shaughnessy. There is no sense in wasting money on something you'll have to do anyways. Why postpone the inevitable? I don't like it that you have to leave Ryan, but I think he'll be okay with Martha."

"No. Owen, if I have to be away from him that long, I want him to be with family. I'm going to have Richard take care of him. He can live at the house where Ryan will be in his own bed. Richard can watch the house and take care of the dogs."

"I would rather have Martha do it so she can bring Ryan down to visit," he pushed. I wasn't comfortable with what he was asking. He seemed too insistent on having her watch him. In my mind, I began to question what kind of relationship they had.

"No," I insisted. "I am having Richard do it. He can come down and visit with you and bring Ryan and anything you need from the motel," I demanded. Richard owned his own barber shop, but he could have someone else run it while he took care of Ryan, ran the hotel, and reported to Owen what was going on.

It was time to go and I hung on to Owen tightly, not wanting to let go. I turned to wipe the tear that began to fall from my eye, preventing the flood of tears that were about to gush out. I walked out of the prison, knowing I was about to walk into one myself.

I was naked, and you gave me clothing. I was sick, and you cared for me. I was in prison, and you visited me (Mt. 25:36 NLT).

CHAPTER FIFTEEN

Back to Jail

Richard drove me to the Justice Center, and I kissed and hugged Ryan goodbye. I held back crying as I walked up the steps to the center to turn myself in to finish the rest of my sentence. I walked to the window and told them I was here to finish my time. The metal door opened, the bars clanging as I walked forward. It slammed behind me. I felt trapped. This was going to be the sound I would hear for the next five months. We rode the elevator to the third floor. I was directed down the hall to stand and wait. An inmate came out, wiping her hands.

"You're next," the guard said. "Let's get your fingerprints."

The guard grabbed my hand, placing it against the blotter containing the black ink. Starting with my right hand, she placed my pinky finger into the ink, then twisted it onto the white square, making my print. She continued until all my fingers were done. She handed me a wet wipe to clean the remainder of the ink off my fingers.

"Step up here to the camera," she instructed.

She placed a number below my chin and asked me to stand still and smile. I had nothing to smile about so I just stood there.

"Come with me," the guard said. I was handed a blue uniform with a pair of huge white underwear along with a pair of tennis shoes. I was instructed to take a shower and wash my hair with a strong soap that was to remove any lice or bugs. They wanted to make sure no one would bring them into the jail. Drying my body off, I felt like I was going to explode. I could picture Richard driving back to the house, taking Ryan by his little hand and going about their day. I had only been there for about a half hour and already, I felt pinned in. I wanted out. I was homesick. I began talking to myself, telling myself that I was going to do this. I had no choice. I was locked in; there was no going back.

We walked through a door at the end of the hall to a large room with a glass sliding door. Outside the door was a camera that displayed everything on a monitor that was in the office by the guards. The door opened by the guards and inside was a large room surrounded by cells on all four walls. In the middle was a bench where a few women were sitting watching the TV mounted on the wall. Their heads turned to see the new girl.

I followed the guard as she led me to my cell. There was a small metal bed with a flat thin mattress with no pillow. The door had a small square hole large enough shove something through if the door was shut. The toilet was silver metal, and there was a sink with buttons to push to get water.

"Make your bed and then you can come out into the dayroom," the guard said.

I wondered what the women were thinking as I took the thin sheets and blanket to make my bed. The metal bed was such a big change from the waterbed I had at home. I could only think that Owen had to have the same kind of set up I did.

I walked out into the dayroom where a few were playing cards and some were reading. I began to get acquainted with the women.

"What are you in here for?" one lady asked.

"I have to finish my time from a contempt of court charge, from my husband's murder trial." They all commented on how twisted the law was. They supported me, saying they were crazy to have me in there. The door opened and in came a cart that held our dinner.

The night dragged on and on before it was finally eleven o'clock and we had to retire to our cells to get locked in for the night. I hated the sound of the door closing, as I knew I was really locked in. I climbed onto the hard bed, putting my blanket close to my mouth, and I cried into it so the sounds would not echo out into the cells. I didn't want to be labeled as a cry baby. Hours went by before I finally fell asleep. Morning came with the clang of the big door, and we went to the dayroom again. Everything was done in the dayroom, and we only got to leave it when we had visitors or went to church.

Owen knew the warden and sent word to him that I was arriving so he could see what could be done to make my time go easier. I was called down to the office, and one of the guards told me that I could be a trustee, which meant I would help them out in the office, checking in the inmates. The other girls were jealous. I never told them about my connections. Working as a trustee made my time go by faster since I wasn't in the dayroom all day, having the time drag. I could also earn good time so my sentence would be reduced.

On weekends we had visits. I told Richard it would be too hard on me to see Ryan, so it would be better if he didn't bring him to visit. I would have a hard time watching him leave. Martha visited me and sometimes Richard came by himself.

Richard was visiting Owen and would return to see me and give me the messages Owen wanted me to have. We would write often, but there were things we couldn't put in our letters, as the guards would read all incoming mail. I began catching Owen in more and more lies. Doubts would rise in my mind, and I questioned our relationship. He was always telling me things would be okay and things would go well for a while, but then everything would collapse on us.

My jail stay was going rather easy. Missing Ryan was the hardest part. I felt stripped of my motherhood. I befriended one of the inmates, Terri, a dark-skinned girl. She struggled with her family. Most of them were taking drugs. She didn't want her daughters around all the drugs, fighting, and even shootings. We would talk about our lives and how we would change them if we could. We got bored with our stay in prison. There was hardly any excitement going on so Terri and I decided to create some. It was lunch time, and we were served spaghetti.

"Did you ever have a food fight?" I asked Terri.

"No," she replied.

I raised my arm from the plate, taking a handful of the spaghetti and quickly threw it directly across the table. It landed right on her face. She immediately responded, throwing spaghetti right back at me and hitting my face. Noodles were sliding down my cheeks. The fight was on, and soon spaghetti was flying back and forth. The other inmates moved away, not wanting to get into our line of fire. Nor did they want a part of the activity, as it would certainly be a lock down if we were caught. One of the inmates watching the door yelled, "Someone's coming. Hurry, clean up." The inmates threw the spaghetti back on the trays while Terri and I ran into the shower stalls to clean up, leaving no trace of the food fight on us. The guard entered the dayroom, collected the trays, and asked where I was.

"I am in the shower," I called out.

"Where's Terri?" she asked.

"I'm in the tub," Terri said.

"It's an odd time to be taking your baths," the guard yelled.

I yelled back, "I just wanted to get it done early."

I could hear the large door slam shut. Knowing that she had left, I took a deep breath. We were okay. Terri and I laughed so hard. That excitement was going to last us for a while.

We often talked about what we were going to do when we got out. I told her she could come and stay with me when she got home; of course, I never told Owen that. No way was he going to let a black girl from the ghetto come to our home. He knew her brother who was in Lucasville, and he was not a good person to know. Owen told me to stay away from her, not to be friends with her. But he couldn't control me while we were separated, so of course I didn't listen to him. With the distance between us, I knew his hands were tied, and there was nothing he could do about who I wanted to be friends with.

Terri was released before I was. She told me to call her as soon as I got out. My release day came, and my excitement mounted as I thought about seeing little Ryan. It was finally my turn to go home. The large door to the dayroom opened, and I was free to leave what had been my home for the past twenty weeks. As I waved goodbye to the women, I turned to walk to the office to receive my release papers and then back to the room that I entered in when I first came to the jail. This time I didn't have to take a shower. I got the street clothes that I wore when I came in and slipped out of the jail uniform into my own clothes. I felt a little freedom just putting them on. Throwing my uniform into the bin, I walked out not turning around to look back. The guard opened the doors with the large keys, a sound I had heard many times. This time, it was my turn to hear them open the door for my freedom.

"Goodbye," I said to the guards with excitement in my voice.

"Be good," they responded.

"You know I will." I smiled back.

I went down the elevator to the main floor where the last door of bars opened, releasing me to freedom. Everything looked like it was popping out at me. The strange faces looked at me as if to say, "We know where you just came from." Suspicion welled up in me. Finally, there was a smile on a familiar face as Richard came toward me with arms open to hug me. I melted in his arms.

"Where is Ryan?"

"He's at the motel," Richard said.

"Let's go," I said. "I want to see him so badly."

"How was your night?"

"It was hard to sleep. I was so excited to get out. Have you talked to Owen today?"

"No, I know he'll be happy to hear from you. Are you planning to go to Lucasville this week?"

"I'm not sure."

"What do you mean?" he asked.

"Richard, I've been doing some thinking, and I'm not sure where my relationship with Owen is going."

We arrived in the driveway of the motel, and I jumped out of the car before he could park. I ran through the back door to the office, and there was the little boy I had missed so badly. He stood there for a moment as I said, "Mommy is here. Come and give me a hug." He looked at me in wonderment. He finally darted to me and I grabbed him, giving kisses all over his little face. His smiles got bigger and brighter as I did my little teases that I would do to make him smile and giggle aloud. I didn't want to put him down. I clung to him as he did to me.

We didn't stay at the motel long as I was anxious to head for home. The dogs greeted me with excitement. They had missed me too. When we went into the house, I put Ryan down so he could get on the floor and play with his toys. I joined him, and we spent hours bonding back together. I repeatedly told him, "Mommy loves you."

The phone rang and the operator asked if I would accept a collect call from Owen. "Yes, I will," I responded.

"Hello, Carol. How are you doing?" Owen asked.

"I'm okay. I'm playing with Ryan."

"Are you and Ryan coming down this week to see me?" he asked.

"I'm not sure."

"What do you mean?" he asked.

"I just got home, and I want to adjust being home. I really don't know if I want to come into a jail, plus make the long trip down there."

"I want to spend some time with Ryan," Owen said.

I was feeling guilty; only part of what I was saying was the truth. Owen convinced me I needed to come to see him.

"I'll be down on Saturday," I finally caved.

"Okay," he said. "I'll talk to you later."

<hr />

A few days had gone by since my release, and I picked up the phone to call Terri. "I'm home," I told her. "How're you doing?"

"Okay," she answered.

"I want to come and get you. Can you get a ride to the motel?"

"I think I can," she said.

"Meet me there in a few hours. I'm going there to do some work."

I drove with Ryan to the motel and went into the office. Everyone was happy to see me back so I could take over running things again. Richard had done a great job, but he needed to get back to his clients at the barber shop.

The clerk buzzed me in the office. "Someone here is asking for you."

"I'll be there is a minute."

I opened the bullet proof door to the lobby and there stood Terri. We gave each other a big hug, and I took her into the back where we sat and caught up on the events in our lives for the past few weeks.

"My brothers are really into the drugs, and I'm afraid for the children," she said, her voice getting choked up.

"Can you get them?" I asked.

"We would have to drive to my mom's."

"Okay, let's go" I said.

I left Ryan at the motel, and Terri and I left. We drove into the inner city of Cleveland where it was rough. But I was with Terri, and I knew she wouldn't let anything happen to me. We got to house, and she was in and out quickly with her girls. They jumped into the car, and we drove off.

Her two girls were older than my boys, but we knew they would get along. We picked up Ryan and headed home.

The next few days we had fun watching the kids playing and getting along so well. I finally got the courage to talk to Owen on the phone.

"What are they doing there?" he asked with a growl in his voice.

"She was having trouble with her brothers, and I wasn't going to let her stay around that."

The arguing began. I tried hard not to be obvious so Terri wouldn't catch on that Owen and I were having a disagreement.

"I'll talk to you on the visit," I said.

"Don't you leave them there in the house when you're gone," he demanded.

"I won't," I promised. "She'll stay at the motel or go home."

"Goodbye," he said. "See you on Saturday."

"That was Owen," I told Terri when I hung up the phone. "When I go to visit on Saturday, he wants you out of the house."

"Okay," Terri responded.

Saturday came, and Ryan and I headed out to Lucasville. When we walked into the entrance to the visiting area, I felt my privacy being invaded again. I had gone through that enough over the past five months, and I was sick of it.

As we waited at the table for Owen to come out into the visiting room,

Ryan began to play with a few of his toys. When Owen came in, I stood to greet him and told Ryan to run to Daddy. Owen picked him up with a large smile on his face. Then he walked to me and wrapped us both in his arms for a hug.

The visit went well until the subject of Terri came up. He did all that he could to convince me she was no good and would only be trouble if I kept her at the house. The argument got intense as I said I wouldn't let her go back to her family. He realized he wouldn't get anywhere at the moment so the subject was dropped, and we went on to talk about the appeal on his case and how it was getting closer to him possibly coming home. He wanted to take all of our property and place it in a new corporation because of the FBI raid and the IRS liens. This way they couldn't touch it. We tossed names back and forth, trying to decide who would be trustworthy enough that we could put our property in their name. We finally both agreed that Martha would be good as she had been loyal to us since she started to work at the motel. Plus, she had stayed with me many times at the house.

"When I get out, I will sit and talk to Martha and see if she agrees to it," Owen said.

"Okay," I responded. The visit ended, and Ryan and I headed for our long drive home.

Months went by, and Terri and I began to grow in our friendship, more than we both expected. Owen demanded more and more that she leave, but I ignored his commands. Eventually, realizing he couldn't control me, Owen resorted to threats. I figured I better listen or I would be heading for some real trouble. I sat Terri down and told her I thought it would be better if she went back home. It was hard on both of us, but I knew that I had better listen to Owen. She became very angry, and when she did leave it wasn't on good terms.

Owen, Martin, and Robert Steele were relentless in trying to get the courts to give them a new trial. They kept looking for a flaw in the court transcripts that would allow them an appeal. As we sat visiting, Owen told me that they were getting closer to an appeal, and my hopes began to rise that he would be coming home soon.

"We are in the court of appeals, and they will reverse the lower courts," Owen said.

"I lost mine," I responded. "What makes you think you will get yours?"

"We have more mistakes in our trial, and the judge will rule in our favor. You watch—I am right," he insisted.

I left from the visit with such mixed emotions. I had betrayed my close friend by sending her back to the wolves, but Owen was telling me he would be home soon. What was next for me?

Moaning and groaning are my food and drink, and my worst fears have all come true. I have no peace or rest—only troubles and worries (Job 3:24-26 CEV).

CHAPTER SIXTEEN

Appeal Won

Five years had gone by, and I finally got a call from Owen's attorney, Ralph Sperli.

"Carol, Owen won his appeal," he said. "I have to take care of the paperwork, but he'll be home in a few days." I couldn't believe what I was hearing. Finally! Owen was coming home, and we would live as a family should.

"Can I go and get him?" I asked.

"No, he'll be escorted back to Cleveland to the Justice Center and released from there," Sperli said.

"Do I have to go get him from there?"

"Yes, Owen will call when he arrives."

"Did Martin get his appeal also?"

"Yes he did and so did Steele."

"Call me when you know more," I said. "Thanks for all you did to help them win the appeal."

I grabbed Ryan, "Daddy is coming home!" My enthusiasm excited him, even though at four years old he didn't understand the legality of his dad coming home. I waited for the phone to ring so I could talk to Owen.

"Hello, Owen."

"Did you hear from the attorney?" he asked.

"Yes, I did."

"I told you we were going to get the appeal. Now do you doubt me?" he asked.

"When can you get home?" I asked him.

"I'll be on the road tomorrow."

"Who will bring you?"

"We come with a guard."

"I can't wait," I said. "I'm so excited."

"Carol, you'll meet me. I'll call you when we get close. Martin will meet with Jenny, and they will go their way and I can come home."

"I'll wait for your call," I said. "Be careful. It's going to be so good for you to be home."

"Bye, honey," he said. "Give Ryan a kiss and tell him Daddy will be home tomorrow."

"I will, and I'll be waiting for you," I said. "Bye."

My heart began to beat faster as I started to make calls to the family to tell them the great news. They bombarded me with questions. "How did he win the appeal? Who gave them the new trial? Does he have to make bond?"

"I don't know all the answers yet," I told my family.

I called Jenny to see if she had heard from Martin.

"Yes I did," she answered.

"This is so awesome. They won their appeal!" I responded.

"I know," she said. "It's going be great having them home."

"It has been a long time," I said. "I'll talk with you tomorrow. Call me if you hear from them, and I'll call you if I hear from Owen."

"Okay, bye," she said.

"Bye. I'm so roused up, I'm going to have a drink so I can knock myself out to get some sleep some," I said, hanging up the phone.

It was so hard to go to sleep, knowing he was going to be coming home. Adrenaline pumped through my body. It felt like I had taken a drug to keep me awake, like the ones truck drivers take when they are on the road at night. I rose before the sun emerged in the morning. Ryan slept tightly, and I let him wake up on his own.

The booking office in the Justice Center closed at five p.m. so Owen needed to get there by that time, or I was afraid he would have to stay at the center until morning to be released. The day went as slowly as a turtle moved. I stayed at the motel waiting for that happy phone call. Ryan was playing with Bobby, and Martha was just as anxious as I was.

The sun set and night approached. It was now after five and I was worried. Seven o'clock came, and the phone finally rang. Owen was on the other end of the line.

"Hi. Where are you?" I asked.

"We're coming into Cleveland. The officer is allowing us to come meet you. The paperwork was done by telephone. The officer said that we could be released in to your custody," he said.

"Where can I meet you?" I asked.

"I'll call you when we get closer to town," he said.

I called Jenny to tell her I got the call. "I'm waiting here at the motel," I told her. "Hopefully it will be in the next hour."

The call came and Owen told me we could get them by the Justice

Center. Jenny and I waited in my car, in anticipation as the day we had waited four long years for was finally here. It seemed like a dream, and time stood so still that the happy moment seemed like it was never going to happen.

Finally the car lights approached, and I could see the image of two men sitting in the back seat of the government vehicle. The door opened, and I could see Owen on the right side of the car. I got out and ran to him as he thanked the men for bringing him and Martin home. Martin walked towards Jenny's car. I clung to Owen's large arms as we walked back to the car.

Ryan was with Martha so we could have a night alone together. We would pick him up in the morning.

"Everything looks so different," he said.

"I know," I said. "When I got out of the Justice Center I felt the same way. Wait till you get to the house. It will look so big to you."

As we drove, we talked and rejoiced that he was finally free. He started to talk about God and how He was the one who let him out. Owen seemed to be clinging to his Catholic faith, telling me that "A family who prays together stays together." I was beginning to believe him. I thought I was looking at a different man, one who behaved differently. I really liked what I was feeling and seeing.

We pulled into the drive, and I warned Owen, "I'm concerned about how the dogs will react to you." Leo and Tippy had died two years ago. Not wanting to be alone in the country, I purchased two German Shepherds, Viking and Butterball. They were very protective of the house.

"I'll just punch them in the face," he said.

"Just sit in the car," I said. "I will have them sniff you, then I can let you in the house."

I pressed the garage door opener and out they came, rushing to the familiar car. This time there would be a new person for them to sniff. Their tails were wagging. I opened my door, and they jumped to greet me until Viking caught the smell of someone different. He immediately ran to the door by Owen, getting somewhat aggressive.

"Put out your hand Owen," I said.

"Okay."

"Just stay in the car until I give you the clear to get out."

The dogs sniffed his hand, and their tails began to wag. "Okay, move slowly out of the car. I will be right by you." I walked in front to protect Owen in case one of them decided to take a sudden leap. I opened the door to the house and we went in, leaving the dogs in the garage.

As we went down the wooden steps into the family room, I could see Owen's eyes look around, leaping from object to object as he recalled his memories of home.

We both were filled with joy. We had anticipated this night for a long time. I watched him as we lay in bed, "Am I dreaming? Am I going to wake up alone again? Is he really here?" The thoughts bounced rapidly through my mind. I melted into his arms of protection. We made up for lost time with a night of romance.

Morning came and with it, the excitement of picking up Ryan at the motel. I drove the usual route, but this time I had Owen next to me. We reached the motel and went to the side entrance where Martha held the door for us. Ryan and Bobby Jr. stared as Owen came in. It took Ryan a moment to process that Daddy was here, and when it sunk in, he ran to Owen's arms. Bobby Jr. wondered who the strange man was that Ryan was calling Daddy. The smile on their faces was such a joy to watch as Owen drew Ryan into his lap.

"Your arms are so big," Bobby Jr. said. Owen let the boys hang from his arms, curling them up and down as if the boys were large weights. They were thrilled with the new game, begging him not to stop.

I talked to Martha for a few moments while the boys were playing. I couldn't help but notice her staring at Owen. Working out for the past few years had made him very muscular.

"Martha, I want to talk to you about the property in a day or so," Owen said to her.

"Carol mentioned it to me," she said.

"Let me spend some time with my family, and then we can talk," he said. "Come on, Ryan. Daddy and Mommy are going home."

"Can Bobby come?" Ryan asked.

"No, we want to spend some family time together. Tomorrow you can see Bobby," I said.

The ride home was full of Ryan's voice, with giggles of excitement. He was going home to play with Daddy. I was thrilled we were going to finally be together. I cooked steak with potatoes, Owen's favorite.

Ryan sat on the floor and called Owen to him. "Come on, Daddy, come and play with me." The sounds of my son and his father playing made my heart fill with joy. Ryan could now share his toys and play cars with his daddy. They played for hours after dinner.

"Come on Carol," Owen said. "Let's put Ryan to bed together."

Owen went into Ryan's room to tuck him into bed for the first time in a long while. I couldn't help but think it was the perfect way to end the perfect day.

"Let me put the dogs out, and I'll be right up," I said.

When I got to his room, Owen said, "Let's pray." We stood over our son's bed and prayed together, as a family.

We kissed Ryan goodnight, "See you in the morning." I felt like my life was finally whole.

Forget what happened long ago! Don't think about the past. I am creating something new (Is. 43:18, 19a CEV).

CHAPTER SEVENTEEN

Old Behavior

After a few days the realization hit me that Owen was really home. It was no longer just an image in my mind; he was really here. Owen started meeting with Martha on a regular basis to deal with the property, and I was beginning to have morning sickness. I felt like I did when I became pregnant with Ryan. We had talked about having another child, so I was hoping I was pregnant. I called for a doctor's appointment and was thrilled with the results.

"Owen, I have good news. I'm going to have another baby."

"That's great! I'm glad. When is the baby due?" he asked.

"The due date is in March, towards the end of the month." My whole life was changing again. My husband was home. Ryan had his daddy, and I was about to add another child to our family.

Six months into my pregnancy, Owen started to show signs of activities that alarmed me. The suits stored in the closet came out. He had been sporting his jeans. His rings, one of a large green shamrock, were placed back on his hands after being in the lock box for the past five years. When he went to the Cadillac store, I really became concerned. The days of me driving him around were about to come to an end. He was stepping out into his freedom, which scared me. Freedom for him meant running with people all hours of the night, sometimes staying out all night and arriving home in the morning. He was discussing less and less of what he and Martha were planning. My fears began to multiply. Behavior traits of his past were surfacing. He told me that he and Martha would spend time together because he was teaching her what she needed to know about going into the banks when they had to. Innkeepers International was formed with Martha as the president, which allowed them to purchase more property. She represented Owen. He was changing her dress code to make her look like a business-woman. Much of the time she wore a suit.

"You don't need to be out late," I said.

"She works the night shift at the motel, and it's the only time we can get together to talk," he would say.

"I wish you would come home to be with Ryan and me."

"Do you want me to make us money so we can do the things we want to do?" he asked.

"Yes, but not all night."

My woman's intuition was kicked into full throttle. I was questioning them both without them knowing what I was doing. Their stories never were the same. I knew they were telling me lies. My pregnancy made me feel so ugly and fat, and having this slender, large-breasted woman around Owen made me feel even more uncomfortable. She would come over a few times a week, but before discussing business, they would work out in the weight room we had in the back of the house. My jealousy toward her was escalating. Was she hot for my husband? No, I told myself, she was my best friend. But the nights Owen spent away from home were increasing. I would lie in bed crying, asking God to take him away if they were together because the pain was too much to bear. I knew my suspicions were real. The signs were adding up

During one of their exercise nights at the house, I was in the kitchen making dinner. The door was closed, and I slid it open to ask what vegetable they wanted with dinner. Owen was holding a weight set over her head and leaning over her. He jumped back, like a kid that was caught stealing a cookie out of the cookie jar. Guilt was written all over their faces. Too afraid to confront it, I walked out and went to the kitchen and continued to cook. When she left, I didn't bring it up. I knew he would lie.

Martha was living on the bottom floor of a house in a neighborhood that wasn't the best. A few months earlier, Owen and I started discussing how he felt Martha needed to move out and into a better place. He thought she needed to buy a house because in doing business with him, she needed to make a good impression on any businessmen they were working with. They started looking for houses and finally found one in Mayfield Heights.

She had lived there for a few months when I decided to investigate where Owen was disappearing to every night. Placing Ryan in the car, I drove to Martha's house. I pulled into the driveway. Ryan was sound asleep in his seat. I got out of the car and walked around to see if there was any sign of Owen. The garage was shut, and the blinds were pulled down on the windows. My mind raced with thoughts: He is in there; he is not in there; he is; he's not. Time froze for a few moments as I stood contemplating what I should do next. I wanted to walk up the steps and knock on the door, but fear stopped me. I didn't want to find him there. I got back into the car and headed home.

Not knowing for sure kept me in denial. I put Ryan in his bed and then went to my own. I lay across the bed sobbing so hard at times I could feel my child within tightening into a ball and kicking me whenever he moved. I tried to relax. I just couldn't. "What am I going to do?" I thought to myself. "He won't admit anything. I can't question him. He won't talk about it. He'll just get closer to her."

I finally dozed off. Early morning the garage door went up and Owen walked in. He climbed the steps softly, trying to avoid waking me. It was too late; I was already awake.

"Where were you?" I asked, a question I was asking several times a week now.

"I was out taking care of business."

"Where?"

"Downtown."

I knew he was telling me a lie. I drew back without another word.

Owen wouldn't go to my childbirth classes. He said he couldn't go into the hospital room and watch me in pain. So Martha said she would be my coach. I still wasn't convinced that things were innocent between her and my husband, but Owen did a good job at trying to convince me that their relationship was purely business. Martha and I began going to birthing classes. March came quickly, but the baby just didn't want to come. My doctor became concerned and scheduled me to come into the hospital.

"I want to induce your labor so I will see you on thirty-first," he said.

I met Martha at the hospital on the scheduled day. I wanted to go as natural as I could without any unnecessary drugs. They injected my veins with liquid to get the labor started and within a few moments I could feel pressure on my uterus getting more intense. My water broke as they probed inside. The labor began to get very strong, and my screams were escalating with each pain.

"You can do it," Martha encouraged me.

It was a hard labor. It didn't help to know that the person who was supposed to help me with the birth of my child was probably having an affair with my husband. I kept convincing myself that they were business partners, trying to banish all thoughts of the affair I suspected.

I wanted to yell at her. But I couldn't, she was my coach. Instead, I tried to stay focused on the birth of my baby. After all, she was there supporting me so maybe what I was thinking about her was all a lie. I didn't think she could be in the room with me, knowing I was having Owen's child and she was not.

Kevin James was finally born and Martha ran to the waiting room to tell Owen he had another son. He finally came in as I was transferred to my room. Kevin was in his little hospital bed. Owen smiled down at him, reaching to pick him up. His 7 pound, 10 ounce son looked tiny in his strong arms.

"I have to go," he said, handing Kevin back to me. Martha came in to say goodbye, and the two of them left for the motel. Kevin squirmed, moving his mouth back and forth trying to find my nipple. He attached to my breast and fell asleep within a few seconds after filling his little tummy. I tried so hard not to let my mind wonder what they were doing together while I was taking care of our newborn son.

Owen came the next day to visit. He only held Kevin for a short while again.

"I have to go to a meeting so I'm going back to the motel," he said.

"You're not spending any time with your son," I protested.

"I have to get these affairs in order so our finances will begin to correct themselves," he said.

"What could you be doing all hours of the night?" I asked.

"Carol, I have to get the IRS off the property, or we won't have anything," he kept telling me.

It broke my heart that his business was more important than taking some time to be with me and his new son. I was frustrated. I wanted to follow him to see where he really was going, but I was stuck.

The doctor came in to tell me I could go home in the morning. I called Owen, "I can come home in the morning. Be here at nine o'clock."

"Okay," he said.

Owen came on time, and we bundled Kevin up. It was winter. The hospital rules stated you had to be wheeled down to your car. As soon as I got home, I laid on the couch. Within minutes Owen was acting restless.

"I have to meet someone at the office," he said, and he was gone again.

Kevin began to grow and six months went by quickly. I finally had to hire a babysitter, Trish. She was such a caring person, and she treated the boys like they were her own. Shirley, her mom, was like an adopted grandma to them. They called her Grandma Shirley. I began to get my strength back, and I could leave Kevin longer times between feedings. I would pump my breasts and leave a bottle. The postpartum blues were hard enough for me, but there was more stress in my life than usual.

December came, and it was my birthday. Owen made reservations at a fancy restaurant in downtown Cleveland overlooking Lake Erie. We were enjoying our night out.

"I have to go and make a call," he said.

When he returned he said, "I have an important meeting I have to go to."

We were really having money problems and owed a lot to the lawyers. Owen said he was going to sell some things, and he needed to meet these people. My life was so full of his lies.

I was at the motel when I got a call from Sonja, the girl from the apartments who turned us in to the FBI. She told me that she was not the only one who helped the FBI send us to jail. I really wanted to talk to her, but Owen convinced me she was the enemy and it was her fault that we went to jail. He ordered me not to talk to her anymore. So of course I told her not to call me again.

Martin was running the carpet cleaning business that we purchased and as business was starting to pick up, my sister Barb began to work for us. Both she and I would make calls to schedule appointments for the cleaners. When she came to work, she would comment to me that she didn't like the way Owen would look at Martha. I responded that they were only business partners. I had to convince myself there was nothing there between them.

Owen was spending less and less time with us. When we did get time together, Martha was always around. I would look through Owen's desk when he wasn't there. I was getting so desperate that I was snooping through everything I could. When he was sleeping, I checked the car to see if I could find cigarette butts in the ashtrays. I knew what brand Martha smoked. I even checked his clothes. I was hoping I would find something to prove they were having an affair, so I wouldn't feel like I was losing my mind. But, at the same time, I was afraid to find proof. I wasn't ready to confront Owen. I couldn't take any more lies. I was so miserable that I couldn't eat right and I'd lost a lot of weight.

Our monthly meeting for the employees at the motel arrived. Ryan begged, as he had done many times before, for his father to take him with him when he left for the day.

"Can I go with you, Daddy?" he asked, his little eyes full of hope.

"Yes, you can come," Owen responded.

They left for the motel, and I drove in separate as I had some things to finish before the meeting. When I arrived late, the meeting was already in progress. Someone had asked Owen for a certain paper, and then the clerk came into the office to ask for a tool that one of the regular tenants needed. Owen walked to the side door, past Ryan and Bobby playing in the office, then out the door. He was out by his car for a few moments when we heard a loud shout from a megaphone. "Put your arms up and get against the car." Not knowing who they were talking to, I ran to the window. They had Owen facing the car with his hands in the air, getting ready to place handcuffs on his wrists.

I ran out yelling, "What are you doing? He is out on an appeal."

"Get away," the officer yelled.

"He is out on bond," I insisted. "Why are you here?"

Owen was getting upset with my questions. He called me to the car and handed me a bag of weed, telling me to give it to Martha. "Carol, call the lawyer right away."

I was so confused. I remembered praying to God one night and asking him to take Owen back to jail if he were fooling around with Martha. And now I was afraid that my prayers had been answered.

"Call the lawyer," Owen shouted again.

I could see on Martha's face that she was just as confused as I was about what was taking place. "Keep calm," she said as she walked towards the car to whisper something to Owen.

The police carted him off, and I walked back inside. Ryan was crying. I picked him up as he kept asking, "Where's Daddy?"

"He had to go with the officers," I told him.

"Why?" he asked.

"I'm not sure, but he'll be back soon." I tried to calm him down.

Kevin was home with Trish so I called her to tell her the horrible news. "They just took Owen off to jail."

"Why?" she asked.

"I'm not sure, and I won't know until I talk to the attorneys. I just want to bring Ryan home. He doesn't understand why his Daddy has been taken away."

Ralph Sperli, Owen's lawyer, finally called back.

"Carol, you should just go home," he told me. "There is nothing you can do. The warrant was for the murder of Arnie Prunella."

"Oh my God," I panicked.

"You need to stay calm. Owen will have to try and get another bond," he said.

"Okay. Call me as soon as you get any details. I'll go home."

Tears rolled down my face as Ryan and I headed for home. What am I going to do now? How is he going to get out of this one? What made them arrest him now? Over and over again, the questions kept repeating in my mind.

I pulled into the garage and opening the door, I was greeted by Trish and her mom, Shirley. I glanced at them, and they knew I was about to break down. Shirley took Ryan to get him ready for bed. Kevin was already down. I paced the floor, hoping that Owen could get to the phone to call and sure enough he did.

"What did the lawyer say?" he asked.

"The warrant was for Arnie Prunella. They have a warrant for Martin also."

"He'll talk to you tomorrow at the arraignment, hopefully to post a bond. I have to get a hold of Martin's lawyer too. Try and be calm. They have nothing," he said.

"Goodnight, I love you," I told him.

"I love you too," he responded.

Ryan was fast asleep and I finally got a second to reflect on the day. I held my stomach as the tears mounted up from deep within. I thought to myself, "What am I going to do? Why, oh God is this happening? He must be having an affair. God, you heard my prayer."

Shirley looked into my teary eyes and tried to console me. But nothing she could say would help. I turned to liquor and went to take a drink to drown the feelings that haunted my mind so badly.

"We'll stay the night so if you need us or have to go, we'll be here," Trish said.

"I'm going to get into the bed," I said, "even though I know I can't sleep. At least I can try to rest. Goodnight and thank you so much for all your help."

"Goodnight," they both spoke at the same time.

I collapsed in the bed, burying my face into the pillow to let out a scream so no one could hear me. I cried until there were no more tears to cry.

Owen called the next morning, "I made my bond early, but I can't come near the house. I don't want them finding me." I couldn't understand if he made bond why he was avoiding home.

"Where can I meet you?" I asked.

"Just stay home, Carol," he said. "There is nothing you can do."

"I need to be with you. Please tell me where I can meet you," I begged.

"Okay, meet me in Chardon at the shopping center in an hour. Make sure no one is following you."

"Okay. Bye."

I called Grandma Shirley, "Can you come and spend the night? I have to do some things with Owen that are very important. I can't take the boys with me."

"Okay," she agreed. "I'll be there shortly."

I arrived earlier than our meeting time and sat in the parking lot. He had the same idea of arriving early. I could see the yellow car that Martha drove on the other side of the parking lot. As I watched him get out of the car, I began to boil inside, knowing she was the one who went and picked him up and not me. As he walked towards my car, I saw her drive off. Owen opened the car door and I smiled, not letting on that I knew how he had got there.

"How did you get here?" I asked.

"A friend dropped me off."

"Why are you driving around like this?"

"I don't want to spend the night in jail, so I'll just go to a hotel for the night."

"Can I go with you?" I asked.

"I think you should go home."

"No," I insisted. "I want to be with you."

As we argued back and forth, I didn't let him know that I knew he wanted to leave me and go with her. I put the pressure on so he would finally give in to my begging.

"Hold on while I go and make a phone call, and I'll be right back." I knew he was going to have to tell her something as she was probably waiting close by. I guessed he had told her that he would get rid of me and be back with her soon. I was putting a damper on their plans. A few minutes later I could see Martha's car arrive across the street. He got in for a moment and then came back toward me. I still didn't let on that I had seen them together. I kept asking the questions, knowing the answers would be lies. I wanted to be with him as I realized that this could be our last time together for a while.

We headed to the hotel, and he already had a key for a room. I knew that this whole set up was planned, but it wasn't supposed to be with me. I tried to stop thinking about her and him. I could see that Owen had a bottle of liquor on the dresser. I took a drink to try and relax. He probably was wondering what was going to happen to him, but I was just relieved that I had him to myself. Early morning came faster than I wanted it to.

"I have to hook up with Martha," he said. "We need to do something in case I have to go back." I wasn't going to argue at this point. I was glad he had been with me last night. I reasoned that they couldn't possibly do anything during the day. He went to her and I went home to the boys.

A few days went by, and Owen had to be in court. They were arguing their bond. It was their second murder charge. This time the Prunella murder was argued. Prosecutors argued their case by telling the judge they were already out on a bond. Prosecutors didn't want them on the streets. The defense lawyers argued for their release. The judge ruled, and their release was denied. I was at the motel, waiting for the call telling me I could pay the bond. Instead the call came with disappointment.

The trial had to begin quickly. Phil Christopher was serving time in the Federal Prison System for a separate crime. For his part in the killing of Prunella, he pleaded guilty to manslaughter, but refused to testify against Martin and Owen. The case was falling apart since the trigger man would not admit to what part Martin and Owen played in the killing. Since they were unable to produce a body, a witness, or a murder weapon, the case was thrown out. They tried to get me to testify again with the statement that I had made to Ressler, but this time I was considered married. But the damage was done. Because they had been picked up for the Prunella murder while they were out on appeal bond, the court ruled that they lost the appeal for the Steele case. They were going back to prison.

I went to visit Owen at the Justice Center, and standing in line I could see Martha towards the back of the line. What was she doing here? I wondered.

I went through the procedure of being searched, then entered the room to wait for Owen. I was excited to see him, even if there was a glass partition between us.

"Hello," he said when I sat down and had the phone to my ear.

"Why is she here?" I asked immediately.

"Don't start, Carol," he warned. "I need to work on getting out of here, and she has to help."

"What am I supposed to do?"

"Don't cause me any trouble. You know the property is in the corporation in her name, and I need her to follow through with certain things."

My gut feeling told me this wasn't a good sign, but I figured I better keep quiet.

The fifteen minute visit went quickly, and I waved goodbye. As I left, I passed Martha again. "See you later," I said to her.

The drive home was lonely, and I knew that I was probably going to be alone for a long time, but I had my boys to keep me going. He got out before, I thought to myself, he could probably do it again.

A few weeks later, Owen was sent back to Lucasville. I was struggling with alternating visits with Martha. One week I would visit, and the next Martha did.

On one of my calls from Owen I asked, "Why do we always visit on opposite weeks? Why can't we visit together?"

"It gives me visits every week this way," was his explanation.

Owen was back in prison and now Martha and I were taking care of the motel. Had God answered my prayer? Was this really what I wanted?

The human heart is most deceitful and desperately wicked. Who really knows how bad it is? But I know! I the Lord, search all hearts and examine secret motives, I give all people their due rewards, according to what their actions deserve (Jer. 17:9-10 NLT).

CHAPTER EIGHTEEN

Life Surrendered

It was beginning to feel like my whole life had been turned completely upside down. I was drinking heavily and smoking a joint on a daily basis. It was getting unmanageable for me. I was miserable. My husband was having an affair, he was in jail, and I was sharing him again. God only knew how much more I could handle. My two boys were all that was keeping me going. I had no idea where I was headed myself. Martha was running the motel at this point. I would go in to help remodel rooms, but I didn't work the check in desk. I did the banking, depositing the money coming in from the businesses. I wanted to avoid Martha as much as possible. She was going to see Owen one weekend, and then I would visit the next.

The carpet cleaning company was not producing income fast enough so we sold the business. Sometimes when I would talk with the cleaning crew they would ask me why I stayed with Owen. He doesn't love you, they said, he's always with other women. They would not tell me it was Martha, nor did they realize I already knew. Once in a while they would throw me some kind of clue concerning Martha. They lost their jobs when the business was closed.

In April of 1974 I received a second phone call from Sonja. She had called me a few months before Owen returned to prison. He forbade me from talking with her. She is the enemy, he would say, reminding me that she turned us into the police. She is not your friend and I do not want you to have any conversation with her at all, he insisted. But this time Owen wasn't there to stop me from talking to her. She called from Tulsa, Oklahoma, where she was attending Bible College under Franklin Graham, who was Billy Graham's son.

I had no idea who she was talking about. Billy Graham was familiar to me because my grandmother watched him preach on TV, but I didn't know he had a son.

"I want to tell you how sorry I am that I participated with Ressler raiding the apartment," Sonja said. "He told me you would be safe. He promised me that only Owen was going to jail, and you wouldn't. I believed him."

"It's in the past," I said. "I forgive you."

She told me horror stories of what happened to her when she was under their protective custody. "I didn't want to turn you in, and I did not want to have them spying on us," she said, "But they had me so scared that Owen was going to kill me if I didn't corporate with them. Especially after you told me about the murders. They kept bringing that up to me. I was afraid for my life. So I gave in to help them. Part of the deal was that they wouldn't harm you and send you to do any jail time at all. They sent you anyways, telling me that they needed to scare you into talking. That's why they put you in Alderson. He used me to get to you. I lost my respect for Ressler after that," she said.

All I could think at that moment was how I could get her to Cleveland and take her to Owen's lawyer. We could use this evidence to show that the Feds messed up. I thought if she turned in evidence against them, we could prove entrapment—that could be the loophole in the case that would win them an appeal for good. The Feds used Sonja to send us to prison, and I hoped we could use her to get Owen out of prison. I had to get her here, I thought to myself. She could visit Owen in person. Let him talk to her. He would know how to approach this with the lawyers. This could be what we needed to get them all out of jail and get them a new trial.

Sonja and I made plans for her to come in a few days. She had no idea of my intentions. I let her think I just wanted to see her. I felt it would be better to let Owen handle what to say to her. He wasn't happy she was coming, but I didn't care. I wanted her to come. I had my own plan to get him out. He would be happy after he heard why I wanted her here, I thought. I refused to tell him my plan on the phone. In person would be the best because our phones were not safe.

Two days passed before Sonja flew in. I picked her up at the airport. It had been ten years since I last saw her. She was so afraid of Owen then that she would sometimes shake. Seeing her now, she was completely different. I looked at her in awe, wondering why she was so peaceful.

"Carol, I go to Bible College," she said. "I'm around Franklin Graham, the son of the famous evangelist Billy Graham. I accepted Jesus into my heart."

"What do you mean?" I asked her.

"I have a personal relationship with Him. I have such peace in my life now, and I have no fear of Owen." I could see the calmness in her, and I knew she was serious. She had changed. If she were coming back to Cleveland to our house, she had to be free of her fear.

"Carol, my life was a mess," Sonja told me. "I was trying to take my life. I worried all the time that Owen was going to send someone to kill me. I was only under the protection of the FBI for one year after you went to jail. After that they said I was on my own. I would jump at the slightest suspicious thing that came my way. Fear controlled my life," she explained.

The next few days we played with the kids. She loved to be with the boys. She was so full of joy. She gave them little Bible books and me some contemporary Christian music. I had never heard that kind of music before. I had always loved to sing. I was in the church choir when I was growing up, and my sister and I would sing solos. My favorite hymn was *In the Garden*. My voice had become deeper over the years from my smoking.

We would put the boys to bed at night and sit on the couch talking about the Bible. She played some tapes by Keith Green, Sandy Patti, and Amy Grant. I would listen to their voices and feel jealous.

"I would love to be able to sing like that," I told Sonja.

"Carol, you can do whatever the Lord has for you to do," she said. "He will give you the desire of your heart."

"Can He get Owen out of jail?" I asked.

"If it is His will, He could do that."

I thought long and hard on that one. I had been praying and here Sonja showed up. Was God sending Sonja to help us to win the appeal, or had she turned into some kind of nut? I asked myself. A strange feeling was coming over me. I could only describe it as if I just taken a good stiff drink, only it didn't get me drunk. I was aware of what I was doing and saying. I wasn't passing out, and I didn't feel like I wanted to go to sleep. But I wanted more of what I was feeling. Something was pulling me. It was a wonderful feeling, and I couldn't explain it. It was not a voice talking to me; it was like some sort of peace that I had never experienced before.

I was impressed when Sonja picked up the phone and called a person on the TV. She told him about our relationship and revealed details of the life we had lived. Sonja handed the phone to me. The gentleman on the other end asked me if I knew Jesus.

"I am learning about Him now," I responded.

"Carol, the Holy Spirit is drawing you," the man said. "He is drawing you to turn to Him."

"I always turned to Owen, my husband," I said.

"Carol, NO! God wants you to turn to Him."

"You're telling me this Jesus is going to set me free? All I have to do is just say a little prayer and that's it?" I asked.

"He died for you, Carol. He took all your pain and sorrow and placed it on the cross. He doesn't want you to carry that baggage any longer. You cried out to Him, and He heard your cry. Now He sent Sonja to share with you her experience so you can have the same."

"I'm not sure that He'll forgive me for all that I've done," I said.

"He wants you the way you are, Carol. He has a plan for your life, and He wants to work that plan through you, if you will let Him. There is nothing you have done that He can't forgive you for." He told me the story of Mary Magdalene and how she was a prostitute in the Old Testament. If she could be forgiven, so could I. It amazed me that there was a story about me in the Bible.

When we got off the phone, Sonja and I listened to Sandi Patty. The music was so soothing to my ears.

The phone rang, and since I was busy with the kids, Sonja answered. "It's Martha," she told me.

"Talk to her a second, and I'll be right there," I called out.

I could barely hear what they were talking about. Owen must have told Martha to call the house to see what was going on. I hadn't gone into the motel since Sonja arrived. Owen couldn't handle it when he wasn't in control. Sonja was talking to Martha about Jesus. Somehow, she convinced Martha everything was okay.

After she got off the phone, Sonja and I sang songs about God. I was feeling something that I had never felt before. It was a high that no drug or drink had ever made me feel. What kind of power was this? Will it go away? I thought to myself.

"Carol, I feel I need to go and see Owen," Sonja said to me.

"For what?" I asked.

"God has something for him," she said. "I'm not sure what I'm going to say, but I need to go."

"Okay," I agreed. "We can go this weekend. I'll have Grandma Shirley watch the kids."

We took the trip to Lucasville. I was nervous, wondering if Owen would respond to her. I knew he wouldn't be as forgiving as I was. No one crossed Owen. We sat at the table and waited for his arrival. I wanted to run into the bathroom and let them meet on their own. I was afraid he would get mad. But I stayed and waited impatiently. He entered the room looking very stern, and I stood, holding my arms out to greet him. He returned my embrace and kissed me hello.

"Hello Sonja," he said as he sat down. "To what do I owe the pleasure of this visit?"

"I wanted to come and tell you that I was not the only one who was responsible for your arrest," Sonja said. "The Feds used me and your friend John to get the information they needed to plan the bust."

"I know that," he responded. "I heard this from another source. Tell me something that I don't already know. What did the FBI tell you to convince you to turn on us?" he asked.

I left to use the restroom, leaving them to talk. I didn't feel threatened by her. She certainly was not after my husband like Martha was. The visit went well. When it was time to leave, she hugged Owen goodbye. I knew Owen must have forgiven her on some level. I hugged and kissed him goodbye.

"I'll talk with you later," I said to him. "Call me. I'm going to call the lawyer in the morning, and I'll let you know what he thinks. Bye, love you."

We left for our journey home. In those four hours, we talked about a lot. Sonja questioned me again about the relationship between Owen and Martha. I told her how Innkeepers International was formed and that Martha and Owen had a business partnership. I wasn't ready to tell her my thoughts about it.

"Carol, do you remember when you got up and went to the bathroom? When you were away, Owen grabbed my hand, asking me if I remembered when we used to be together and how it used to be. I told him that I was a Born Again believer and that I'm not that same person and that I didn't want to talk about it anymore. I pulled back my hand," she said.

I had enough to deal with when it came to Martha. I didn't want to believe what Sonja was telling me. Could I trust her with what she was saying? I asked myself. Is she really my friend? Was she really here to help me, or was Owen right, women just wanted him? Did she fall for him again and now she was going to try and get him for herself? By the time we arrived home she had talked enough to convince me to believe her instead of what Owen was saying to me.

Martha had called the house and left me a message to call her when I got home. Owen had time to contact her, and I wondered what he had told her. I knew he told her to call. I told Sonja to call the motel. Martha answered, and Sonja asked her questions. From what Sonja was saying, it made me think something was going on. She handed me the phone.

Owen was worrying. He wanted me to hide some money that we had in the house. "Owen wants you to bring me the suitcase you have with the money in it," Martha told me. "He's worried that Sonja is going to steal it. He doesn't trust her in the house with it." I had no intentions at the time of even showing the money to Sonja. But Owen was so worried that I was going to that I finally showed her, out of spite. She didn't care about it. We took the suitcase, jumped into the car, and drove it over to Martha's place. Sonja would see what my competition was. I struggled as we drove to Martha's, wondering if I was doing the right thing. Does Owen have some insight about Sonja that I can't see? Am I a fool for trusting Martha? Who should I trust? I met Martha at her door and handed her the suitcase. She walked over to the car so I introduced her to Sonja.

"Hello, Sonja, nice to meet you," Martha said.

"Nice to meet you too," Sonja replied.

"I better go," I said. "Owen is calling back. I will talk with you later."

We listened to the Christian radio station on the drive home. I felt like my life was an open book. The pastor's message spoke directly to me. It was if my body were injected with spirituality. I felt like I was floating through this situation I was now facing.

I went to pick up the boys at Grandma Shirley's.

"Hello, Shirley, how're the boys doing?"

"They played hard today," she said. "And now they're sleeping on the couch."

"Do you mind if they stay there for the night?"

"Sure, they're asleep anyway. Why wake them?"

"Great, I'll see you in the morning. Goodnight, kiss them on their cheeks for me."

I listened to some more preaching on the way home. My mind pondered over everything I was hearing. I focused on only what the Bible was telling me.

When I walked in the door, the phone rang. It was Owen.

"Owen, I've been doing a lot of thinking lately. You better go back to your cell and repent for all that you've done. You need to get right with God," I told him.

His voice rose as he yelled at me. "What is going on over there? What is she doing to you? Are you drinking? Or smoking pot?"

"I'm not doing a thing. I am high on God," I said.

"I want her out of the house right away and don't give me any more of your lip."

"Where am I going to take her? It's late."

"I don't care," he said. "Just get her out of there." Fear gripped me. I knew I had better listen. I hung up the phone and panicked.

"I need to take you out of here," I said to Sonja. "You need to go back to the airport and go home."

"I can't, Carol. My flight's not for two more days. I can't stay at the airport."

"I don't care. I have to listen to Owen." She sensed my fear.

"Carol, I am not your enemy," she said.

Of course she was, I thought. I didn't want to believe what she was trying to tell me. "Let's go I have to get you out of here."

The whole way to the airport I could see her out of the corner of my eyes, staring at me in disbelief. I was going to take her to the airport and just drop her off. What was wrong with me? I asked myself. I was supposed to be her friend. I had to make my heart hard again so I could do that to her, so I could do what Owen told me to.

"Carol, you need to think about what you're doing," she said.

"I'm doing what Owen has asked me to do." I pulled up to the entrance of the airport. "Just get out," I said. "Hurry, I have to get back home."

"Carol, if you think about it, Owen has control over you, and you're responding to him even while he is locked up. Look how scared you are," she said.

"I am not scared," I said. "I'm just listening to my husband. Now, just go!"

She got out, and I pulled away. Driving home, I couldn't stop the battle in my head. I questioned what had happened to me while Sonja was here. Was this Jesus thing real? Did I really experience His presence around me? Was there a part of my heart that was starting to trust someone other than Owen? What really had happened to me in the past few days?

The house seemed lonely with Sonja gone. I started feeling guilty for the way I treated her. I listened to the Christian music and picked up the Bible she left behind for me. Lying on my bed I began to read. A few days later, I called Sonja.

"Sonja, I'm so sorry for what I did to you," I said to her.

"Carol, it's okay. I made it home okay."

We talked for hours. We couldn't stop. The Bible stories she shared were so interesting. I wanted to hear more. Over the next few weeks we would talk daily, running up a phone bill well over five-hundred dollars.

"Sonja, I'm going to send you a check to cover the bill."

"Thanks," she said. "I didn't realize it would be this much."

"I'm going to cool it for a bit," I told her. "I know Owen is going to be upset when he knows I sent you the money. I'll call you in a few days. We can't talk every day."

Owen did a lot of the paperwork from prison so when I did send him the checking account information, I heard from him. "What the hell did you pay that bill for? She is ripping you off," he said.

"I am responsible as much as she is, and I'm not going to stick her with the bill. I called her," I said.

Owen placed Martha in control of the money we were taking in. He didn't trust me anymore. Whatever money I needed, I had to go through her. I was not happy with the fact that I was now accountable to her.

I, the Lord your God, will make up for the losses caused by those swarms and swarms of locusts I sent to attack you (Joel 2:25 CEV).

Chapter Nineteen

Faith Grows

I struggled each day I had to go into the motel. It was getting very difficult to be there, especially around Martha. Our friend Jan called me and asked me to stop by her house because she wanted to talk with me. She lived two streets away from Martha.

"Carol, I'm having a problem with jealousy of Martha," she told me.

"What do you mean?"

"I think she is after my husband."

"Jan, you don't have to worry," I told her. "She is already after mine." I don't think she knew what I knew. "Jan, I just became a Christian. Sonja came from Tulsa, and she talked about Jesus and how I can have a relationship with Him."

"That's great," she was excited for me. "I have a friend I think you should meet. Her name is Faith."

"I'd love to. Tell her to give me a call."

"She's going to be at my daughter's shower on Sunday. You can meet her then. You both have a lot in common."

"Okay," I agreed. "In the meantime though, don't say anything about our conversation about Martha. Let's keep it between us. I'm going home to the boys. I'll see you."

I didn't go to the motel for a few days. I worked in the yard, tending to my flower beds, something I love to do. I was looking forward to the shower and meeting Faith. When Sunday finally arrived, I left the boys with Grandma Shirley.

I walked in, and Jan came to me with a friend next to her.

"Carol, I want you to meet Faith," Jan said.

"Hello, Faith, I've heard a lot about you," I said.

"Same here, I heard you just became a Christian"

"Yes, I did." We enjoyed our time together, sharing and laughing like I hadn't done in years. She was so different from those I was used to being around. There was peace.

It was only a few days later that I took Ryan and Kevin over to meet her kids. She had two daughters, Joy and Jena, and a son, Ricky. They were a bit older. We started spending a lot of time together, and Faith would minister to me. Sometimes I would sit at her dining room table, holding my head, crying from the confusion I felt.

"I'm going to a Bible study on Tuesday," she said. "I'd like for you to go. It will do you good, and you'll grow spiritually. It's called Bible Study Fellowship where women get together for fellowship and to study the Bible."

"Okay, I'll go," I agreed. "I'll come by your house, and we can drive together."

I enjoyed the Bible studies, and I was becoming sociable. I would look at these women who I thought had it all together, as they shared their testimonies of what they had been through. I was amazed at what God had done in their lives. I could see a glimpse of hope for me. I was beginning to believe He could change me too. I felt accepted, and my past was fading away.

On one occasion, a speaker shared the story of Mary Magdalene, reminding me of the phone call Sonja and I had made to the TV show. This time tears flowed down my cheeks, and I began to weep. The more the speaker shared about her life and how that story helped her, I realized her message was that God had come into her life and transformed her. I felt a release inside of me as I finally accepted my past. These women will understand, I told myself. I was not going to be judged for what I did. However, I was still not ready to tell them. Each week I became stronger and stronger in my faith. I was becoming a new person.

The Bible studies were opening up my eyes, showing me that I was doing things that God did not want from me. The motel where I spent so many hours was used by many people who were having a one-night affair; men were cheating on their wives, women cheating on their husbands. The place really had a reputation, especially after the article in *Playboy*.

Listening to the Christian radio station while driving to the motel helped me to hear God clearly. When I would get to the office, I tuned into the radio station, filling myself with the word of God. Martha would come into the office. She must have heard what I was listening to, but she never asked me what it was. She would stay for just a moment and go back to the front desk. I got the feeling she was uncomfortable with it.

I realized that I had such a trash mouth in the past. I would say the "F" word every other word. But as I let God in my life, I was losing the foul mouth and becoming a young lady. I didn't try to stop the words from others, but I just couldn't say them anymore. They disappeared from my vocabulary. The Lord took away my urge to smoke too. After all that I was going through, not once did I break down and smoke. I didn't even want to be in the same room with smokers. Only God could've given me the strength to quit. When Jesus started to clean me up, He took the filth out and replaced it with purity.

I attempted to tell Martha what was happening to me. She looked at me with eyes of disgust. I knew she could not receive it. I was becoming convinced that the movies that were shown at the motel were trash. The movies were the main attraction of the motel, and without them, the place was a dive. People were addicted to the adult films. We had regulars that would come every week. I was at a point in my walk with the Lord that I wanted to tell them all to repent and go home to be with their wives and husbands and stop cheating on them. I refused to work the desk any longer. I finally told Owen I was not going to put one more of those trash movies on for anyone to see. That really made him mad, after all that was what the motel was all about.

As I read more of my Bible, I began to see all the sin I was involved with. I was helping these people to do the things they were doing.

On Wednesday evenings I was taking Ryan and Kevin to the Baptist Church that Faith and her family attended. The boys attended a club where they learned about Bible characters through playing games and having fellowship with other children their ages.

Faith's church was like one big family. The men would help the boys and me. They were the family I never had. I felt loved and accepted. I was finally helping my boys have stability in their lives. I could not get enough of church. I attended every event I could and took my boys with me. The potlucks were the best. The food we had was made for a king.

I used to think that Christians lived a boring life. I was beginning to get my true identity back. For years I followed exactly what Owen wanted me to do. I lost my desires along with what I enjoyed doing. Everything revolved around the business. I never had any free time to do something fun. There was no balance in my life. I would sometimes take the boys places, but we spent so much more time trying to keep the business going.

Owen was really losing his control over me at this point. I was letting God be the one who was in control of my life. Owen couldn't fight against it; he didn't know how to. All that mattered to him was making money. He transferred more responsibility onto Martha because he knew he could control her. I went to the motel one day, and Martha had lost a paper that she was supposed to have for Owen. She was frantically going through the trash trying to find it. She was so afraid that if she didn't find that paper, something would happen to her. I looked at her and in a very peaceful voice I said, "What do you think he can do to you? He's in jail." She gave me a look as if to say, "How dare you talk against him! What are you nuts?" I left her at the motel with her fears.

Even though Owen was losing his strong hold over me, I would still question whether I was right or wrong. He would say things to me, and I would go over and over the conversation in my head, questioning my knowledge. I felt dumb next to him. I would journal our conversations after I hung the phone up from talking to him. Then I would read it back to myself so I could reassure myself that I was the right one and he was wrong. He had twisted my words for so long that I would start to doubt myself. Owen had told me for so many years that I was wrong that I now doubted my own thinking. He was the smart one and I was so stupid, so of course what I thought had to be wrong.

But now I was starting to think for myself. Many times after I talked to Owen, I would call Faith right away and go over my conversation with her. She would be the one to tell me he was twisting things. "He is trying to control you," she would remind me. The Lord began to strengthen me, and I saw the control that Owen had over me. I would cry when I was with Faith because as the word of God began to work on my heart and mind, I saw how my life had been manipulated by a person, not God. I started thinking on my own, thinking of Christ. And I stopped thinking about what Owen tried to get me to believe.

For many years I wanted to crawl under a rock and stay there. If only they would stop bringing up our name. Wherever I went, the Kilbane name would come up, and the shame would rise up in me again. Just when things started to settle down, the media would dig up the case again, once again splashing the Kilbane name across the front page of the paper. The local news channels carried the story every time. I couldn't escape my shame.

Tuesday's women's Bible study helped build my self-esteem back up. My identity was who I was in Christ, not what the world had to offer me. My heart softened, and I let go of the shame I held onto for many years. I had always been ashamed of whom I was married to, that he was my pimp before my husband. God opened my eyes to the reality of our relationship. I had been ashamed for my children so much so that I had told Ryan to tell his friends his daddy was away at school. Owen was enrolled in college at the prison, so I justified it to myself by thinking we were only telling a little white lie.

The more and more I read my Bible, the more my eyes opened up to the truth of my life. I had told one lie after another to cover up what I was doing with my life. When I found God, I was able to let go of the lies and fill my life with His love.

One night, after leaving Faith's, I took the boys home and settled in for the night. I had many nights of restless sleep. This night I woke up at 2 a.m. I heard a small voice inside of me, telling me to reach for my Bible that was on the nightstand next to my bed. I started flipping the pages coming to a book of Joel. I had not studied this chapter yet. I was just beginning to memorize where certain books were in the Bible, and I didn't know this one existed. Joel 2:25. I started reading. It looked like the words were bouncing off the page and jumping out at me. God was speaking directly to me; He was telling me to read it. The scripture read, "Then, I will make up to you for the years, that the swarming locusts have eaten." I began to weep. I knew that this was my first ever experience of God talking directly at me. He was telling me He was going to make up for all the lost years. He loved me so much that He cared about helping me restore my life.

I know perfectly well that what I am doing is wrong, and my bad conscience shows that I agree that the Law is good. But I can't help myself, because it is sin inside me that makes me do these evil things (Rom. 7:16-17 NLT).

CHAPTER TWENTY

Friend's Betrayal

Jan called late one Friday night, "How are you doing Carol? How are you and Faith doing?"

"We're doing great," I told her. "I love the Bible study I am going to. I am learning so much. Faith is like family. The kids and I go over there all the time."

"Carol, I like you a lot, and I care about what happens to you," she said. "I don't want to see you hurt anymore, and I want to share something with you."

"Okay, I'm listening."

"Remember our conversation a while back when I told you I thought Martha was after my husband?"

"Yes, I told you she was after mine."

"You were right. Owen and Martha have been together for some time now. Right around the time you told me, they began seeing each other even more."

"I've tried approaching the both of them," I told her. "They both deny it. They say they are business partners, and that's it. Sometimes I think I'm crazy."

"Carol, what if you had proof? What would you do? I know they write letters to each other, and there are times when they take pictures together in the visiting room. She would come home after a visit and show them to me."

My mind began scheming. How could I find this evidence? Martha was visiting Owen this weekend, and I had access to her house. I knew how I could get in. If I go over there, maybe I can find the letters or pictures, I thought to myself.

"Jan, I am coming over. I have a plan." I took the boys over to Grandma Shirley's so she could watch them.

When I arrived at Jan's, I tried to figure out where Bobby would be because I didn't want to walk in the house to find him. I wouldn't be able to explain why I was there. We finally realized he was at his grandma's, and I

146

was free to go. I knew I could get into the house quickly and easily because many times I had watched Martha when she didn't have her key. She would climb into the window on the side of the house. I had been over there so much that Tippy, her dog, wouldn't bark at me. And the neighbors always saw my car over there, so they wouldn't be suspicious either.

I left Jan's and drove to Martha's, two streets away. Pulling into the drive, I turned off my lights. I got out of the car and approached the window. Tippy started to bark, but I calmed her as I spoke out her name. I climbed through the window into a pitch dark house. I knew my way around, and I felt my way to the steps and upstairs to her bedroom. I began by searching the tables next to her bed, finding nothing. There was, however, a cigarette pack, the same kind Owen smoked.

I began to feel such a pain in my heart that I had never experienced. I opened different drawers, looking for whatever proof I could find. I could imagine them sleeping here together, and it made me feel sick. I turned to the large wall that had a closet built in. I opened it up and reached my hands under a stack of sweaters. I felt something like paper and pulled it toward me. I was so anxious I could feel my heartbeat in my fingertips. It was a large, manila envelope. I was afraid to open it up, knowing what I might find. Slowly, I pulled the metal clasp back, opening the top of the envelope. I pulled out a handful of papers. There was a picture directly on top of Martha and Owen in an embrace. I felt like a knife ripped my heart down the middle. I started to shake. I opened a letter and read: "Dear Martha, I love and miss you, and I can't wait until we can be together again."

My heart sank. Every emotion I shared with Owen, he had shared with Martha. He was sharing his love with her the same as he did with me. I slammed the closet shut. Tears gushed so fast down my face I couldn't read the rest of the letter. I wiped my tears with my sleeve, grabbed the envelope and raced down the stairs. Passing Tippy, I flew through the front door, slamming it behind me. I felt like I was dying. I sat for a moment in the car, trying to compose myself. The tears were still gushing. The thought of her and him together was overwhelming me. Tears made it hard for me to see as I drove back to Jan's. I pulled into her driveway and sat for a minute. I was paralyzed with an emotional pain that was unbearable.

When I finally knocked on Jan's door, she opened, eager with anticipation to see what I found. "Carol, what did you find?" she asked as she reached to hug me.

"Jan, here it is," I showed her the envelope. "The proof I needed. Oh, it hurts so bad. My heart is beyond broken."

"Come, let's sit down."

I tossed the envelope on the kitchen table. Jan reached to open it up. We both sat at the table, reading letter after letter of the words they wrote. The tears just would not stop. I folded my arms on the table, grabbing my head. I let out a scream.

"How dare she lie to me! I was her friend. How could she face me? She knows how much I love him. What kind of person is she anyways?"

"Now you know," Jan said. "It's out in the open, and they can't lie to you anymore. I know this hurts, but it is better now than for the both of them to keep playing with your head," she paused. "Carol, I want to tell you that Owen started writing me a while back," Jan confessed. "I got rid of the letters, feeling bad that he would do something like that to you. I wish I would have saved them now."

He had a game going, I realized. He would tell all the women the same thing. None of us talked to each other out of jealousy. It was his way of keeping us under control. We all knew he was with someone else, but we were afraid to confront it head on. I picked up the phone finally to tell Faith that I had the proof I needed. I was going down to Lucasville to visit Owen.

"Faith, I don't want to drive alone. Do you think you could drive with me?" I asked her.

"Sure. I don't want you to drive by yourself with the state you're in."

"I'll go home and get my things together, and we can leave in about an hour. I will call Grandma Shirley and ask her to keep the boys for me."

I knew Martha would be on her way back from the visit. I only had a little time to confront him to make sure they didn't have time to come up with a story together. I needed to visit Owen by the morning. I knew he would be calling the house to talk, and I wouldn't be there. Martha would usually call Jan after her visits with Owen. I warned Jan that she couldn't act suspicious, or Martha and Owen would figure something was up. We had to really play our cards right so the whole thing would work in my favor. I didn't realize at the time that it was the Lord who orchestrated all that was happening, including leading me right to the closet to get the proof I needed. Without that, I may never have had the strength to confront Owen.

Faith and I left that evening. I was in a hurry, even though I knew I wouldn't be able to visit until the morning. If I arrived the night before, I could be closer to finally confronting Owen with the evidence that I had, proving that I was right all along. It would put an end to the games he played with my head. The closer we got to our destination, the clearer my mind became. I was able to take a clear look at our relationship. All my suspicions were coming to the light.

I was startled when there was a police siren and lights behind me. I stopped the car and the officer approached. "Do you know how fast you were going?" he asked.

"No sir. I was talking and not paying attention."

"Hold on, I'll be right back."

"I bet he's giving me a ticket," I told Faith.

"I think you're right," she said.

A few minutes later, the officer again approached the car and handed me my license and a paper telling me I could pay the ticket now or go to court. I handed him my credit card to pay the ticket.

"Be careful and drive slower," he warned me.

We drove on as darkness set in, and we couldn't see the make of cars that were driving around us. Sirens went off again.

"Don't tell me he is stopping us again," I said.

"I wonder what they want," Faith said.

I stopped on the brim and the policeman approached my car. I rolled down the window. It was a different officer. "Miss, do you know how fast you were going?" he asked.

Not again, I thought. I better let Faith take over, I thought to myself. I am not doing very well this evening.

"No sir, I'm upset and I haven't been paying attention to my speed. I am very sorry."

"I need to see your driver's license and registration of the car," he said and I handed them to him. "I'll be right back."

"I know he's going to give me a ticket," I said to Faith. "Let's change seats. You're going to drive."

The officer came back and handed me the papers. "You can waiver this," he told me. "You don't need to come to court, just send a check to this address below."

We finally arrived at the hotel and called Jan to make sure she followed the plan.

"Did Martha call?"

"Yes, I acted like nothing was up," Jan reported.

"I'll see you when we get home to let you know how the visit went. If Martha asks where I'm at, you don't know."

I took my shower and tried to calm myself for sleep, but my mind was racing. I rehearsed what I was going to say to Owen over and over. I became really pumped up. I wanted to take a baseball bat into the visiting room and slug him as hard as I could. When I finally fell asleep, I only slept a couple hours before the alarm went off. Faith drove me to the prison.

I tried so hard not to draw attention to myself because I didn't want the guards to become suspicious of me. I really wanted to shout to the whole world, I found out!

I got through the check in and past the guards with a fake smile plastered on my face. Entering the visiting room, I got assigned to a table. I was placed directly in front of the guards' table, in the middle of the room. I thought to myself, we won't be able to hide this quarrel. All eyes will be on us. How am I going to do this without attention? I needed to be able to vent my frustration.

Owen would be strip searched before entering. The guards were determined to keep anyone from smuggling drugs in and inmates sending out contraband. As I waited for him to come out, my heart beat fast. I could hardly sit still. I didn't take my eyes off the door he would enter. I wanted to see the expression of surprise when he saw me. A few inmates came out first, and then his face appeared. I could tell by the look on his face that he wondered why I was there.

I held the envelope behind my back, my hand sweaty from nervousness.

"What is going on? Why are you here?" he asked as he leaned down to give me a hug and kiss. I turned my cheek to refuse his kiss. Pulling the envelope from behind me, I threw it across the table.

"What is that?" he asked.

"My proof. You can't lie to me any longer."

"What're you talking about?"

"Open the envelope. You'll see." I stood back. I didn't want to sit next to him. I was so disgusted with the lies. He pulled out the first picture of them together and I growled, "Now are you going to deny this affair?"

"No, I'm glad it is out in the open," he said. "I have wanted to tell you. I was afraid."

Part of me was relieved he didn't try to deny it, but the other part of me just wanted to rip his head off. I asked him all the questions that had played over and over again in my head. I just kept shooting question after question.

"Why did you lie to me?"

"I didn't want to. It got out of hand, and I was going to end it."

"When did this affair start?"

"About six months after Martha and I spent a lot of time together."

"Do you love her?"

"I have feelings for her," he said. "I don't love her like I do you."

"Then why did you tell her in the letters you loved her?"

"I had to keep her happy. I was doing my job."

"A job?" I said. "You are playing with people's emotions."

Sitting next to him, I felt secure enough to make my demands. I couldn't tell him I wanted out of the marriage. Instead I told him I wanted the property and business placed back into our names. I wanted Martha out of our lives. The visits from her must stop. He agreed. At the end of the visit he had me convinced I was all that he wanted, and he didn't want to lose me. He wanted the kids and me to stay with him. I thought to myself that God hated divorce, and He must want this marriage to work out. As I left, Owen said he wanted to work things out. I kissed him goodbye.

"Call me later," I said. "I'll wait for your call."

Faith met me as I left the prison, and we started our drive back home.

"He loves me," I told her. "We are working it out."

"Is he getting rid of Martha?"

"Yes. He said it will take a little time. We have to get the liens off the property and put the businesses back in our names. The paperwork will take the most time, and I have to be patient. I told him I wanted the visits to stop, and he said they would after he had the property transferred."

I dropped Faith off and went to pick up the boys. I was so happy to see them. I made my call to Jan.

"The visit went great," I told her. "I'm tired. I'll call you tomorrow to give you the details."

"Okay, have a good night," she said.

I called Martha the next morning and informed her that I wanted to meet with her. I told her to meet me at the restaurant down the street from her house. When I arrived, she was already sitting at a table. I slid into the booth. Tears started to run down my cheeks.

"Martha, I visited Owen yesterday, giving him the proof of your affair. He didn't deny it. He said he was glad it was out in the open. I want you to leave my husband alone. I don't want you in our lives any longer than it takes to get things back in our name."

I never gave her the chance to say a word. I got up and walked out, leaving her sitting there to ponder what just happened.

As time went on I could see that Owen was not doing his part. Things were not getting moved over to our names. He kept telling me it was going to take some time, and he couldn't get things done quickly. He needed her to come down on multiple visits so he could get her to sign certain papers. I knew what they were really doing was planning how they could stop me from what I was trying to do. We had $90,000 of tax liens against the property, and I wanted to start selling things. I had a person from the city mission who wanted to purchase the motel, but Owen wouldn't consider the offer. He wanted way more than what it was worth. I looked into selling our house, even having a realtor show the house. I had power of attorney and could act on Owen's behalf on any business transaction, so he couldn't stop me. He spoke with his lawyer and voided my power of attorney. It stopped me from doing anything.

I could finally see that he wasn't serious about the demands I had made. I had told him I would file for divorce if he didn't do what I asked, but it made no difference. I had cried wolf before and would always come running back after he gave me a smooth line. This time I had the Lord behind me, and I refused to back down. Owen didn't know how to handle this control over my life that I had. He probably thought I would grow out of it, and he would have things the way he wanted them. But the stronger I got in the Lord, the more I could stand up to Owen.

Things got so bad, all we did was fight. He wouldn't agree with anything I said. I finally went into the motel one weekend while I knew Martha was on a visit. I grabbed what personal things I wanted from the motel, taking as much money I could and I walked out of there, saying to the Lord, "If you are really real, I need you to show yourself to me and my children. I am walking away from all of this. I am going to completely trust you all the way." I got in my car and pulled away, playing my Christian music, weeping with the knowledge that I was taking a big leap of faith, trusting someone that I couldn't even see. But I knew the Lord had guided my life to this day and He was building my faith so that I could trust Him. I was about to start a new life.

> "I cried out to you, O Lord: I said, 'You are my refuge, my portion in the land of the living. Attend to my cry, for I am brought very low; deliver me from my persecutors, for they are stronger than I" (Ps. 142:5-6 NKJV).

CHAPTER TWENTY-ONE

Hitchhiker

The fear that had controlled my life for so many years was losing its grip on me. I began to trust in God instead of Owen to take care of me.

On one occasion, I was coming home from a Bible study and stopped by to pick up the rent from one of our properties. I was full of joy from a day spent with the Lord, and I was singing along with the music. My singing voice had been getting stronger, and my confidence in it was growing. I loved to sing along with the radio as I drove.

As I was headed home, I saw a young, clean-cut guy standing on the street with a radio in his hand and his thumb out for a ride. My girlfriends often heard me say I would never pick up a hitchhiker and neither should they. But something made me stop to pick him up. I asked him to get in.

"Where are you going?" I asked.

"I need to go to Cedar and Som Center." I was already on Cedar and there were only a few blocks until we would reach Som Center. I didn't see a problem taking him that short distance.

"What's your name?" I asked.

"Jake."

"I'm Carol. Glad to meet you. Why are you hitchhiking?" I asked him.

"My apartment had a fire last night, and it burned to the ground. I lost everything except the clothes on my back and this radio," he responded

"I'm so sorry. What are you going to do?"

"I'm going to stay with my friend who has his own place on Som," he said.

At Bible study that day, we discussed what God was doing in other people's lives, including my own.

"You know you need to get right with God," I started preaching to him and telling him what the Lord was doing for me. He listened to me without comment.

"What do you do for a living?" I asked.

"I work in a bar," Jake said. "I play the music people request."

I turned on the radio to show him some Christian contemporary music.

"This is what you and everyone needs to hear."

He shook his head. "Here's the house," he said. I pulled in the drive as the drizzle of rain turned into a downpour.

"I'll wait to see if you get in." He ran out quickly. Peeking around the corner, I could see him knocking at his friend's back door, getting drenched. No one answered. He dashed back into the car.

"I don't know where he's at. Maybe he's at work," he said.

"Can you get in?" I asked.

"No, I better wait until I can reach him on the phone."

"I have to go into my tax man's office to get some papers," I told him. "I'll take you with me, and we can try to get ahold of your friend at the office. Is that okay? I really don't want to leave you in the pouring rain."

Jake agreed, and as we drove, I continued to share how God set me free. We arrived at the office, and he sat in the lobby as I went in to see what I could do. Owen was fighting me with the tax issues, and I was trying to see what rights I had. I needed to know how the tax liens were going to affect me.

By the time I left the office, I was running late. I needed to pick up Kevin at the daycare center right down the road.

"Do you mind if I go and pick up my son?" I asked Jake.

"Sure," he said. "Do you want me to wait here?"

"No, you can come with me. You can call your friend from my house."

I continued talking about God as I drove to the daycare. I shared with Jake how my husband was incarcerated and that I was fighting him in a divorce.

"I'll be right back," I said when we got to the daycare. "I'll run and get him, and you can wait here." Kevin was taking his nap so I motioned for Jake to come in.

"I can't carry him. Do you mind lifting him and putting him in the car?"

"Sure," he agreed and lifted my son like he weighed only a couple of pounds. He placed him in the back seat and we strapped him in. I lived only ten minutes away from the daycare, but I was hoping Kevin wouldn't wake so he would get through his nap. When we got home, I opened the garage and the dogs ran out. I explained to Jake how they were my protection, and I needed to introduce them slowly to him. I placed the dogs outside and closed the garage door.

When we went inside, I pointed Jake to the phone so he could make his call. He left my number for his friend. Kevin woke and we took him outside to play in the yard while we waited for Ryan to get home from school on the bus. When the bus arrived, one of our dogs, Viking, ran to greet Ryan as he approached the end of the drive. I walked down to meet him.

"How was school honey?" I asked.

"Who is that guy by Kevin?" Ryan asked.

"That's Jake. He is visiting us for a bit," I said. "Do you want to go on your slip and slide?"

"Yes, Mommy."

"Jake, this is my son Ryan. He's going to go on his slip and slide. Do you think you can set it up for them while I go and start dinner?"

"Sure, glad to meet you Ryan," he said. "Come on."

I could hear the boys laughing as they slid down their slide. Jake was enjoying playing with the boys.

"Come and eat," I yelled.

"We're coming, Mommy!" Ryan called out.

"Go and clean up, then come and sit down."

Jake tried his friend one more time, still no answer. We sat at the table.

"Let's say a prayer." We all bowed our heads, including Jake. "Thank you, Lord, for this day. Bless this food to nourish us and thank you for bringing Jake to us today. Amen."

The boys finished their dinner and went into the family room to play with their G.I. Joe soldiers. Jake joined them while I cleaned up the dishes. The phone rang and I answered. It was Faith.

"Guess what I did? I picked up a hitchhiker," I told her.

"What do you mean?" she asked. I told her how I met him and brought him home.

"I'm going to call Pastor Murphy and tell him what you did. He needs to go somewhere. He can't stay there. I hope you didn't tell him you are alone, and Owen is away in prison," she said. "I'll call you right back."

"Jake, that was my friend calling. She said she's going to call our pastor to find a place for you to stay if you can't get ahold of your friend. Try and call him again before she calls back."

He quickly called, but there was still no answer. The phone rang again. It was Faith.

"Pastor says he can get him to the City Mission in downtown Cleveland. It's a Christ-centered place for homeless. They won't take anyone without a social security card," she said.

"Jake, my pastor found you a place to stay, but they need your social security card."

"I lost it in the fire," he said.

"Faith, it burned up in the fire."

"Ask him if he knows the number," Faith asked.

"Jake do you know your number by heart?" I asked.

"Yes," he told me the numbers, and I gave them to Faith.

"I'll call back in a minute after I give this to pastor," she said.

The phone rang seconds later. "Yes Faith," I answered, but it wasn't her. A strange male voice started speaking. "Carol, this is the Madison Police department calling. I want you to just answer yes or no. Do not let the man in your home know who you're talking to."

"Okay," I responded.

The officer proceeded to ask me questions, "Does the guy have blonde curly hair?"

"Yes."

"Is he tall? About six foot or more?"

"Yes," I answered, wondering how he could be describing Jake. How does he know he's here? What is going on? I dared not ask.

"Carol, I don't want you to panic. I need you to get your two boys and immediately get out of your house!" This must be serious, I thought. "I will meet you at the end of your road in the shopping plaza in five minutes," the officer said.

"Okay, see you then. Goodbye," I replied.

How was I going to pull this off? I picked Kevin up and placed him on my hip. Ryan was in the living room playing with his toys. Jake came from the bathroom and stood in the kitchen.

"That was Faith. Pastor is sending someone to get you. The street is hard to find so I have to go and meet them at the end of my drive. I'll be right back."

I walked to the door that led to the garage and looked down at Ryan, waving my hands for him to come with me. "I'm playing with my toys Mommy," he said. Jake was out of my sight, and he couldn't see me give Ryan a mad look that he knew meant you better come here right now. Ryan finally grabbed his toys and ran to me.

"I'll be right back," I called out as we walked out the door. I pushed Ryan into the car. "Get in and don't give me any back talk. Just listen to Mommy," I yelled and practically threw Kevin into his car seat, not stopping to buckle him in. I started the car and backed up quickly and drove off without looking back, leaving the dogs alone in the yard. I arrived at the end of the road and pulled into the shopping plaza. The only vehicles were from the karate place. No police cars were in sight. A car suddenly came flying into the lot. It was Faith's girls, Jana and Joy.

"Where's your mom?" I asked.

"I don't know," Joy responded.

"What the heck is going on? Who is playing a trick on me? Here, take the boys with you. I have to find out what's going on." I buckled the boys in their car and went back to my own. Before I could shut my door, the lot instantly filled with police cars. They had their sirens off. One officer jumped out of his car and came running up to my car.

"Where is he, Carol?" the officer asked.

"He's in the house."

"We need to know where you left him standing. Give us the layout of your house. We're going to go in and arrest him."

"What the hell is going on? Why are you after this guy?" I asked, demanding answers.

"He's a suspect we've been looking for. He robbed the local Dairy Mart store in Madison a week ago. He tied the worker up and raped her. He also is a suspect in burning down a church in Kirtland."

"Oh my gosh. You need to get him out of my house. Please go get him. The house is wood, it will burn in seconds. My dogs, I have to go get them. You won't get in the yard; they are watch dogs. I will get them, and then you can go right in." I got in my car and raced to the driveway, calling the dogs out my window until I could see them both. I jumped out and ushered them into the back door of the car, then sped backwards almost hitting the police cruiser behind me. I opened the garage door with the opener so the officer could go in and get Jake, but instead he came towards my car.

"It's okay," the officer said. "They got him."

"What do you mean? You never went in the house," I argued.

"He was next door at your neighbor's, knocking on their door to ask if he could use their phone. The neighbor was suspicious and asked him where he came from. The guy told him he was jogging down the street when it started to rain, and he needed to make a call to get a ride to town. Your neighbor offered him a ride. We had the road blocked so they were stopped."

A police car pulled up beside me and glancing in the rear, I could see Jake was there. I jumped out of my car to yell at him, but the officer put his hand out, blocking me from reaching into the car.

"Carol, next time, make sure you don't pick up any strangers."

"I will never do this again," I promised. I pointed my finger at Jake,

"You lied to me. And how you dare mess with a child of God? You will never get away with these things because the Lord will get you," I shouted. He looked at me like I was nuts as they drove away.

I let the dogs out of the car and went to Faith's to pick up the boys.

"What a close call for you," Faith said. "I bet you were scared."

"Faith, for the first time in my life, I really wasn't scared. I had a peace when I spoke to him about God," I said. "I need to go gather up the dogs and get the boys to bed. I'll talk with you later."

Viking and Butterball were jumping with excitement as we pulled into the driveway. I took us all into the house and breathed a sigh of relief. We were safe at home.

Faith called me in the morning and told me to grab the newspaper. Jake's picture was on the front page.

"You are darn lucky he did not hurt you and the boys,"

"Faith, I believe I had some big angels all around me yesterday. Where I live, I could have screamed, and no one would have heard me. The Lord used this crazy experience to show me I have nothing to fear of man. I no longer have to fear Owen. I know God doesn't want me trying to test His protection. I know He protected me and the boys. I know that if someone were to try and break into my house, even though I have the dogs and my gun, God would really be my protection."

"Pastor Murphy said everyone's prayers were answered when they found out you all were safe."

"I'm going to clean, so I'll talk with you later."

Jake called me from jail about a week later to tell me that someone had come to his cell to bring him a Bible. He began reading it. I told him it would be the best book he ever read. I told him, "Jake, I believe our paths will cross again someday. At that time you will be walking with the Lord."

There is no fear in love, but perfect love casts out fear, because fear involves torment. But he who fears has not been made perfect in love (Jn. 4:18 NKJV).

CHAPTER TWENTY-TWO

Moving On

During the summer of 1988, I was trying get some money out of the property Owen and I owned, but no matter what I did, Owen would block me. At one point I had the house up for sale, but Owen claimed it was his, and he wanted me out. My hands were tied because it wasn't in my name. How could he simply kick me and the boys out into the street? I started packing the things I knew I could take with me. I was so angry at how Owen was treating us so I had a large garage sale to sell his things. I thought, if he were going to act like this, I would show him. I was desperate to get me and the boys some cash and leave that house.

Finding homes for the dogs was going to be the hardest. They were attached to me and the boys. They protected us. I placed an ad in the local newspaper and received a call from a guy name Bill who told me he was looking for an aggressive dog. Viking was just that dog. He wouldn't let anyone hurt the kids, and no one could come into our yard. I had been afraid that I would not be able to get him a home because he was a biter. I put Viking in the car and drove to Bill's house. I told Bill that I would have to bring Viking out of his territory to see what he would do. Bill's house was located only half a mile away from where we were moving. I knew God was finding our dog a home near my boys to make it easier for them. When I got out of the car, Bill came out of the house.

"Bill, stay there on the porch," I called out. "Let me see what he's going to do."

As I pulled him out of the car he pranced around the yard and lifted his leg to mark his territory. He didn't care that Bill was on the porch. I slowly moved toward Bill with Viking on his leash. He didn't even bark. I couldn't believe what I was seeing. He had never acted like this. No one but me and the kids could even get near him, but here he was with this stranger right by him. I knew then that Viking was going to be staying here. The peace on Viking could only come from God.

"Bill, the boys and I really love this dog. It's breaking my heart that I have to give him away. The boys are going to be crushed when they get home from school and see he is gone."

"You all can come back and visit him whenever you like," Bill promised.

We tied Viking to a tree and Bill went to him, handing him treats. Their friendship was beginning. An hour later it was time for me to see how he would react when I left. Bill slowly pulled the leash closer to the walkway, toward to the front door, so Viking could go in on his own. I hesitated to get into the car. I knew I had to get home for the boys, so I yelled to Viking to be a good boy and that I would be back to see him soon. I felt like I was his mother, leaving my child with a complete stranger. The tears began even before I could start the car. My heart broke even more when I realized I'd have to tell the boys that I found him a home. I had to pull over a few times on the way home when my crying made it difficult for me to see. By the time I reached home, I had settled down. I was grateful because I didn't want the boys to see me crying.

When Ryan got off the bus, I said to him, "Ryan, you know how Mommy said we have to find Viking a new home because we're moving and can't take him with us? Well, Mommy found him a great home. He'll be living right down the street from where I want us to live. We can go and see him all the time."

I could see the sadness on Ryan's face. I could see his little heart was broken. But I had no choice. His father wasn't helping us, and I had to act fast to get us a place to stay. We drove to daycare to get Kevin.

"Viking is gone," Ryan said to Kevin.

"Where'd he go? We can keep Butterball, can't we Mom?" Kevin asked.

"Mommy had to give him to this nice man who is going to take care of him for us," Ryan said.

"We'll find a nice home for Butterball too," I told them. They were too young to realize what a mess my life had become. I was trying to be a single mom and wasn't getting any help from their father. He would only help if I did what he wanted me to do. I wasn't going to be under that control anymore, no matter what the cost.

Bill called that night, "I kept going up to the tree and giving Viking bones. I took him out a rib bone, and he wagged his tail some. I didn't go near him and let him chew for a while. I kept calling his name so he would get familiar with my voice. I finally took his leash and pulled him slowly into the house. I left the leash on so when he needs to go out, he doesn't run off. I'm going to keep him on the leash until he knows this is home. He sniffed everywhere, and finally he laid down at my feet." I was so relieved to hear that Viking was adjusting to his new home.

A few days later, I heard from Bill again. "I have a friend in Cleveland who likes Viking, and he wanted to know if he could have your other dog."

"Sure," I said. "He can come to the house to get him. I want him to come when the boys aren't here so it isn't too hard on them."

An hour went by and I received a call from Bill's friend, and we made arrangements for him to come. It was easier to let Butterball go. I had worried more about Viking adjusting. Butterball was friendly with everyone. A young man and his mom arrived. Butterball immediately went over to sniff them, and they bonded quickly. There was no question in my mind about letting him go with them.

I was attending a church in Willoughby, and I had started to like a man I met there named Rog. We hung out often and soon began talking marriage. My divorce still wasn't final. Rog went through divorce himself, and he knew the ugliness that takes place. He told me I could come and stay at his place. This way I wouldn't have to put up with the way Owen was treating me. I finished packing our belongings, and we made the move to Rog's. At the time, I was working for an interior landscaping company, making minimum wage and struggling to pay the bills. Owen didn't seem to care. Our lawyers were battling the divorce. I was frustrated it was taking so long. I wanted it over; I wanted to get on with my life. I wanted to start a new life with someone else who was going to care for me and love me for me and not use me. Rog and I were getting very close, and I thought he was going to be the one for me.

Finally on December 7, 1988 my divorce became final. I didn't get near what we needed. I received only $10,000. That was such a small amount compared to what all we had. Owen acted like he was giving me so much. All the years I had worked, all the money he had made from me and the other girls was so many times more. Once again, he was only thinking about himself and his money. He was not thinking about the boys and what they needed or what he could do for them. He just wanted to get rid of me. We had agreed on a disbursement so we wouldn't have to go to court to fight back and forth. We settled on child support and visitation and the money that I received. Since he had put all the property in Martha's name, I couldn't fight for it.

After my divorce was final, I thought I was going to get married to Rog, but the longer we lived together the more we began to fight. I told him that we needed to be right before God and get married. I felt like I was letting God down. Even though I was a Christian, I had fallen back to my old life of being sexually active. I wanted more than the feeling of being used. Even a Christian man wants sex. Why can't it be different? I asked myself. I was really struggling with guilt and shame again.

Martha and her son Bobby ended up moving into the house Owen and I had shared. She and Owen were married in prison. She was now the new Mrs. Kilbane, taking on the lifestyle I had left behind.

At the Interior Landscaping Company, there was one house I took care of on a weekly basis every Wednesday. I would water and maintain the plants. The owner of the house had an Amish girl named Martha who cleaned the house and did the laundry. She would occasionally be in the kitchen doing the ironing when I was there. One particular week she approached me, and we talked about Amish traditions and how she struggled with them. I shared with her my beliefs. We talked more and more as the weeks went on. She asked me how I could be a Christian and have bright nail polish like I was wearing.

We both started to look forward to Wednesdays when we would take lunch breaks together. I told her about Rog and what it was like living together. She convinced me I shouldn't be living with him. Living with him was really starting to bother me. Here I was, supposed to be an example to the unsaved, and she was telling me what I was doing wrong. The more I thought about my situation, the more convinced I became that she was right.

I finally told Rog I was leaving. But where was I going to go? I began to cry out to God, telling Him I wanted to serve Him; I wanted to do right for my boys. I prayed daily that I could get a mobile home. But how was I going to do this? My credit was shot; Owen's tax liens were on my credit report. No way could I get a loan. I couldn't borrow the money. I didn't know anyone with that kind of cash. Stepping out in faith, I approached four different banks, receiving no from all of them. I wasn't going to quit, I needed to get out of Rog's house and start living for God. I told myself I would try one more. I called a bank in Indiana and put in my application.

A few days later I received a call approving me of a loan of $26,000, which was what I needed to get the mobile home. I hung up the phone thanking God for what He did. He must have put blinders over the bankers' eyes. They wouldn't have given me the loan if they had seen the liens. I know that the Lord had heard my cry. He wanted me to move on, and I knew He would begin to put my life together the way He wanted to, not the way I was trying to.

I had all our boxes ready to go. The mobile home was on its way from Indiana. I ordered a brand new trailer to be delivered to the park. I got to pick out colors and different things I wanted. The boys and I were going to get a fresh start in life. I knew they both were young and didn't fully understand what had been going on in their lives. But I also knew they were hurting because they had given up their home and now they were moving again.

The day came for the move, and I took a few days off work to get us settled. Our house had arrived. I was so excited. I drove out to the mobile home park. The truck was backing our home onto the concrete slab where it would be parked on Leader Lane. It was two-tone gray with white shutters, all vinyl. I was so proud of it. I went back to Rog's to begin loading up the car. I knew by the time I was done, the kids would be getting home from school and we could head out. I had to register them for the Chardon school district so they would miss school for a few days.

We moved all of our things out of Rog's and into our new home. The boys ran into the trailer when we got there, wanting to see what their very own rooms would look like. Ryan was given the room on the end and Kevin went in the room next to the hallway. My room was on the other end with my very own private bathroom. We all jumped with excitement as we raced to explore. The boys ran outside to check out our lot.

We unpacked a bit and spent our first night surrounded by boxes—no dogs for protection, and no loaded gun. I didn't care. I was at peace in our home. I told my boss at the Interior Landscaping Company I needed to quit because I had to bring in more income. He hated to see me go, I was his best worker. But he understood my reasons. I never got to say goodbye to Martha, and I was sure she would wonder what happened to me. I asked my boss to tell her I was getting another job and told him to give her my number.

I started a new job at a Medical Billing Company in Chagrin Falls, a quaint town that had large waterfalls on both sides of the road. When I was a little girl, my grandparents would take us for a ride in the country to get ice cream and popcorn at the store right over the falls. Now I was taking a job in that same town.

My job paid me more than the landscaping job, but I had to travel more. On my lunch hour I would walk around Chagrin Falls to get exercise and spend my time talking to God. The people I worked with didn't share my beliefs. There was only one other girl there who was a Christian. She lived in the same mobile park.

Ryan and Kevin started in their new schools and rode the bus to and from so I didn't have to worry about getting them to school. Kevin began acting out in school so they put him in a special program. He was bused to another school. I was taking both boys to counseling. At one point I went to a church where they had a divorce recovery workshop for me and a program called Mended Rainbow for the boys. I wanted them to know what happened between me and their father wasn't their fault. I was still trying to cope myself, as well as trying to hold us all together. I continued to grow closer to the Lord. He was healing my heart and the deep wounds that I had.

All I could give my children at this time was God. I had nothing else to give. I had missed out on God for so many years. I knew I had to give this to them. I got involved with as many Christian programs as possible. I embraced a scripture that says, "Train up a child in the Lord and when he is old he will not depart from it." I wanted to make sure my children would not miss out on the Lord like I had.

Owen was granted visitation rights with the boys in our divorce. I didn't want them going to a jail, even to visit their father. But the courts did not agree with me on that. It was declared that since Owen was their father, he had the right to see them.

He wanted me to let my boys come down to the jail with Martha. There was no way I was going to allow them to go with a woman who had betrayed me. I told Owen I would only let them go with someone that I trusted. The divorce papers said it had to be someone that we both agreed upon, and I was not about to agree on Martha. After a time we finally agreed to allow the boys to go with a pastor we knew named Ernie. I would drive the boys over to meet Pastor Ernie, and he would take them down; then I would go and get them after their visit.

The tension was building at work. I was asked to double my work load. When I was accused of stealing stamps, they fired me. I cried on the way home. I lay across the bed crying out to God. What was I going to do now? I had my beauty license so I opened the phone book and asked the Lord to lead me to a place under beauty salons. I called and a lady answered the phone.

"My name is Carol, and I live here in Chardon," I told her. "I worked in a salon back in my teens. I recently went through a divorce, and I need to find a place to work. I wanted to get back into doing hair again. Do you have an opening?"

"As matter of fact, I do," she said. "Can you come in to see me within the hour?"

"Yes, I'll be there," I said. I couldn't believe it.

An hour later I went to Fazios Salon in Chardon. A rather jolly redhead asked, "May I help you?"

"I'm looking for Karen. I have an interview with her. My name's Carol."

"Hi Carol," she said. "I'm Karen."

The interview went well, and she asked me to start in two days. Friday was one of her better days, and Saturday was the best. She wanted me for any walk-ins that would come in on those days. I was going to be under her supervision until she could see my work. I left, thanking her for the opportunity.

On the way home, I thought about my life. I had met Owen when I worked in a beauty shop. After all the years in between now and then, here I was, back to working in a beauty shop again.

It was uncomfortable at first because I felt like I was back in school again, being trained. The hair cutting technique had changed, and I had to learn the up-to-date cuts. It was like beauty school all over again. I did that for a few weeks while Karen watched over me until she felt comfortable to let me cut on my own. I eventually built my own clientele, but the business was just not moving fast enough and the child support I was getting wasn't covering what I needed for the boys. I worked there for over a year, and it didn't get better. I finally told Karen that I had to move on.

* * *

Things were starting to change in my life again. I wanted more and more of the Lord, and I was going to different churches. I could see that God moved in different ways at each church. I was going to Faith's church, and the boys were involved with the programs. They were in Bible programs that taught them how to deal with life. Ryan was in Royal Rangers, a Christian program that was like the Boy Scouts but based in Christ. I sang in the choir at Riverview, and we became a part of the church family. The church embraced me and the boys. They would actually come and help me out at home. One time I stood in my driveway and cried because one of the men from church heard that my tractor had broken, and he came over with his tractor and began to cut my grass. I never before had people help me like this. I had always had to do things all on my own.

I attended Riverview for a few years, but one Wednesday night I decided to go to Dayspring, a charismatic church that was holding a sermon on speaking in tongues. I heard a few of my friends speak in a language that I had never heard before, and they told me it was a gift from God. After the message they had an altar call and asked if anyone wanted to come forth and get the baptism of speaking in tongues. I practically jumped up and ran down the aisle because I wanted to experience more of this. I wanted to get closer and closer to God in any way that I could. So when I went up, the pastor and his wife came over, and they laid hands on me and said just let the spirit take over. The woman placed her hands on my upper stomach and a heat went through me like I had never felt before. I began to speak a language that I had never heard before out of my mouth. It sounded so strange at first, but they kept telling me to just keep speaking and as I did, more and more would come forth. As time went on, it became natural for me to pray in this language that the Lord had given to me. I experienced God in a whole new light.

I began visiting Riverview less and less and attending Dayspring more. I went to the singles events often. We had a lot of fun getting together each week. I made friends through the singles groups, including Debbie and Wade. Debbie had a son named Ty who attended youth group with Ryan while Kevin attended the kid's church. I joined the worship team. A Christian woman gave me voice lessons, and I started to build up my voice.

A missionary came to the church with his family. They were having prayer over families so I went to get Ryan and Kevin. I had never experienced God this way. I could actually feel His power in the room, and I was drawn to it. Standing in the prayer line, the closer to the front we got, I could feel myself becoming weak, like someone was trying to take me to the ground. I had no control over it. I felt like I was going to melt to the ground. The boys were watching as people were dropping to the floor one by one. The man would slightly touch their forehead and down to the floor they would go, falling like a feather to the ground. Ryan and Kevin never experienced this for themselves. We got to the front, and as the guy came toward us he placed his hands on both of the boys at the same time, and they both fell to the floor in unison. I wept before the Lord as I knew He was doing something with them. I didn't go down that time as I had many times in the past. When Ryan and Kevin got up and we walked away, Ryan

166

told me that he went down on purpose. I just smiled at him and said, "You went down under the power of the Lord."

———•◆•———

Jill, the pastor's wife, asked me to speak at a women's fashion show we were having at the church. "Carol, please don't take this personally," she said to me. "I want to show how God can take a life and transform it. I want to use the theme Ashes to Beauty, and I'd like to use your story as the illustration of what God can truly do."

This would be the first time I would speak in front of a large room of women, sharing my dirty laundry. I prepared for the next few months. The fashion show was beautiful. Women of different age groups from the church modeled. The clothes they modeled were elegant. The tables were decorated with beautiful flower arrangements. The lunch we had was put together for a queen. I was then introduced to speak. I placed a large framed portrait of myself on the easel next to the platform. I pointed to the girl with the blonde wig and thick false eyelashes.

"This is a picture of what I used to look like," I said to the women. "This person looks beautiful, but inside she is dying. This was me." I continued to tell the women my story. There were moments I would cry because of God's mercy and what he brought me through. Parts of my past were still sensitive; parts of my heart were still healing. The Lord was using this talk to heal me even more. Moments when I would get choked up, Jill would walk up and put her arms around me to console me. When I felt I was ready to go on, she would sit back down. I had an altar call at the end, asking any woman that wanted to come forth and turn her life over to God to pray with me. Several women came, and we prayed. Many of them told me how I inspired them to go on. They told me that they were so glad they came to hear my wonderful story of God's redeeming love.

One lady had received a basket of flowers as a gift. She walked up to me and handed me the flowers, telling me that the Lord said I was a sweet fragrance to Him. She made me feel blessed. Women were talking to me for weeks about how they were inspired by what I had shared. My road to recovery progressed when I could tell my story aloud and see that these women would accept me, despite all that I had done.

I don't mean to say that I have already achieved these things or that I have already reached perfection! But I keep working toward that day when I will finally be all that Christ Jesus saved me for and wants me to be. No, dear brothers and sisters, I am still not all that I should be, but I am focusing all my energies on this one thing: forgetting the past and looking forward to what lies ahead. I strain to reach the end of the race and receive the prize for which God, through Christ Jesus, is calling us up to heaven (Phil. 3:12-14 NLT).

CHAPTER TWENTY-THREE

My Daughter

I received a phone call from Sandra, who had been at Scioto Village with me when I was a kid. We had made a pact when we were teenagers that someday we would get together.

"Carol, do you know how long it's taken me to find you?"

"Where are you at?" I asked her.

"I'm on the west side of Cleveland."

"I live in Chardon with my two boys."

"What ever happened to your daughter?" she asked.

"I gave her up for adoption."

"That's too bad. Do you ever wonder about her?" she asked.

"Many times. I just hope she's in a good home."

We talked for hours, catching up on our lives and making arrangements to get together. My life was filling with people I cared about. I started thinking about where my daughter Toni might possibly be living.

———•◦•———

The day came for my reunion with Sandra. Her husband drove with her to meet me. It was as if time stood still for a moment as we reflected on the time we were at Scioto Village together when we were only in our teens. We laughed, cried, and shared many memories. It was a happy day for the both of us. She handed me little angels, telling me they were a gift. I felt bad that I didn't think of getting her a gift.

"Carol, you know I looked for my father, and it took me a few years, but I finally located him."

"How was that?" I asked.

"I went to the library and did my research."

"Did you go and see him?"

"Yes, he really didn't seem happy to see me. I never went again, but it helped me to put closure on our relationship," she said.

We sat for a few more hours and made plans to get together again soon. I hoped to see her again.

Then one day Sandra called me, "Carol, have you done any more thinking about trying to find your daughter?"

"Yes, but I'm not sure if she wants to find me."

"Give me the name on her birth record, and I'll see what I can do." I gave it to her.

"Sandra, are you sure we should do this? What if she's married, and I have grandchildren? I don't know if we should approach her. Maybe she never told her husband," I said.

Sandra hung up, telling me she would call me if she found anything. I didn't have as much hope as she had at finding her.

Sandra eventually called. "Carol, you better sit down," she said.

"Why?"

"I have some good news for you. I've contacted an organization who helps find children that have been adopted. You can go to one of their support groups, and they'll help you."

"What do I have to do?" I asked her.

"Just go and see what it's about. The next meeting is Tuesday at 7:30 in the evening."

"Okay, I'll go. Talk to you after the meeting."

Tuesday came quickly, and I arrived at the meeting. A circle was formed in the center of the room. Men and women were there. The meeting started with a woman telling the story of how she researched finding her daughter and was finally united with her last week. She stood up and introduced her daughter to us. The tears were flowing from everyone, including me. We all clapped. Throughout the rest of the meeting different people shared their stories. Some were children looking for their biological parents and others were parents looking for their children. One lady told us how we could look up records at the library. The information they shared would help me a lot in my search.

After the meeting I approached one of the ladies who searched for her child, asking her what steps she took to find her. She gave me the number for someone who she said could find anyone. I tucked it safely into my wallet. I left the meeting feeling very inspired and hopeful.

The next morning I called the number.

"Hello, my name is Carol, and I received your number from the support group I attended last night. I was told you could help me find my daughter."

"I will need her full birth name, her father's name, and your name on her birth record. And any other info you can give me," the woman said.

"What if I have her original birth certificate?" I asked.

"If you have that, it'll cut my work in half."

"Hold on. I'll get it. I will be right back."

When I received the picture of her at Scioto Village, I had placed her birth certificate behind her picture in the frame. I was supposed to hand in all documents I had when I turned her over to the state, but they never asked me for it. I kept it all these years safely in my belongings. I took it everywhere I went. I went to my closet and pulled out the box of my important papers and took the picture out. Opening the frame I took out the certificate and went back to the phone.

"Grab a pen," I said. "I have the number on the certificate." I gave her number on the right-hand corner at the top of the certificate.

"I'll call you when I have some news."

When the following Tuesday arrived, I didn't feel like going to the support group, but I forced myself to go. I reminded myself that I needed to support them. They would be taking part in my reunion with Toni if we found her. New faces arrived. New stories were shared of a few more reunions. I couldn't wait for mine.

When I finally got the call, I was in shock. "Carol, I have the address where your daughter is at," she told me. "I also have a phone number. The name on her birth record for her adoption is Lynn; they changed her name. They do that for her protection and the adopted parents. When you call her just give her the facts of her adoption and then let her talk. You will know then if she is ready to accept you or not."

"Thank you so much."

"Good luck, Carol. Come to the meeting, and let us know how it went."

"Okay, I will. Bye."

I stood in my kitchen frozen; I didn't know what to do. Should I call? Should I drive over to the house? What if she wasn't there? What if, what if, what if? It played over and over in my head.

I called Sandra to tell her the great news. I was pacing back and forth. I just couldn't stand still.

"Thank you so much for getting this whole thing started," I told Sandra. "I don't know what I'm going to do next. I'll let you know. I will call you to let you know what I decide."

I wanted to shout to the world what we discovered. I got in the car and drove to the address in Wickliffe. I pulled onto the street, shaking as I got closer to the right house number. I didn't know how I was going to react. I didn't even know what I was going to do. The house was quiet; no one in sight. I parked in front, hoping she would walk out. I stayed for over an hour and no sign of activity. Eventually, I pulled away disappointed.

———————◆·◆·◆———————

A few days later, Sandra called me back and pushed me to make the call. Kevin and Ryan would overhear my conversations with Sandra so I sat them both down in the living room to tell them what was going on.

"Mom has something I have to share with you boys. When I was seventeen years old I became pregnant by a guy named Larry, and he didn't want anything to do with me. He got what he wanted and was gone. I would not have an abortion, so Mommy had a baby girl. I couldn't take care of her properly because I was a child myself, so I turned her over to the state, and she was adopted. You have a half-sister. Her name is Toni. I've been searching for her for the past few months, and I believe I know where she's at. I need to call, and I'm really scared."

"Mom, just make the call," Kevin said. "She'll understand. Tell her what you just told us."

Ryan got up and walked to his room. "Mom, just make the call," he yelled back.

I stood in the kitchen. I picked up the phone, and then I put it back down. I picked it up again. I felt like I had five hundred pounds in my hand, and I wanted to just drop the phone.

"Mom, just do it," Kevin said. "Here, I will dial the phone." He grabbed the paper from my hand and proceeded to dial. He shoved the phone to my ear. I heard the ringing. A young woman answered the phone.

"Hello, may I speak to Lynn?" I asked, trembling inside.

"This is Lynn," she said. I wanted to hang up, but Kevin was staring right at me, with his little hands cheering me on.

"Lynn, my name is Carol, and I'm calling from Chardon, Ohio. When I was seventeen years old I gave birth to a baby girl, and her name was Toni. I had circumstances in my life that took place where I couldn't take care of her, and I proceeded to give her up for adoption. I've always wondered how she was doing. I started a search a few months ago, and my search has led me to you." I took a breath.

Silence hung for a moment, then she asked, "How do I know you are not a prank?"

I could hear a man in the background yelling for her to hang the phone up. Get rid of the solicitor, so we can watch our movie. Just hang up, I heard him say.

"Honey, it isn't a solicitor. This is important," she told him.

"Lynn, I have longed to find you and now I have so much to share."

"I still don't believe you. What proof do I have you are really who you say you are?"

"Do you have a copy of your birth certificate? I have a copy here in front of me. I will give you the number, and you will see that they match. The numbers never change, only the name changes when you are adopted."

"Honey," she yelled, "Go get my birth certificate."

"You're not going to give a person on the phone your information," I heard her husband say. "Hang up or I will."

"Just go get it!" she screamed at him. "Hurry, hurry."

I could hear her husband in the background, getting frustrated with her. "I want to watch our movie. Here's your certificate."

"Okay, you read your number first," she said to me.

As I read the number, I could hear her saying, "Oh my God."

"Lynn, they're the same, aren't they?" I asked.

She blasted away at me with her questions, "Why did you give me up?

"I was young, and I couldn't take care of you."

"Why are you calling now?"

"I recently got up enough courage to start my search."

"Why did you wait so long?"

"I was afraid you would reject me and not want anything to do with me."

The questions were coming so fast, I didn't have the chance to think about my answers. I let her go until she had no more questions to ask. The support group had prepared me for this. I was told to let her vent. Let her say whatever is on her heart.

"I have waited for this moment all my life," she told me.

"I am so glad I kept your pictures. I would look at them often. I can still see the day you walked out of my life. It is embedded in my mind forever. You are like a fingerprint in my mind. It can never go away. You had your little teddy bear tucked tightly in your arms. I told you, you were going bye-bye." I wiped away my tears and took a deep breath. I didn't want to break down on the phone. She couldn't hear me cry just yet.

"I am still collecting bears," she told me.

"That is amazing," I said. "I have collections of bears all over my house."

"Do you know my dad? And where he is at?" she asked.

"I know who he is. His name is Larry. I'm not sure where he's at. He bailed out on us. He listened to his parents. They said I was a whore, and they didn't want him with me. Do you want to find him?"

"No, maybe later. I told my husband that I wanted to start to look for you; now here you are calling me. There was a part of my life that was missing, and you were it. Do I have any brothers or sisters?"

"Yes, you have two brothers, Ryan and Kevin. They're younger than you are. They know about you. When you are ready, I hope that we can get together."

"I would like that too," she answered.

"I have your address. I drove over to your home last week," I admitted.

"I'm not in Ohio," she said. "I live in Virginia, but I had my phone number forwarded since my husband and I moved here. It was supposed to be only for six months. You're lucky you were able to get ahold of me," she said.

"It wasn't luck," I told her. "God wanted me to find you. I needed to be healed just as you do."

"That house is my adopted parents' home."

"What does your dad do?"

"He's a detective on the Euclid police department."

"Oh, Lynn..." I said.

I knew I'd have to spill my story to her. I didn't want her to hear it from anyone else.

"I didn't want to tell you this over the phone. I wanted to see you face to face. When you tell your adoptive dad my name, he's going to tell you to stay away from me. He'll think I want something from you. He knows me only from my past. He doesn't know that I am a changed person. I'm a Christian now. Back when he knew of me, I was a monster. I am no longer with my ex-husband."

"I'll tell him you have changed. It's my choice. I will not even tell my mom and dad I'm meeting you."

"That's up to you, Lynn. My last name is Kilbane, and your father will know the case as the Judge Steele murder trial."

"I remember that case. My dad talked about it."

"When he hears I've contacted you, he'll say I have a motive. Lynn, my only motive is to start a friendship. I can't take the place of the woman who raised you. I only want to start to build a relationship from now. I am not a threat to them. I appreciate all that they have done for you. They raised you to be a young lady. I was always worried I would find you, and you would be in some kind of trouble. I am grateful to them."

"I'm going to see when my husband and I can come up. It'll be a few months before he can get off work. I would love to meet you."

"You call me, and I'll be looking forward to meeting you."

"Goodbye," she said, and I hung up the phone.

Kevin looked at me, "Mom, how did it go?"

"It went better than I could have hoped for."

He ran off to his room. I sat down at the kitchen table, laid my head down and began to weep. I had dreamed of this day for so long. Now I would get to see my baby girl after all these years. I wondered what she looked like. Did she look like me or her father? Was she skinny like me? Did she have my eyes? My color hair? I could not stop the questions from racing through my mind.

You saw me before I was born, every day of my life was recorded in Your Book. Every moment was laid out before a single day had passed (Ps. 139:16 NLT).

CHAPTER TWENTY-FOUR

Double Date

I finally heard from my Amish friend, Martha, when she called me to tell me she had left the Amish faith completely. She had been away from her family going on three years and was getting her own place. I was so excited for her. She told me she was born again and had started going to church. I invited her to come to church with me. She attended a few times, but life got busy and I didn't hear from her for a while.

The pastor was having an affair with his secretary, and the church was splitting up. I needed to move on. I started to attend a small church down the street from our home. It wasn't the same, but it was still a family church.

Slowly other people were leaving Dayspring and coming to Chardon Christian Fellowship. Debbie and Wade followed not too long after I left. The services at the new church were a bit reserved. I was used to feeling the Spirit really move me. The worship leader at Dayspring had really known how to bring us into the presence of the Lord. I missed his worship.

Ryan was fighting me because he wanted to go back to Dayspring. He was too young for me to explain why we had to leave. The youth group was different at Chardon Christian. It was hard for them to handle the kids that were hurting that came from Dayspring. I tried to get Ryan involved, and although he did join in to a certain point, he had his walls up.

I started to settle into the church and attended almost all the family events trying to get the boys involved. I was curious about one man in particular. His name was Joe, and he was very attractive, with a full head of pure white hair. He was always by himself. He was one of the ushers that collected the offering. I asked Sherry, the pastor's wife, what she knew about him, and it turned out that his daughter Tara was friends with her daughter Ginny. She told me he was single and raising two girls on his own. He had left the Amish when he was sixteen. Word quickly spread that I was interested in him. His two daughters and Sherry were trying to play matchmaker. I knew they were trying to get us together, but I wasn't sure if he knew. Whenever I talked to him at the church socials, he would respond, but had his head down. We were so opposite, I was afraid my outgoing nature would scare him off.

Pastor Wayne approached me to ask if I would join a few others on Sunday to give my testimony of what God had done in my life, how He had changed me. I agreed that I would. When Sunday came, I watched as two members shared their stories before it was my turn. I stood behind the pulpit, shaking. I began my story, and eyes were glued to me. Tears ran down my face when I told the sensitive parts of my life. I wiped the tears and continued on about the murders I was involved in. When I looked to the back of the church, I saw Joe standing there, and I looked away with embarrassment. I finished my story but couldn't bring myself to look at Joe. Everyone clapped as I walked off the stage. I felt completely beat up. As I sat down next to Sherry, my mind raced with thoughts of Joe. He is never going to be with me now that he knows my past and who I was involved with, I thought. No one wanted to mess with Owen Kilbane. I told myself, he will never see you especially when he knows how many men you have been with. I left quickly after church. I wanted to crawl into bed and never come out again.

Martha called me one day, upset over the religious struggles she was having.

"Carol, my parents won't talk to me. I'm living in Burton where I rent a room. Why don't we get together?" she suggested.

"Let's do it today," I said.

"Where at?" she asked.

"Do you know where Leaders Trailer Park is? You can come to my home."

We began spending a lot of time together, and I invited her to come to my church. She was struggling with the Amish and told me she felt they were a cult. The bishops were giving her a hard time for leaving. I told her about how Joe had left the Amish. They had a lot in common. Martha tried to play matchmaker, telling me she would help get the two of us together. She was dating a guy named Rob, and he started coming to the church with her. I could see she was becoming free of the Amish customs. I couldn't see any traits in Joe, and I figured maybe he had been out of that religion for so long he lost them. Martha just left, so all the upbringing was still attached to her.

Martha began talking about getting married to Rob. She didn't have her father to rely on so she asked Pastor Wayne to take him out to lunch to make sure he was suitable for her to marry. He passed the test with flying colors. Rob asked Martha to marry him, and she asked me to be her maid of honor. She started planning her wedding for July 24, 1993, just a few months away.

———•◦•———

Ginny, the pastor's daughter, was getting married to a man named Adrian. I was going with Joe's daughters, Sherry and Tara, to Ginny's rehearsal dinner at the buffalo farm where Adrian's mom lived. This was the first time I had been around his daughters without him. Sherry was driving. The girls were giving me the inside scoop on their dad.

"We'll help you get a date with our dad, but you can't go too fast. He hasn't been on a date in years. Take it slow and I think you can get him to go," said Sherry.

"I'll take it slow. I don't want your father to back off," I said. "Martha said she is going to talk to him. Leaving the Amish herself, she can relate to him."

When we arrived at the farm, cars were lined up everywhere. We approached the garage where the dinner was being served. Ginny's parents, Sherry and Pastor Wayne, greeted me, telling me they were glad I could come. It was the first time I had tasted buffalo. I mingled among the people I knew. The rehearsal dinner came to an end, and the girls and I went home. They dropped me off.

"Goodnight girls. I'll see you in the morning," I called out.

"Goodnight," they replied in unison.

———•◦•———

The day of Ginny's wedding arrived. Rob, Martha, and I went together. I was thrilled I was going to see Joe at the wedding. He hadn't asked me to go out on a date with him yet, but he knew I had my eye on him. He liked me too but was too shy to do anything about it. I figured I would have to be the forward one here and push for the date. With everyone working behind the scenes to get us together, he had no chance. The date was going to happen.

"When we get to the reception, I'll get Rob to have Joe come and sit with us," Martha said.

"That will be awesome," I replied.

"Rob and I are going to the movies after this. I can have Rob ask if he wants to join us," she said.

"I hope he'll go." I wanted to spend time with him.

The wedding was beautiful. It made me think about how I never had a wedding like that. I hoped the person I would marry in the future would let me have a romantic Victorian wedding.

We drove to the reception hall. Martha, Rob, and I sat on the end of the table. When Rob walked over to Joe to ask him to join us, I felt giggly inside.

"I wonder if he'll come," I said to Martha.

"Rob will get him to," Martha replied, but when Rob walked back to the table alone, I was disappointed.

"Joe said he would come over after he finishes setting up the last of the few tables," Rob said. The butterflies came back. Martha and I laughed. She made fun of my girlish behavior. When Joe finally walked over, he pulled a chair out and sat next to Rob, on the other end, not close to me. I had to talk across Martha and Rob for him to even hear me.

"The wedding was nice," Rob said to Joe.

"Yes, Ginny looked nice," he responded.

"Martha, Carol, and I are going to the movies later. Would you like to join us?" Rob asked.

"I don't think so," Joe said. "I have to take the tables down, and then I have to do something at home."

My heart sank. I was not worth a date, I thought. After that, I didn't even try to talk to him. What was the point? I thought. He wasn't even interested in me. I wanted to leave.

"Martha, can we go?"

"Wait until they throw the bride's bouquet," she said.

"Okay." Joe stood up to leave, saying goodbye, and Rob went with him. He told Martha he was going to help with the tables, and she decided to come with me back to my place to wait. Rob would pick her up when he was done.

They announced the throwing of the bouquet.

"Go and see if you can catch it," Martha urged. I walked over to the group of ladies all bunched together. I removed my shoes and stood in a crouching position. I was determined to catch those flowers. Ginny yelled, "Are you ready? One, two, three!" The bouquet flew high into the air towards the crowd. I leaped to my feet, as though I was Michael Jordan wanting to catch a ball. My hands spread, I could see them heading in my direction. I pushed my way through the crowd and caught the flowers. The women around me laughed at my enthusiasm. "She really wanted them," they remarked, "we had no chance." I was smiling so hard my cheeks ached.

Martha and I left, going back to my house. I was so disappointed that Joe stayed behind. Kevin and Ryan were playing video games. Martha and I stood in the kitchen. and she grabbed my hands and said, "Let's pray."

"Dear God, if You want Carol and Joe to get together, then You will have to make it happen. You give us the desires of our heart, and she truly wants to get to know this man. If You want him to go to the show, then bring him here. Amen."

We laid across my bed while Ryan played his games in the living room. Kevin came in and heard me talking about Joe. He wanted to hear what was going on so he stayed. We began to read the Bible and talk about David and Goliath, the boys' favorite story. Martha kept hinting she was hungry.

"Let's go to Burger King and get a hamburger," she said.

"Rob is coming soon," I reminded her. "You better wait."

"I'm really hungry. I guess I'll just grab a snack from you," she said. She walked out into the kitchen, grabbed some chips, and walked back to sit down on the bed when we heard Rob walk in the front door.

"Are you ready to go?" he yelled. Martha and I looked at each other puzzled.

"What are you talking about?" she yelled. Rob was standing in the middle of the living room, and Joe was directly behind him. Martha and I looked at each other. She jumped up, closing the bedroom door behind her. I could hear through the door as she walked to the living room.

"Carol's getting ready. She'll be right out," she said.

Kevin and I started jumping up and down, excited. "He's here! I can't believe he's here." I settled down long enough to change into something I felt would really make me look good for my first date. I freshened up my makeup and hair. I took a deep breath to gain composure and opened the door. I walked slowly toward the kitchen.

"Where are we going?" Kevin asked.

"Only your mom is going with us," Rob told him.

Kevin continued to whine until Ryan finally yelled, "Mom is going on a date, and you're not going. You are staying here with me."

"Should I grab a coat? Do you think it is going to get chilly?" I asked, then ran back to the bedroom as they were walking out the door. I grabbed my light jacket and ran to the door to catch up.

"Ryan, make sure you feed Kevin. I'll see you later."

"Have fun, Mom," Ryan yelled as I walked out the door.

I was so excited about my date that I excused myself to run next door to share the news with my neighbor, Robin. I had told her about my interest in Joe, even going so far as to tell her that I was going to marry him someday. I went inside her place and jumped up and down with my excitement, not seeing the man on her couch. It was her father. She introduced me, and then I told her I had to go.

I regained my composure and walked back to the car, opened the door and climbed into the backseat, sitting on the opposite side of the seat from Joe. Martha looked back at me and smiled. She knew I was trying to control my excitement. I let Joe and Rob do most of the talking. Once in a while I would throw in a question. We arrived at the deli, next door to the movies. We sat down at a table and I ordered a Ruben, one of my favorite sandwiches. Joe ordered the same.

Martha shared a funny story with us, "When Rob and I went on one of our dates to the movies, he snuck in a bottle of pop. I told him not to bring it, but he did anyways. We were sitting halfway through the movie, and Rob dropped the bottle and it went clunk, clunk, clunk, rolling down the floor. I wanted to slide under my seat, I was so embarrassed."

We walked to the theater and Joe was a complete gentleman, opening the door for me. We decided to see the movie *Groundhog Day*. We sat close to the back, and Joe sat next to me. I was pleased with the way the date was going so far. It would be even better if he felt the same. But he was so quiet. I had hoped he would open up more. The movie began, and we laughed at the comedy that was taking place. We laughed even harder when someone dropped a bottle of pop, and it rolled down the floor. We looked at each other and giggled out of control. People in the back of us said, "It's not that funny." They didn't get our inside joke. When the movie ended, we headed home.

"Goodnight," Joe called out as he walked towards his truck.

"We're going to go also. Rob has a long way home back to Stow, an hour away," Martha said.

"Goodnight," I said and walked into the house. The lights were out and the boys were sound asleep. I climbed into my pajamas and jumped into bed. I laid there smiling, reflecting back at the great night I had just experienced. I hoped we would do it again and soon. I was determined to make it happen.

A few days later, I called Martha telling her I was going to have a cookout after church and asked if she and Rob could come, and I would invite Joe. Sunday came and after church I walked up to Joe, "I'm having Martha and Rob over for a cookout. Can you join us?" I asked.

"Sure. What can I bring?" he asked.

"Just bring some chips. I'll see you in a bit."

Martha and Rob were at the house, waiting when I got home. "Rob can you start the grill? Joe's coming over shortly," I said.

"That's so exciting," said Martha.

Joe arrived with a bag of chips. He stood by the grill with Rob while Martha and I set up the table inside. I went to gather up the boys who were riding their bikes. "Time to eat," I yelled. We gathered around the kitchen table while Rob said a short prayer. After dinner we settled in the living room to relax. I listened as Joe opened up more and more throughout the conversation. The evening went too quickly, and one by one everyone had to leave.

"I have to get up early," Joe said. "I need to get to sleep. I better get home."

"It was nice having you here. We'll have to do this again," I said.

"Yes, we all do," Martha said as she and Rob walked out the door.

"Goodnight everyone," I said, shutting the door.

Delight yourself also in the Lord, and He shall give you the desires of your heart. Commit your way to the Lord, trust also in Him, and He shall bring it to pass (Ps. 37:4-5 NKJV).

CHAPTER TWENTY-FIVE

My Daughter

My relationships were growing. Lynn and I spoke often, a few times a week, and Joe and I were spending more time together. He would come over, or I would stop over at his place. I loved to walk and so did he. We would walk the roads around the trailer park. It felt so natural; we locked hands. I knew he wanted to be with me. I asked him, "Do you remember when I gave my testimony at church and you were standing in the back of the church against the wall? What were you thinking after you heard it?"

"I thought about how much you loved the Lord, and it made me more attracted to you," he admitted. When he told me that, I knew he was a godly man.

Lynn called to tell me she and Vince, her husband, were going to come up for the Fourth of July to her parents' house. It was 1993, and it had been well over twenty-five years since I held her in my arms. We planned to meet on the square of Chardon in the large, white gazebo in the middle of the park. I counted the days to her arrival. I told Robin I wanted her to be there on my special day. Pastor Wayne and his wife, Sherry, would also come for moral support. He said he would take a video for me so I could have it for my memory. I gathered a few more of my special friends that I wanted to be at my joyous moment. My boys were my top priority to meet their sister for the first time. Joe, Martha, Sylvia, and Debbie were just a few I wanted to be there.

The morning came, and the sky was perfect. Joe came over to get me, and he kept me calm. I had so many emotions stirring inside. I could feel the pain so deeply of what I did to her so many years ago. Was she going to truly forgive me? What was our relationship going to be from here? Joe kept holding onto me, letting me pour out my emotions.

"Come on," he said. "It's time to go."

We walked outside, and Robin was waiting in the drive, a smile on her face. "Carol, this is your day," she said. Joe drove us to the gazebo. I knew Lynn loved bears so I had searched for just the right one for this occasion. The bear I found for her was all dressed up in a pink dress, the same color dress Lynn had on when she left me. I held onto the bear tightly as I walked to the gazebo. Pastor stood there with the camera, and Sherry began to pray.

"God give her peace for this special day. Let Lynn have peace also. Let them embrace each other's love. Amen," she said. Martha gave me a hug.

I couldn't stand still. I never asked what kind of vehicle she was coming in so I turned my head at each vehicle that went by. The cars kept going by. I knew I would know her. A van pulled into a parking space across the street. A gentleman got out and walked around the van to open the door. Out came a slender young woman clutching a teddy bear. Oh, she thought like me, she was bringing me a bear, I thought to myself. I watched as Vince held her arm and led her across the street. I walked slowly to the edge of the gazebo.

My knees were shaking, and I hoped I wouldn't faint. The walkway was so close, yet she seemed so far from my reach. I slowly went down the first step, moving closer to her. She came to the curb and onto the grass. I couldn't hold back any longer, and I rushed to her. She let go of Vince and at that moment we fell into each other's arms, and everyone else around us seemed to disappear. I was flooded with tears, and I saw that she was too. Here she was, here was my baby. After all these years, I had my baby in my arms again. I didn't want to let go. I wanted to hang on forever. I had let her go before. I didn't want to let her go this time, and I swore I would never let her go again. If I just hold on, she can't leave. I finally had to pull back, and I looked into her eyes.

"I am so glad you are here. I've waited for this day forever," I told her.

"Me too," she said. "I need a Kleenex. My face must be a mess."

"Your face looks beautiful to me. Stand back," I said. "Let me take a look at you."

"I have to sit down before I fall down," she said. I turned around to direct her to the stairs so we could sit. I could see everyone around us wiping their eyes. There wasn't a dry eye. They were feeling our joy.

She took my hand and placed hers next to mine. "Your hand and wrist are exactly like mine," she said.

"Here, I have something for you," I said, handing her the bear. She smiled at me.

"We think alike. I have one for you." I grabbed her closely again, and we started crying all over. Holding her felt so good. It was like time had stood still for us, and we picked up where we had left off. There was a bond, a natural mother's bond, that I felt deeply. It had never gone away, even after all these years. I had always held her close in my heart, and now I could hold her in my arms.

"Vince, come here," she said. "I want you to meet my husband."

"It's so nice to meet you." I yelled for Ryan and Kevin. Kevin met her first.

"Kevin, this is your sister Lynn." She gave him a hug. "Ryan this is your sister." They hugged too. I was thrilled to have all three of my children together.

Lynn stood up to look around, amazed at all my friends that were there to support our reunion.

"Lynn, I want you to meet Joe," I continued with the introductions.

"Great to meet you," he said. "I've heard a lot about you."

I reached to hug Joe, and I told him how grateful I was for his support. I continued to introduce Lynn to everyone that was there.

We couldn't stop looking at each other, comparing. I stretched out my leg next to hers. Our legs were the same, chicken legs. It ran in the family. Our feet, our body shape, our wrists—all looked the same. She was a blueprint of me. We sat, we stood, we hugged, we cried, we smiled, taking in all that we could of each other.

"Do you want to come over to my place?" I asked.

"Sure, we'll follow you," Vince said.

Everyone scattered in different directions. I hung onto Joe's hand, and we said our goodbyes to everyone, thanking them for their support. I continued glancing back at Lynn as she approached her car. I was still in amazement at what she looked like. I clutched the teddy bear tightly in my arms as we walked to the car, parked on the opposite side of the town square. We waited for Lynn and Vince to come around the corner to follow us back to the mobile home. I could see Lynn coming. I smiled at Joe.

By the time we got home, Ryan and Kevin were getting somewhat antsy. I took Lynn by the hand and we went inside. We couldn't be separated, only long enough for each of us to go to the bathroom. I hugged her again. We sat on the couch. I took out the picture of her I was given at Scioto Village. I smiled.

"This is what I held onto for all these years. I have your birth certificate right here," I said, handing it to her.

"It's amazing you have been through so much, and yet you still have this."

"God wanted me to have it for this day."

I took out the baby pictures I had of her holding onto her little teddy bear. Her face was so sweet and innocent looking. I could see the tears flowing down her cheek. I placed my arm around her and held her close. I knew there was pain.

"This is your Grandma Braun," I told her, pointing to one of the pictures.

"How could she? How could she not accept me?"

"My mom has problems," I tried to explain. "She never should have had children. She never cared for her own children." As I showed her more pictures, I could see it was becoming too much for her.

"I need to go," she said. "I'm overwhelmed."

"We'll catch up tomorrow. I have a party for us at the church I go to. We passed it on the way down the hill. It's at 4 o'clock. They want to celebrate our reunion," I said.

"I need to go home and rest. This has been a lot to absorb today. I'll see you tomorrow at 4."

I reached to hug her goodnight. "Have a good night. Take good care of her Vince." She walked out to the drive and got in her van. I waved until the van was out of sight. When it finally disappeared, I turned around, and Joe took me in his arms.

"She has had an emotional day, and so have you," he said.

"I know. I hope she's okay."

"I'm going to go home also so you can rest," he said.

"Goodnight, I love you," we both said.

I went in to see how Ryan and Kevin were doing. They had slipped into the background while all of this was going on. My attention had been focused on Lynn, and I wanted to make sure the boys weren't feeling left out. I gave them both hugs,

"You both know you are very special to me, you will always be my boys. Lynn was a stranger, and I'm just building a friendship. You all are my children now," I told them.

They slipped down under the covers. "Goodnight, Mom, we love you too."

I called Martha and asked her, "So what did you think of the day?"

"It was one of the most emotional days of my life. I can't imagine how you're feeling."

"I am emotionally drained. But it's a good drain. I will remember this day forever. I am so glad Pastor did the video so I can go back and look at it later. There were so many emotions flying, I couldn't take them all in. I will later. I'm going to bed. I'll see you tomorrow. Goodnight."

Morning came quickly. I waited for Joe to get home from work. He came over as soon as he changed, and we got ready to head to the church for the reunion party.

"I am so excited for this party. I hope it's not too much for her," I told him.

"I think she will let you know if it is."

I stopped next door to ask Robin what she thought of my outfit. She was pacing the floor more than I was.

"She looks so much like you. She is beautiful. What an emotional day. Thanks for letting me be a part of it," she said.

"Thanks, I'm glad you were part of it. I can't wait for everyone to see her at the party. Do I look okay?"

"You look wonderful. Go and enjoy your reunion. I'll see you there," she said.

Joe was sitting on the couch when I got back to my house. I asked him to pray for me. I was a basket case. My nerves were shaking up a storm. He took my hand and asked God to give me peace.

"We need to go. It's close to the time," Joe said.

"Come on, Ryan and Kevin, we need to go," I called out and the four of us piled into the truck. As we pulled into the parking lot of the church, I could see familiar cars there. I knew who had already arrived. I didn't see Lynn's van. As Joe parked, she pulled in. I waited for Vince to park before jumping out and rushing to her side. We were both wearing the same color green. That's scary, I thought, we hadn't even asked each other what we were going to wear. I grabbed her hand as tight as I could, and we started to the door. As we went in, the hall was lined with my friends, strangers to her, yelling and clapping. We went through the archway of hands into a large room filled with more friends. The camera was going as we made our way to the end of the room. On the table were two yellow teddy bear cakes joined by holding hands. One had Lynn written on the chest and the other had Carol written on it. We smiled. People were beginning to come up to us. I introduced her to each one as they came. There was no way she would remember all of the names. Pastor said a prayer, and Lynn and I started the line to eat. We both were so nervous we didn't have an appetite. We grabbed a little food and went to sit down. Vince was standing back by Joe. He was taking it all in.

After a while, Lynn excused herself. A few moments later Vince came over and whispered in my ear that they were going. Lynn wasn't feeling very well.

"I hope she'll be okay," I said to Vince.

"I think the last two days have been a lot for her. I'm going to take her home and put her to bed."

"Tell her just she and I will get together tomorrow before you head back to Virginia."

"Okay, goodnight."

I sat there, looking at everyone in the room. I wondered if someone said too much to her. Maybe it all had been too much. Maybe I should have waited to do this. I walked over to Martha and Robin and told them she left. "I hope I didn't scare her off," I said.

We cleaned up and Joe took me home. We went inside and sat on the couch, going over the events of the day.

"I hope she'll be okay," I said.

"She will be, just take it slow from now on," he said.

I pulled out her pictures and flipped through them. She had grown up. Look at all these years I have lost, I thought to myself, now I have to find out all that I missed. Joe kissed me goodnight, and I went to check on the boys. Ryan was playing his video game and Kevin was watching a TV show. I let them be, knowing they needed their space. I went back into my room and placed a worship tape on and let God touch me after a long emotional draining day. I needed a touch from my heavenly Father. He was the only one who could fill me up after being emptied of so many emotions today. I drifted off to sleep.

I woke up the next morning to find Ryan outside with Robin's boy, and Kevin was playing his Nintendo. I made them breakfast and sat for a moment and talked with them.

"You know boys," I said. "This has been very hard on Mom for the past couple of days. I have put all my attention on Lynn. We are going to do something special this weekend. We can go roller skating at the rink."

"Yes, Mom," Kevin said. "We'd like that."

"Can I bring a friend?" Ryan asked.

"Sure. I have to see if I can meet up with Lynn before she goes back to Virginia so you boys let me know your plans for the rest of the day."

I called Lynn to see how she was doing.

"I got so sick," she said. "I don't know if it was my nerves or what."

"I hope I didn't put too much on you. If I did, I am sorry. I was so excited you came I wanted to celebrate."

"I do want to take it easy," she said.

"I know. I just want to get together with you alone today. There are things I want to talk about in person. Why don't we meet at the park where we met? We can sit on a picnic table and talk."

"Okay," she agreed. "What time?"

"What's good for you?"

"Let's meet at 1 o'clock. That's good."

I told the boys I was going to town in an hour, and they needed to stay close to the house. I made lunch for them, then got dressed and ate quickly myself. Before I knew it, it was time to go. I headed to the square, parked my car, and walked to the picnic bench by the gazebo. Flashbacks of our reunion bounced across my mind. I could only smile. I watched for the van to swing by. Vince was going to drop Lynn off, then he had some business to take care of. He would come back in a few hours to pick her up. I watched the van pull up, and Lynn jumped out. Vince kissed Lynn goodbye, then waved to me. She walked toward the table and sat directly across from me. I felt I better give her some space so I stayed where I was at. Maybe I had been smothering her too much.

"Are you feeling any better?"

"I think so," she said.

"These last two days have been overwhelming to me," I said. "I can only imagine how you feel."

"Carol, I have so many questions I need to ask," she said.

"I'll answer anything."

"When I was little, did I have a broken arm?"

"Why do you ask that?"

"I remember a cast on my arm."

"You were only two years old! That is wild that you can remember when you were that young. I left you with Owen and when I came back, he told me that you had fallen. He said he took you to the hospital to get checked. They took an x-ray and said it was broken. You were afraid of men for some reason. I often wondered if Owen did something to you that night. Our friend Sy was with him. You would hide under your crib when men came around. You were only okay with my dad. It was one of the reasons I felt you would be better off in a stable home. Your fear of men was something I didn't know how to deal with."

"Why did you really give me up?"

"I was involved with prostitution, and Owen told me that our lifestyle wasn't good for you. I let him convince me to give you up. I called the state agency, and they came to pick you up. I told you I have that day imprinted on my mind."

"I wonder if that's why I am attached to bears like I am."

"It could be. I have my collection too, and maybe we both have hidden reasons for collecting bears."

"Tell me more about my father," she said.

The questions went on and on for a few hours. I answered her truthfully. I hoped she could handle the truth. I had lived with lies for so many years, and here I was, sitting with my daughter, telling her my whole life story.

"I talked to my adoptive dad. My mom is feeling uncomfortable with me meeting you. I told her I was going to meet you anyway."

"If you want, I can meet her. I would love to thank her for taking care of you and raising you to be the young lady you turned out to be. She raised you. I could never take that away from her. She is your mother. I am your mother by blood only. I only want to build a friendship. She needs to know I am not a threat to your relationship with her."

Eventually Vince showed up to get her.

"I'll call you when I get home to let you know I made it home safe," she said.

"It has been wonderful. I'm looking forward to us building a great relationship for many years." I stood and hugged her gently, being sure to give her space. "Have a safe trip. I'll talk with you soon." I hugged Vince and thanked him for bringing her to see me. I watched as she climbed into the car, waving goodbye as they drove off, not knowing when I would see her again.

On my way home I cried until I hit the driveway. I sat in the car for a few minutes, took a deep breath, then went inside.

Children are a blessing and a gift from the Lord (Ps. 127:3 CEV).

CHAPTER TWENTY-SIX

Marriage Proposal

My heart was heavy with the knowledge that I didn't know when I would see Lynn again. I tried to focus on what I had ahead of me. I had Martha's wedding to help plan, and I was building my friendship with Joe. I called Martha to make plans to get together.

"Do you want to go looking for dresses tomorrow?" I asked her.

"Sure," she said. "How was the day with your daughter?"

"It was difficult. I shared some hard truths with her. I hope she can handle them. I gave her a lot to think about. We're going to work on our friendship. I don't know when I will see her again. Now we need to plan your wedding—come over after work and we can start looking. I'll see you tomorrow."

"We need to figure out the bridesmaids' dresses and colors too. We can get some ideas tomorrow when we're out. Goodnight," Martha said.

I took it easy the next day and slept in. My emotions were drained. Kevin must have been tired too. When I woke up and looked in on him, he was still sleeping. Ryan had spent the night at a friend's.

Martha had a certain look in mind for her wedding dress. She wanted a flower print for us bridesmaids—something we could wear again. We stopped at a couple of places. The dresses were so expensive. Even though she knew exactly what she was looking for, none of the stores had her style. When we stopped in a small bridal store, she finally found exactly what she was looking for in her price range and ordered the dress. And she picked out dresses for us that were pastel and knee-length.

Joe stopped by one day after work while the boys were playing at their friends' houses. He asked me if I wanted to go to town. We ended up at Taco Bell. He ordered while I grabbed us a table. He would always say a prayer before each meal—I loved that about him. I took a bite of my taco and looked up at him. He looked directly at me with his puppy brown eyes.

"What do you want to do with the rest of your life?" he asked, catching me off guard. I almost choked on my taco. Why was he asking me this?

191

"What do you want to do with yours?" I countered, not sure how I should answer him.

"I want to travel, and I don't want to be by myself. I want someone to travel with me."

"I'd like to travel too, and I also don't want to be alone the rest of my life," I said. I bent down to grab my taco, trying not to give away that I was questioning his motive. What is he up to? Why is he asking me these questions? Is he going to ask me to marry him? I was afraid to look at him in case he might ask me another question, one that I wasn't sure how to answer. I tried not to look obvious. I kept my head down, mostly looking at the ground so I could avoid making eye contact.

We left Taco Bell and drove back to my place. We pulled into the driveway, and he turned off the car. We sat for a moment in silence. I started to open the door to get out, but he took my hand to stop me.

"Carol, I meant it when I said I wanted someone to travel with me," Joe said. "I don't want to be alone. I want to know if you will marry me."

I didn't think twice. "Yes, I will," I said, grabbing him tightly and kissing him. I couldn't believe it. Had he really asked me that? Was I going to really get married? Was I going to have the Victorian wedding I always wanted?

"Carol, I want you to have the wedding that you never had," he said. We tried to figure out what to do next.

"Let's wait and tell the children together," Joe suggested and I agreed. I couldn't wait to tell the boys.

"Okay, I'm going to call Martha and tell her the great news. I'll see you tomorrow. Goodnight, I love you," I said.

I rushed past the boys to the phone. I couldn't let the cat out of the bag to them. I shut my bedroom door, leaving them to watch their TV show.

"Martha, Martha, guess what just happened!" I said, almost out of breath. "Joe asked me to marry him. I guess I caught the bouquet at that wedding for a reason."

"That's wonderful," she said. "When are you planning the wedding for?"

"We talked about next year around May. You and Rob will be married this year so you can help me with mine," I said. I had a vision of what I wanted for my special day. I wasn't working, and I wanted to do everything myself to cut back on expenses. It was like we were sisters, planning our weddings together. I was so happy I wanted to shout it to the whole world. I ran next door to Robin to tell her my news.

"Carol, you said you were going to marry him, and you were right," she said. "I'm so happy for you. He seems like a good man for you. It's about time you got a break in life." I told Robin the Lord had changed my life and brought me all the happiness that I had. I wanted her to have some peace too. She worked a lot and was home late many nights. She was married to her career.

Joe and I decided he should tell his girls about our engagement by himself. He had raised them by himself for sixteen years. And then I came along, and I knew there were some jealousy issues, just as Ryan and Kevin were having of him. They hadn't shared me with anyone since their dad left. Having a man around the house was going to be a challenge. I wasn't going to try and be a mother to Joe's daughters. We would all have to make adjustments as we blended our families together. The girls and my boys had spent time together at both of our houses, and they seemed to get along. I hoped that they would accept me and my boys, and that my kids would accept Joe and his girls. We were going to find out. Joe sat his girls down at his house, and at the same time I sat down my boys.

"Ryan and Kevin, Mom has something very special to tell you. We've been spending a lot of time with Joe and his girls. Joe and I have become very close. How would you feel if Joe and I were to get married, and Sherry and Tara would become your sisters?" They both yelled at the same time, "Yes!" I leaned over and gave them both a big hug. "I love you both, and you will always be by favorites."

"We love you too, Mom. Is Joe coming here to live with the girls?" Kevin asked.

"I'm not sure what we'll do. We wanted to make sure you boys were okay with us becoming a family. I have to see what his girls are saying, and then we can start to make plans. I'm going to call Joe now to see what happened over there."

"Joe, the boys are very excited," I told him when he answered.

"The girls are happy for us. They were worried about me. With Tara going off to college in St Louis and Sherry gone a lot, they wanted to make sure I wouldn't be alone."

I was so glad they had all accepted our engagement.

Martha's rehearsal night came before we knew it. I was so excited for her. Pastor Wayne had counseled them, and they were ready for their commitment. Martha's dad had passed away so she had the father of a close family friend stand in for him to walk her down the aisle. Her mother, brother, and sisters remained in the Amish faith and refused to come to the wedding. Martha was being shunned.

Rob's mom wanted to have us all for the rehearsal dinner so we went to Quail Hallow Resort, a real ritzy place. After the dinner, Rob and his dad stayed at the local Chardon Motel. I went home, and Martha went to her place. The evening ended late, and we needed to get rest for the big day.

I met Martha early the next morning at the church where we admired the decorations. Sherry and some other ladies of the church had chipped in to decorate it for Martha, and it looked beautiful.

"You're going to be walking down here very soon," I told her. "Let's go get dressed."

We all gathered at the entrance of the building. We hung a sheet so no one could see Martha before it was time. The church pews filled and Martha's day began. The wedding was beautiful. Her reception was immediately after in the social room. My friend left for her honeymoon in Toronto, Canada, and I was starting to put my own wedding together. Our lives were changing quickly.

> *"When the Lord first began speaking to Israel through Hosea, He said to him, 'Go and marry a prostitute, so some of her children will be born to you from other men.' This will illustrate the way My people have been untrue to Me, openly committing adultery against the Lord by worshiping other gods"* (Hosea 1:2 NLT).

CHAPTER TWENTY-SEVEN

Wedding Plans

Tara, Joe's daughter, was granted time to go to Costa Rico as a college exchange student. She would leave in August and return in December, just in time for our first family Christmas together. Joe, Kevin, and I took her to the airport and went into the observation tower to watch her depart. Kevin enjoyed watching the big airplanes flying right above our heads. Sherry had graduated from high school and started working at the dollar store.

Martha came back from her honeymoon, and Rob moved in to her apartment in Chardon. Joe was coming over weekly, helping me make decorations for our wedding. I didn't want to count on him to pay for everything. I returned to my beauty trade, cutting hair at home for friends and family so I was making a little cash. I cut Joe's hair for the first time, and he told the guys at work he had the prettiest barber in town. Martha and Rob would come by and we went to dinner or a show. Debbie and Wade would pop in once in a while. Ryan would hang out with his friends, and Kevin was all over the park, spending time entertaining himself. I was involved with a couple of Women's Organizations. I tried to share my story often. The boys were visiting their dad regularly with Pastor Ernie.

Martha stopped by one afternoon, and we started to look at bridal magazines to help me get an idea of what type of wedding dress I wanted. My heart was set on a Victorian dress. Everywhere we went and looked, we ended up discouraged. I didn't have that kind of money to spend.

"Let's go and drive up and down Euclid Avenue. They have to have something out that way," I said. As we headed down the main road, we reminisced on how our lives had changed. We laughed as we recalled how we went to a self-confrontation course. Both of us were single at the time and had prayed for God to bring men into our lives. And now here we were, her married and me looking for a wedding dress.

As we drove, I kept my eye on the shops, looking for a place that would carry wedding dresses. I caught a glance of a large sign plastered in the glass window of a store with huge letters that read, "GOING OUT OF BUSINESS—EVERYTHING 75% OFF."

"Martha, stop," I said. "Look over there! Turn around, go back." She pulled the car into the lot, and we both stared at the sign. "Wow, I wonder why they're going out of business?"

We walked in and a woman greeted us. "This is our last day sale," she said. "Everything here is another 50 percent off the prices marked at 75 percent."

Martha reached for a dress, lifting it up. "What do you think of this?" she asked.

"No, I'm looking for something Victorian."

The woman overheard me. "There is a whole rack of Victorian dresses over there," she said, pointing to the back of the store. I rushed with excitement and was dazzled as I looked at all of them on the rack. I picked one up, placed it back, then another. My eyes settled on a lacy style, and I knew I wanted it. My creative juices started to flow as I visualized what I could do with the dress. I would have to add a few pearls, and it could be exactly what I wanted. I held it up.

"Martha, look at this. What do you think?"

"It looks like you," she said.

I looked at a couple more, but they didn't catch my eye the way the lacy one did. I looked at the tag. It was $400.

"I can't afford this," I said. The woman overheard me again.

"You need to take 75 percent off, then another 50 percent," she said. "That dress would cost you $58."

I screamed, "You are kidding! Martha, can you believe this? Look what God is doing for this wedding."

The woman was drawn to what we were saying, wanting to know why I was so excited. I leaned over the counter to tell her my story and how God had brought Joe into my life. It was a fairy-tale story. Dreams do come true, I told her. When I was a little girl I had dreamed of my wedding. She smiled at me.

"Do you have a hat to match?" I asked her.

She led me to the counter of hats she had on display. I started to try them on, but nothing was quite right for what I was looking for. The woman told me about a bridal place on the east side where they get their accessories. She told me to mention her name, and I could get a hat designed just the way I wanted. I was so grateful to her.

I looked at the other accessories. The gloves were lacy. I tried them on.

Martha was circling the store making sure I wasn't missing anything. I picked up a hoop to make the dress poof out and went to try on the ensemble. I walked out to show Martha.

"That dress was waiting for you. It fits you perfect, and you look fantastic," she said.

I raced back to change and then paid the bill. I couldn't wait to tell Joe about the great bargain we found. Of course I couldn't show him yet. I would have to hide it away for our special day. Martha and I chatted all the way home about how God had blessed me with my heart's desire.

She dropped me off and headed home to Rob. Joe was off work, and he had stopped by. He was stretched across the couch taking a nap.

"Joe! Joe, guess what the Lord did? Guess how much I paid for my dress?"

"How much?" he asked.

"$58. We ended up at a store that was going out of business."

"That's wonderful."

"Joe, what do you think of me calling Lynn and asking her to be my maid of honor?"

"Call and see how she feels about it."

"Okay. I'm going to call and see if she's home." I went in my bedroom to dial the phone. I was about to ask my daughter a special question.

"Hello," she answered.

"Hello Lynn. It's Carol. Can you talk at the moment?"

"Sure, what's up?"

"I want to ask you something and if you feel you can't do it, please let me know," I paused. "I would be very honored if you would be my maid of honor in my wedding." I took a deep breath and waited for her to respond.

"Carol, I'd love to be your maid of honor. I'm honored that you asked."

"I can't wait for you to come. We are planning on a May wedding next year. So I'll let you know the exact date when Joe and I figure it out. He's sitting right here. He's glad that you accepted too!"

"I'll tell Vince we'll be coming up in May. We both will have to take off work, but we'll be there. I wouldn't miss it for the world. I've got to make dinner so I'll talk with you later. I love you."

"I love you too, honey. Talk soon, bye."

As I hung up the phone I turned to Joe, "That is amazing. I would have never imagined my daughter being in my wedding. We're going to have a large bridal party. We need your daughters and Lynn, Martha, and Debbie."

"I want my nephew Danny to be my best man," Joe said. "I'll ask him the next time I see him."

"I want my brother Richard and Rob and Ryan and Kevin too. I don't want my dad to walk me down the aisle. I want my two boys to do that. I want one on each side of me as I walk to you. My dad has never been there for me. I feel a little guilty, but it would mean so much more for all that we have been through to have them give me away." Joe and I continued making our plans until it was time for him to head home.

"Goodnight, I'll see you tomorrow," he said, kissing me goodnight. Our kisses were becoming more passionate. I had told him I wanted this marriage to start out right. I would not want to sleep together before our honeymoon. I wanted God to bless us. He agreed and although we became tempted, he was strong when I was weak, and I stayed strong when he was weak.

I started going to the craft stores looking for ideas of things I could make for the wedding. I loved dried flowers. I would make all the arrangements for the girls. I wanted my niece Joc as the flower girl and my nephew Justin as the ring bearer. There were the Brason twins in our church that I wanted to throw rose petals before I came down the aisle. My friend Sylvia loved to dance before the Lord, and I wanted her to come down the aisle and dance to "Candle of the Bride." I decided to check out the bridal craft shop the woman had suggested to me when I bought my dress. When I walked in the store, I was amazed. They had everything I could imagine for a wedding. My eyes focused on the hats lining the shelves, and I walked over to see a large Victorian hat. It was very plain, with nothing but the frame of a hat. I would need to add some lace, pearls, and my veil. I selected some of the pearls at the store and got enough that I could add some to my dress. I walked out with everything I needed and spent less than $50. I was set to start my alterations and make the hat and dress the way I had visualized them.

I had to do some schooling since I was getting help from the state. I never graduated from high school so I had to take my GED. Growing up in the Amish faith, Joe had only finished eighth grade, so he decided to study with me to get his high school equivalent diploma. We studied together often.

We went to the library and took classes to get ready for the test. I hated school. I wanted to throw my book across the room several times, but Joe kept encouraging me, telling me that I could do it. English was my worst subject. We had a tutor that came each week, but I still had problems trying to comprehend and retain what I had just finished reading. I kept on going, only because Joe was there to tell me not to quit. We would tell everyone we went to school together, even though we were in our 40s when we graduated.

After a few months of studying, we both decided to take our test. It took all day. We had to sit for hours and only had a break to use the bathroom. We all sat in a room under supervision. I struggled with some of the math problems. I guessed at some. I was relieved when I walked up to the teacher and handed him my test. I walked out, realizing they had my fate in their hands. I had to wait to get my test results by mail in a few weeks.

Joe followed shortly behind me. "How do you think you did?" I asked him.

"I think I did okay. We'll know in a few weeks," he said.

We walked out of school holding hands. At least we could say we tried our best, I told myself.

A few weeks had gone by when I went to the mailbox and saw that I had received a letter from the state. I was so excited I tore it open. I knew it had to be my test scores for the GED. I had passed all the courses, and I received my high school diploma. I ran to the phone to call Joe.

"Joe I got my test results back. I passed my GED!"

"You said you flunked," he said. "I told you that you could do it. Great job. I wonder where mine is?" he asked.

"Are you coming over tonight?" I asked.

"Yes, we can go for a walk," he said "See you in a bit."

When Joe finally received his scores from the GED, he was pleased to find out he had passed and would receive his high school diploma too. We framed our diplomas and placed them side by side on the table. We both were proud of what we had accomplished together.

————◆————

It was the middle of December, a week and half before Christmas, and Joe's daughter Tara was coming home from Costa Rica. Kevin, Joe, and I went to pick her up at the airport. We watched from the tower as we waited for her plane to arrive. Joe was so anxious to have her home. We were so excited she made it home for Christmas.

Tara was so glad to be home. When she walked into her house, she immediately ran to her room, wanting to lie across her own bed. Then she dashed out into the living room, dropping to the floor and moving her arms and legs back and forth as if she were making a snow angel on the carpet. She was so excited to see carpet after living in a hut with only a dirt floor for the past four months. She was able to speak Spanish fluently with the family.

Christmas was going to be a fun holiday for us. We decided to go as a family to get our first Christmas tree together. The kids were all excited. Joe's place was bigger than mine so we decided to have the tree at his place. We all bundled up and went to a tree farm to cut it down ourselves. The boys were running here and there yelling, "Let's get this one!" The girls would yell right back, "We found one!" Joe yelled, "Here is the right one!" And there it stood, a fat, round tree that was just perfect for us. We all clapped, jumping for joy.

Joe and the boys dragged the tree to the truck and tied it up. We couldn't wait to get home to decorate. The girls were so thrilled to have a real tree. We made hot chocolate, and Sherry and Kevin started making a gingerbread house at the kitchen table. Joe dragged the tree in and placed it in the corner of the room while I brought over my decorations to add to what they already had. Ryan crawled under the tree to tighten it to the stand. All four children gathered around, reminiscing about childhood Christmases as they placed ornaments on the tree. "I remember this one, I remember this one," they would yell as they shared memories with each other for the first time.

Joe and I sat back on the couch, watching the children's joy as they decorated their tree together. We looked at each other and smiled, so happy to bring this family together. Christmas morning would be a few days away. Joe and I left the kids to their bonding so we could get some shopping done. He was going to help me figure out what to get the girls. Christmas had always been a special time for my boys, and I wanted it to be just as special for Joe's girls.

On Christmas Eve, we attended the candlelight service. We wanted to remind ourselves of the reason behind the holiday and to celebrate Jesus' birthday. After service, we went back to Joe's place and relaxed, watching TV. The night went by too fast and as we got ready to leave, Joe and I made plans for Christmas morning. We decided I would take the boys home and bring them back early in the morning. They were way past the stage of believing in Santa, so it made our job easier. Kevin was eleven while Ryan was going on sixteen. The girls were in their upper teenage years, almost adults. We could place the presents directly under the tree and wait for morning. We kissed goodnight, and the boys and I drove home.

Kevin was the first one up the next morning, yelling, "Come on we have to go to Joe's!" Ryan was like me, not a morning person. He rolled over in bed, yelling at Kevin to be quiet. But Ryan didn't stay in bed long when he realized it was Christmas morning, and he didn't want to miss out on his gifts. We jumped into our clothes and hurried out the door. The girls greeted us when we arrived, and Joe had breakfast ready, his famous blueberry pancakes. We ate quickly and then dashed into the living room to open gifts. Kevin was peeking under the tree, shouting out names on the packages. He was the most excited. He couldn't wait to see his presents. Joe had bought Ryan his first rifle and was excited to teach Ryan to hunt. I could see Ryan's eyes light up when he opened it. Kevin ripped open his gift, ecstatic to receive the video games he wanted. Sherry and Tara smiled when they saw their gifts of girly things, like makeup, shampoo, and hair products. I gave Tara a Bible promise book.

Joe surprised me when he walked into his room and came back with a large box. He handed it to me. "What is this?" I asked. "We said we would only buy for the kids and take our money and use it towards the wedding."

"Just open it," he said.

I tore the paper back on the box, opening slowly. Kevin got impatient and reached over and ripped the paper. "Come on, Mom," he said. "Just rip the paper."

I couldn't believe my eyes. It was a suede coat, just like the one that Joe wore, only a lady's style. I jumped up and give him a hug,

"Thank you so much. You didn't have to get this."

"I wanted you to have one like mine. Now we can look alike," he said. I handed him a small box. "I thought you weren't getting me anything," he said.

"I lied."

He opened the box and pulled out a key chain. I had inscribed it with "I Love You" and the date. "You can remember this Christmas forever when you look at this keychain," I said. He kissed me, thanking me.

It was a perfect Christmas spent together as we became a family.

The long winter set in, and we spent a lot of time indoors. I worked on making wedding invitations. I wanted the colors to be ivory and peach. Martha and I went to Jo-Ann Fabrics where they were having their biggest sale of the year. Everything in the store was 50% to 75% off. I needed to start the flowers for my girls. We picked out the ribbon, flowers, and lace. I once again was blessed with savings.

When we got home, Martha and I placed all the items on the table, trying to decide where to start. I wanted to make the Brason's baskets to carry the rose petals in so I had bought two small identical ones in ivory. I wanted a banner to be hung on the altar in front of us, saying, "If we love one another, God dwelled in us." I asked Sylvia if her sister could make one for me. She said she would love to help me out.

I wanted my girls to wear peach dresses. I found them in a JC Penney's catalog. All I needed to do was get their sizes. I also wanted them all to wear hats, and the catalog showed hats that matched.

Joe came over in the evenings to help me make the favors that we would place on the guest tables. We used a gold pen and wrote on all the napkins, "Joe & Carol May 28th 1994." I was having so much fun being creative. I only had five months left to get everything ready. I hid everything in my closet to make sure things would be safe.

The winter went by quickly and spring arrived. The tulips and flowers emerged, bringing life back into the earth. Joe and I were attending our pre-marriage classes taught by Pastor Wayne. The classes were to help us to prepare for our union together.

Joe got a ham from work at Easter. We decided to save it and then get another one, so we could serve them at our wedding. We were planning our menu. We couldn't afford much for food, so we asked our family and church friends if they would help out with the meal. Everyone was so excited to help out. We made a list of scalloped potatoes, salad, green beans, and rolls. When I hung up the list at church, the donations were filled immediately. Someone even offered to buy the extra ham we needed. Everything was falling into place.

Before we knew it, the wedding weekend had arrived, and we were all gathered at church for the rehearsal dinner. My bridesmaids were showing up and the best man, Dan, arrived along with my brother, niece, and nephew. We were waiting for Lynn to arrive. I had ordered her dress and we were hoping that it would fit. Pastor asked everyone to come forward, and we prayed before we got started. Lynn walked in and I rushed to greet her. We hugged and I thanked Vince for bringing her up.

We were ready to rehearse. I couldn't believe our day was here. It didn't take long before we were through and headed to a small dinner in the social hall of the church. We all gathered there, laughing and sharing a good time together before I would become Mrs. Carol Byler. At the end of the night, I kissed Joe and went home.

Ryan and Kevin had been acting out a bit, and so they needed my attention. I sat with them on the couch. I would be leaving for my honeymoon tomorrow, and I thought they weren't sure how to deal with me going off with Joe for a couple of weeks. I reassured them that they would always be the first men in my life. No one would ever take their place because they were my priority. I kissed them goodnight and went to my bedroom. I pulled out my diary, writing that this would be my last night as a single mom. I was getting married tomorrow, and the boys would have a stepfather. I took my dress out of the closet and held it up to me. My special day was finally here, and I was going to wear my dream gown. I prayed, thanking God for bringing Joe into my life. Then I finally tried to get some sleep.

Respect and honor your wife. Don't be a slave of your desires or live like people who don't know God (1 Thess. 4:3-4 CEV).

CHAPTER TWENTY-EIGHT

Dreams Come True

Morning came and Martha called, "Did you get some sleep?"

"I think I slept a few hours. I remember looking at the clock around 2 a.m. and I was still up. I'll be okay. I'm so excited my day is here!" I said.

"I'll meet you at the church around noon," Martha said.

"Okay. I'm going to get the boys up and get all my things together. I need to do my hair and my makeup here. I can't wait to put my dress on."

"You deserve this day," she said. "I'll see you later. Bye."

Lynn called next, "Are you doing okay? Are you staying calm? What time do you need me at the church?"

"I'm going at noon. If you want to come then, you can. All you girls are getting dressed in the nursery with me."

"My dress fits perfect. I didn't have to alter it at all," she said.

"I'm so glad. How does the hat fit?"

"Perfect."

"Okay. I'll see you at the church. Vince can hang with some of the guys there. Bye for now."

I wanted my makeup to look just right so I took my time and applied it as perfectly as I could. I was wearing my hair under my hat so I needed the curls to hang below the brim of the hat. I had to do my hair and then place the hat on so I couldn't do that until I went to the church. I ran next door to Robin's place real quick for a second opinion.

"Does my makeup look okay?" I asked her.

"Carol, your face is radiant. You will make a beautiful bride. I can't wait to see you in your dress," she said.

"I'm going to get the boys, and we're going to head for the church. I'll see you there." I went back home to gather up the boys. "Ryan, Kevin, let's go guys. It's time to go."

"Okay Mom, we're ready," Ryan said.

"Grab your tuxes and make sure you comb your hair neatly."

I grabbed my hat and dress, and we were out the door. I would be returning as Mrs. Byler in two weeks. Joe and I had decided we would live at my trailer. The boys were younger, and Kevin was still in school. Tara was in college and Sherry was working. Joe wanted someone to stay at his trailer until we sold it. We planned on putting it up for sale if the girls didn't want it.

I stepped into the church and went to the nursery where I hung my dress across a chair. Sylvia was walking around, looking at the decorations we had placed. Martha, Debbie, Tara, and Sherry arrived and joined us in the sanctuary to admire the bridal sashes on the ends of the pews. Everything looked perfect to me.

Lynn arrived. "Carol it looks gorgeous in here," she said. "You placed the flowers just right in front of the altar." I had made two large baskets of flowers that sat on the steps where Joe and I would be standing. They matched the arrangements I made for the girls. I called them into the room to show them what they would be holding. Their eyes lit up as they looked at their bouquets.

"These are beautiful. I can't believe you made these. They look so professional. You must have put a lot of time in the past few months working on these. They match our dresses perfectly," Martha said.

"I'm so glad you made something we can keep," Lynn said.

It was getting close to 2:30 p.m. and the wedding was supposed to start at 3 p.m. Pastor's wife, Sherry, came to see how we were doing. "Some of the men in the bridal party are arriving. Joe will be coming soon. So you need to stay in here, and I'll have the rest of the girls come in," she said.

Sylvia and the twins were dressed in off-white dresses with baby's breath braided in their hair. Their baskets were full of rose petals. Joc came in dressed in a little peach dress that her mom had made. She looked so cute. I was starting to get nervous. When Tara and Sherry finally arrived, everyone was here. The clock was getting closer and closer to the hour. As everyone got dressed, I sat in a chair in front of a long mirror. I placed my hat onto my head, making the adjustments I needed so it wouldn't fall off. Tara helped me, talking to try and keep me calm. I was having a problem getting the hat as tight as I needed it. I couldn't imagine walking down to Joe and my hat falling off. We finally got it secure. I stood up, looking at all of my friends and I couldn't stop the tears. I wiped them back. My friends were about to walk down the aisle, and I would be right behind them.

"I can't cry now," I said. "I'll ruin my makeup." I turned away to distract myself and slipped into my hoop slip and fastened it to my waist. Martha and Debbie helped lift my dress to pull it over my hat. It slipped down across my slender body, flowing to the floor. The lace on my hat sat perfectly across my shoulders. Tara reached to zip me up. Everyone had tears in their eyes as they looked at me, dressed for my wedding to Joe.

"You look like a fairy-tale bride. Wait until Joe sees you. He won't be able to take his eyes off you," Martha said. I looked in the mirror, pleased with how I looked. It was my day, and the focus was going to be on me. Pastor's wife Sherry came in. "Your mom and dad are here," she told me. "They want to come in and see you."

"Send them in."

Dad walked over to give me a hug, then Mom leaned in to hug me. I held onto my hat, I could feel it slipping some. I hoped I wouldn't have to deal with that all day.

"Let's give it some more bobby pins to make sure," I said. Martha reached under my hat with the pins to tighten it. She knew I was struggling with my mom being there. Everyone was aware of the tense relationship with my mom, except of course, my mom. She was in her own little world, one no one could enter. Hugging her had been like hugging a stranger. She had no emotional attachment to me.

I refused to let her emotional detachment rob me of my special day. My friends were my family now. I was starting a brand new life with a whole new family. I let Sherry walk my parents out to be seated.

I finished saying hello to some of my friends who came in to see how I looked. The music started and the bridal party began lining up. I waited in the nursery as one by one they departed to the hallway. The pastor's wife, Sherry, orchestrated the lineup. She called each person when it was her turn. Debbie, Martha, and Lynn proceeded down the aisle. Kevin and Ryan had to walk Joe's daughters, Sherry and Tara, to the altar and then come back down the aisle to stand next to me. I wanted to see Jos and Justin walk, but I had to stay hidden. I could hear the music I picked for the twins as they walked down the aisle, tossing rose petals onto the white bridal carpet. Sylvia stood at the back and I lined up behind her as Ryan took one of my arms and Kevin took the other. We stood as Sylvia began her dance down the aisle. The song was a representation of Christ and the bride coming to the groom.

Sherry the pastor's wife shut the door to the sanctuary and waved me to come and stand behind the closed doors. We waited for the music to end, letting us know Sylvia had reached the altar and was standing among the bridal party. Sherry opened the door when the music started for me to enter. I wanted to cry, but I couldn't. I couldn't contain my smile. I could see Joe at the end, and I hoped my knees would make it all the way down the aisle. It seemed to go on forever. I looked at the girls standing there as I took my first step, and everyone stood up. I could see the faces of those I knew and loved. They smiled at me as I walked slowly towards Joe. He was smiling, his eyes locked on mine.

"Mom, are you okay?" Kevin asked.

"Yes, I think my legs are trembling," I said.

"Mom, you'll make it. Just keep walking," Ryan told me. We reached the altar. Pastor was standing with Joe next to him. I couldn't look at him just yet, afraid I would cry.

"Who is giving this bride away?" Pastor asked.

Kevin and Ryan answered in unison, "We both do." Joe reached out his hand, taking mine. The boys walked to stand in the bridal line. Joe and I turned to face Pastor while everyone was asked to sit. He began talking to us. I could only focus on the words that were coming from his mouth. When we had rehearsed, I didn't hear these words. They were now music to my ears.

"Do you, Joe, take Carol as your wife?" he asked.

"I do," Joe replied.

"Do you, Carol, take Joe as your husband?"

"Yes, I do." I gazed into his eyes and smiled, he smiled back. I was lost in the moment as time seemed to stand still. I didn't want it to end. I could hear Pastor's message clearly.

"Who has the rings?" Pastor asked.

Justin approached the altar with the heart-shaped ivory and peach pillow I made for the rings. I didn't want them lost so I attached them with the ivory and peach ribbon. Pastor reached down to untie the ribbon. He handed me Joe's ring, and Joe took mine.

"Joe, take this ring and place it on Carol's finger and repeat after me." Joe gently took my hand and slid the ring onto my finger. I looked at my ring. I had wanted a Victorian style. Joe and I used the diamonds we had from our previous rings, combining our pasts to make a promise for the future. I looked up and smiled, listening to him repeat Pastor's words.

"Carol, take this ring and place it upon Joe's finger." I slid the band onto his finger and repeated the words. We grabbed hands and turned towards Pastor.

"I now pronounce you husband and wife. You can now kiss the bride." This was the moment I had been waiting for. I felt butterflies like the first time. Joe leaned over and placed his arms around me, kissing me gently.

It was then time to take our first communion together. We walked to the altar, which was set up for us with our special communion cup. I had wanted two hearts on a glass with our names and the date engraved. Joe and I reached down to take a piece of the bread and as the song played, he gently placed a piece into my mouth. As I reached toward his mouth our arms crossed, and I placed the bread into his mouth at the same time. He reached down to take the glass and held it to my lips as I took a sip. He then took a sip himself. Placing the glass back onto the table, we paused for a moment, gazing into each other's eyes. I wanted to hug and kiss him. The music ended, and we turned to walk down the steps of the altar.

"For the first time, I want to introduce Mr. and Mrs. Byler," the pastor said. Everyone stood and clapped. The pianist played the Charlie Brown theme song as we headed down the aisle together, as husband and wife. When we got to the back of the church, I turned to look at Joe.

"We did it," I said. "I'm your wife."

"Yes, we're a married couple now," he said.

We walked back to the first pew at the front of the church to greet our guests one by one, thanking them for making our day special.

We walked outside into the sunny day as the crowd showered us with birdseed. A friend of ours had loaned us his antique car. We jumped into it and circled the block, heading back to the church for pictures.

Sharon, one of the ladies from our church, told us for our gift she would take the pictures for us. We posed at the altar with the bridal party. I was consumed with my day, but every once in a while I noticed Lynn had vanished from the group. I thought to myself that she must be having some emotional issues with the day.

After we finished with pictures at the church, we dashed over to one of the neighbor's yard. I had called her earlier to ask permission to take some of our pictures among her beautiful landscaping. The yard had a pond and the most amazing rhododendrons and azaleas that were in full bloom. The sunlight falling on the flowers made them sparkle. It was a magnificent picture. A wooden swing sat in front of the flowers, and I had long imagined Joe and I in that swing, newly married. We walked over to the swing and I placed my dress neatly on the seat as we embraced. I snuggled next to him, and he placed his arms around my waist. I put my left hand across his leg, grabbing his right hand with mine.

"Smile," Sharon said and we both looked at her. She took a few with different poses. I wanted this scene to be the best picture.

Finally, we stopped at the gazebo in the Chardon square to finish up the photos. The boys were anxious to take their suits off. "We're almost done. Wait until we get to the reception, then you can change clothes. Mom needs to get all the pictures done first," I told them. We finished up and got into the limo to head to the reception hall, which was located at Faith's church, where the boys and I had previously attended. Omen Hall was dedicated to a pastor that was in his 90s when he had passed. He had often made a house call to see me and the boys.

We decorated the hall the day before, and the place was stunning. The limo pulled up and we were greeted by the rest of the bridal party. Everyone else was inside, waiting for us to arrive. We walked in and the party was announced. Everyone stood up when Joe and I came in.

"Here is Mr. and Mrs. Byler," they announced. It sounded so good to hear our names together.

We walked over to the bridal table set in front of the fireplace. Mr. Omen's picture was above the mantel. I thought to myself that if he were looking down at me right now, he'd be so proud of me. I sat for a moment and took a deep breath. Guests approached me to tell me that it had been the most beautiful, inspired wedding they had ever attended. They enjoyed watching Sylvia come down the aisle, commenting that it was so spiritual and the music I picked pulled it all together. I couldn't wait to see the video. I couldn't see all that was taking place, and I wanted to see how it looked to everyone else.

We were motioned to start the line for the food. We took our plates and our friends served us. I thanked them all as I walked by. We sat to eat, but I could hardly swallow a bite. The excitement of being married finally hit me. I looked around, watching everyone enjoying themselves. Joe was doing okay. He looked very relaxed to me, which wasn't surprising. He was the laid back one, and I was the emotional one.

Mom had heard how Lynn and I reconnected. I knew what kind of welcome Lynn would receive from her. I had spared Lynn the emotional drama up until now. I couldn't bring myself to having my mom meet her on the day of our reunion, so today would be their first meeting. I walked over, taking Lynn's hand and locking it tightly with mine.

"I know you're having a hard time with this, but you need to meet your grandmother. It will be just a quick hello. Trust me, that's all it will be." We walked slowly over, and I kneeled down on my knees between my mom and dad.

"Mom and Dad, I want you to meet Lynn, Toni, your granddaughter."

My dad looked up, "Hello."

My mom looked up, and said, "How do you do?" That's it? I thought. Neither of them gave her the hug she deserved.

"Where are you from?" Dad asked. Mom continued eating her food, looking up a few times as she listened to the conversation. As usual, she didn't connect. I spared Lynn any further pain.

"We're going over to meet more people. We'll talk to you later."

"Okay," they both said.

What a shame, I thought to myself. It was just a casual hello from my mom to Lynn, not even a hug. I wanted her to be happy for me and Lynn, but she showed no sentiment at all. Not one tear flowed from her eyes. I had to let it go, or I would have blasted her. How could a mother not care about her daughter's reunion? How could a person have no feelings? I was the complete opposite of her—I wore my emotions on my sleeve. I was not about to let her rob me of all the joyous feelings I was having today.

"Lynn, go and enjoy yourself. Don't let her get to you. I'm not going to let her affect me," I said.

"How could she be so cold?" Lynn asked.

"It's her loss, so just let it go," I said.

Some of our friends wanted to play a song for us on their guitars. We sat back listening. Then, it was time for Joe and I to have our first dance. We held on to each other tightly, as everyone watched.

When I threw the bouquet, one of the little girls caught it. We laughed. It would be awhile before she was old enough to get married. The reception was coming to a close. People were leaving, and the food was getting put away. Joe took out his wallet, showing his friends he was broke. We all laughed.

Sherry and Tara were heading home. We put our gifts in the back of the truck for the girls to take home. Hugging them, we said our goodbyes. Kevin and Ryan were headed back to our trailer. Ryan was responsible, so I knew I could trust him to manage the homestead. He could drive and take care of himself, but I didn't trust Ryan and Kevin together. I might come home to a broken up trailer. My two boys alone was not a good idea so Kevin was going to stay with my brother. I hugged Lynn goodbye, she was heading back to Virginia in the morning.

My darling, you are lovely, so very lovely—as you look through your veil, your eyes are those of a dove (Song of Solomon 4:1a CEV).

CHAPTER TWENTY-NINE

Honeymoon

One of our wedding gifts, from Debbie's mom, was a night in the bridal suite at the bed and breakfast where she worked. We were headed to the Blue Ridge Parkway. Joe wanted us to enjoy the drive. He owned a Chevy truck, but his daughter Sherry let us borrow her Nissan Pulsar sports car with a t-roof for the two weeks of our honeymoon. Joe loved to travel. He had mapped out the route we were taking. Our first stop would be the bed and breakfast. I was so nervous to spend my first night together with my new husband.

When we arrived, we were shown to our room. Debbie had left us a basket with some goodies. The lights were dim; the fireplace was so romantic. I lit some candles and slipped off my shoes. Joe took off his jacket. The sliding doors led to a private patio overlooking the field behind the house. As we stood on the patio, we kissed in the moonlight. I took the bag of cards we received from the reception, and we both climbed onto the bed and leaned back against the headboard.

"Joe, look at this card. It's from Martha and Rob."

"Look at this one from Debbie and Wade," Joe responded.

We took turns opening the cards and sharing the generous gift inside each of them. We were so blessed. I gave him a kiss. We lay there, thanking God for the beautiful day we just had. I was a nervous wreck, thinking about the fact that this was our wedding night. He reached out to hold onto me as we talked about what we like best about the wedding.

"I loved the look on your face when I started to walk toward you," I said.

"You looked gorgeous," he said.

"I thought I was going to lose it when I started to walk with the boys. Kevin and Ryan were talking to me to keep me stable."

"Joc and Justin looked so cute coming down the aisle," Joe said.

"We had all our friends there. There is so much to reflect on. I can't wait to see the video when we get back," I said.

"I think I'm going to get comfortable," Joe said.

"Me too. I'll be right back. I'm going to the bathroom." I grabbed the bag I had packed and headed to the bathroom. I closed the door and looked at myself in the mirror. I began to think aloud, "I'm so nervous. I hope he's getting ready. I hope he'll be excited when he takes a look at me." I couldn't get out of my dress, so I yelled through the door that I needed help to unzip my dress.

He walked to me with his shirttail out and touched my back, slowly unzipping my dress. He was a perfect gentleman. Thanking him, I walked back and shut the door to prepare myself for my husband. I slid the dress off, placing it on the hanger, and hung it on the door. I pulled on the long ivory gown I had bought for this special night over my head and put on a long, lacy, flowing robe. I looked like a princess. I felt so special. I had waited a long time for this night and so had he. Taking a deep breath, I opened the door. Joe was waiting for me in his long bathrobe.

"Oh, Carol you look gorgeous," he said. He grabbed me and we embraced with a kiss. We fell into bed together and got lost in our love for each other.

Morning came and we laid in bed awake, looking at each other. It was our first morning together. I jumped up, dashing to the bathroom to get ready for the day. Joe had our whole trip planned out but hadn't told me the plan. Each day was going to be a surprise for me as he was not going to tell me until that day where we were going.

We walked to the kitchen to have breakfast but instead were led to a small, private patio overlooking the rolling hills. There was a table set for the two of us. We sat down and talked about where we were headed that day. My brother and his wife, Kelly, gave us a gift of a two-night stay at a bed and breakfast in Bedford, Pennsylvania.

We looked at each other and bowed our heads to pray. Joe said, "Thank you, God, for our day and bless our trip as we travel. Bless this meal and the hands that prepared it for us. Amen." I had always been impressed that he would take the time before each meal to pray for us.

We finished our breakfast, packed up our stuff, and got ready to head out on our two-week honeymoon. Joe opened the car door for me. The sun was shining brightly, and there was no rain in the forecast. We could enjoy the ride to Bedford, just a couple hours away. We stopped along the way, looking at points of interest. As we passed through the old-fashioned town of Bedford, I could see the craft makers making brooms and blowing glass. Things like that had always caught my interest.

"Can we go and see them after we get to our room?" I asked Joe.

"Sure, I like things like that too."

We pulled into a circular driveway in front of a sign that read, "Bed & Breakfast." The old stone structure had a wrap-around porch that reached all the way to the back of the building. The porch was lined with handmade rocking chairs, and large plants hung from the porch ceiling. The place looked like something you would see in a magazine. As we entered the front door, we couldn't help but chuckle at a wooden bear dressed in a suit. The foyer was filled with antiques. A long wooden staircase led to the second floor. I walked over to admire a picture on the wall when a woman came in from the other room.

"Welcome. We're glad you're here," she said.

"We have a reservation. Our names are Mr. and Mrs. Byler. We're on our honeymoon."

"Oh, yes. We've been waiting for you. Let me show you around." We followed her. "This is the dining room where breakfast is served. Over here is the living room. You can sit and relax anytime you like. I'll take you to your room now."

We followed her up the wooden staircase to the top of the stairs and down the hallway of the left wing. The doors to the rooms were open. Each room was decorated completely differently. It seemed like the place was empty. I noticed how close the rooms were to each other, and I hoped we were somewhere by ourselves. The walls were thin, and I didn't want anyone hearing us in our room. After all, we were newlyweds.

"This is your bathroom. Make sure you lock the door behind you, so no one can come in on you. Here is the library in case you're interested in a book or magazine to read."

Then she led us into a beautiful, frilly room, all decked out in lace. The bed was filled with pillows, and the walls had old-fashioned pictures. A large window faced out to the front of the bed and breakfast. We could see our car parked in the drive.

"I'll let you settle in. If you need anything, don't be afraid to ask," the woman said, shutting the door to our room as she left. Joe and I looked at each other and smiled.

"What a nice lady. I think it'll be fun to stay here," I said. It was still early, and we realized we'd have some time to kill before dinner.

"Let's go back and check out that tourist town and see what all it has to offer. We can make plans for the morning," I suggested.

"Sure," Joe agreed.

We left our luggage and went down the hall to the first floor. I kept looking at the empty rooms wondering why they weren't filled. When we got to the dining room the same woman greeted us again.

"I want you to know that I'm only filling the rooms on the right wing of the house so the two of you can have your privacy," she said, answering my question.

"Thank you."

"Dinner will be served at 6 o'clock," she said.

"We're going to check out the town. We'll be back in time for dinner."

As we drove into town, we couldn't help but notice how beautiful the surrounding land was. The rolling hills were filled with farmland, and there were horses running wild in the fields.

Joe pulled into the lot of the Bedford Museum. We walked to the information booth and gathered literature that listed events taking place. The picture of the broom-making caught my eye. The presentations were held early in the day.

"We're going to have to come back tomorrow so we can take the tour and catch all the exhibits," Joe said.

We walked around, enjoying what little we could see before leaving to return to the bed and breakfast.

Dinner was served in the formal dining room. All the guests came in and sat at the different tables. Joe and I sat in the back of the room. We were introduced to everyone as the newly-married couple on our honeymoon. We were congratulated by complete strangers. After our meal, Joe and I walked to the porch and sat in the rocking chairs where we held hands and gazed up at the stars. When it got late we returned to our room and settled in for the night.

The next morning, after breakfast, we headed into town and arrived at the Bedford Museum. After purchasing tickets, we walked into a large building that was filled with crafts—everything from glass blowing to quilting and broom making. We entered each place amazed at the talent we witnessed as each crafter showed off their skills. We enjoyed the day. That evening we sat alone on the porch with the owners of the bed and breakfast.

The next morning we headed for Virginia where Joe wanted me to see the Blue Ridge Parkway. The road was lined on each side with rhododendrons and azaleas. "It's as if God just drove down Himself and planted them along miles and miles of this parkway. This is a sight everyone must see," Joe said. I couldn't take my eyes off the flowers as each bush seemed to get bigger and bigger. The blossoms were magnificent to look at.

I felt so complete, knowing I was driving with my husband. He wanted me to have a special honeymoon, one that we both would never forget. We stopped at a large antique place along the way. Some of the things we saw brought memories of our childhoods. We planned to do nothing but sightsee for the next couple of days.

In some places, the roads were so windy I felt queasy so Joe decided to pull off the side of the road. We took a blanket and lay on the grass. I put my head in his lap and fell asleep. I woke up to a smiling face. Joe was looking down on me.

"Did you have a good nap? You slept for over an hour."

"I can't believe I fell off to sleep," I said. "I wasn't feeling very good when we stopped."

"How do you feel now? Are you ready to get going?" he asked.

"Yes, let's try this again," I said.

We got back on the road. Along our drive Joe and I shared with each other some of our dreams.

"Someday, I'd love to own a cabin in the woods with a babbling brook outside the window, where I could hear the water from my bedroom window," he said.

"That would be nice if we could," I responded.

We drove along the parkway most of the day, stopping to look at Mabry Mill, and Cones Mansion, a large vacation home overlooking a valley.

Before we knew it, it was time to find a place for the night. There were signs all over, directing travelers to stay at a cabin. We followed the arrows that pointed us down a dirt road leading us back into the mountains. We pulled up to the office, and Joe went in to ask about staying for the night. He came out smiling. He got us a cabin down the road a bit that sat right next to a creek. The bedroom faced the water. I looked at him, amazed.

"God heard you," I said. "He knew what you said, and He directed us here. He wanted to bless you."

We drove up to the front of the frame cabin and grabbing our luggage, we climbed the stairs to the front door. We let ourselves in and Joe walked to the back and opened the sliding door. He walked out onto the patio and there it was—a creek flowing right under the patio. We could sleep with the door open and Joe would hear the water, just like he had talked about.

There was a small kitchen on the first floor of the cabin. "Why don't we go and get something to make for dinner and come back here and enjoy the night on the porch and have dinner?" I said.

"We could go back to the store down the road and grab a few things. We can even get something for breakfast," Joe said. We headed to town and bought some chicken, dessert, and rolls for breakfast. We came back and cooked our dinner and sat at the small table on the deck to eat our meal. We listened to the water and looked up into a sky filled with stars.

"What a perfect night," I said.

"God really blessed us tonight," he said.

I had seen pictures of Biltmore Estate so we looked forward to seeing the place in person. It was mammoth. It looked like a castle. It was so large it took us most of the day to take the tour.

The next day we arrived in Louisiana, a state noted for their plantations. My favorite movie growing up was *Gone with the Wind* with Clark Gable. I wanted to live back in those days with the dresses that flowed to the ground and the petticoats. I was excited we were going to re-live that era by visiting some of the largest plantations that had been preserved.

Over the next few days we traveled from Mississippi to Alabama and Tennessee. I had talked to Lynn before we left and told her we would be coming right through her town as we traveled. She told us to make sure we stopped. We decided we would stay in her town for the night so we could visit her. I would be able to finally see where she lived. When we got there, I knocked at her door. She greeted me with a hug.

"Glad you're here. Come on in," she said. Her house was very country, like mine.

"Vince will be home soon," she said. "He's just leaving work."

We enjoyed a meal and spent the time getting to know each other even better. The night ended too soon, and we were ready to get back on our way. Joe and I didn't want to impose on them so we stayed at the local hotel. We were anxious to get back to the kids. We had been on the road twelve days, and I couldn't wait to get home.

The next morning we decided to head straight home without any stops. We finally arrived and were greeted by two lonely boys. Kevin came running. "Mom, you're home!"

Ryan, being a teenager, waited for me to come to him. He had to act cool. I gave him a hug. We walked in and I was amazed everything looked okay. Joe brought in the luggage and presents we had bought for the kids, along with the souvenirs we purchased for ourselves.

I sat down to look around for a bit. Although I had been on my honeymoon, there was nothing like being at home. Joe called the girls to see where they were. They drove over right away, excited to see their dad. We had dinner together and gave the children their gifts. Their faces lit up.

"Speaking of gifts, all your wedding gifts are at Dad's place," Tara mentioned.

"We should all go over, and we can open them up," I suggested.

Sherry was so happy to get her car back. Joe and I hopped into his truck and Tara and the boys drove, as we all headed over to Joe's place. Sherry waved her hand out her t-top as if to say, "I have it back, yeah!"

All the gifts were piled in Joe's room, so the kids took turns carrying out a gift and placing it in the center of the living room. I sat on the floor next to Joe. We anxiously ripped the paper to see what was inside the boxes. We had mentioned to everyone what we really needed. Towels were a must, peach and ivory was the color theme I wanted to use. We also got a crock-pot, knife set, and electric can opener. With each box we opened, someone blessed us with what we needed.

The girls were excited for their dad to be home. I could sense some quietness as Joe went and grabbed some of his things to bring to my place. We decided we would come back later to get the rest. Sherry and Tara would be staying at Joe's. We were starting our family in separate homes.

My darling, I am yours, and you are mine (Song of Solomon 6:3 CEV).

CHAPTER THIRTY

New Home

Joe and I had been married for four months when I decided to sell my trailer. Joe's daughters didn't want to live in his trailer, so he also put his up for sale. I had a few people stop to inquire so Joe and I started looking at houses in the Chardon area. A couple from our church, Fran and Regina, were working on their century home and wanting to put it up for sale. They wanted to move up the street into his mother's home. I decided to take a look one day while Joe was at work. I pulled into the driveway of a blue house with red heart shutters. The walk up to the door was made out of brick, but I couldn't help notice the flower beds looked sparse. I glanced around as I knocked on the red front door. Regina opened the door.

"Come on in," she said. "I'll show you around." I walked into the old country farm house and immediately my attention was drawn to the wide plank floors in the dining room. The wallpaper was very country, just my style. The large window in the center of the spacious kitchen overlooked a field across the road. There were no neighbors in sight. Regina led me to a room off the kitchen that she and Fran used for their bedroom. They were in the middle of putting up new drywall. The ceiling was high and looked up at a small attic. There was a wood burning stove against the back of the room.

We continued into the living room. The fireplace against the back wall was made of brick, with a large beam running across the top, and the old windows still had the original wavy glass. Off the dining room, there was another small bedroom where Fran's mother was staying. We walked up the old, steep, narrow wooden staircase to the second floor. The walls were open with the old lattice where dry wall was starting to be applied. The first room on the left was a long, narrow room with windows like the living room. All the doors to the rooms were original, with the original hardware too. The second room on the left was another spacious room running the same length as the first room. To the right was a smaller room. Down the hall, Regina led me to an unfinished bathroom. I stared at the open walls with only lattice. A toilet and sink were operable, but there was no bathtub or shower yet. A small window, halfway up the wall looked out into the backyard. A small door opened into the attic that I saw from the wood burning room. It was the only storage place in the house.

We went back downstairs where Regina showed me another bathroom next to the kitchen. The door to the basement was across from the bathroom. We walked down the steep steps to an old sandstone basement. The large boulders had been hand-cemented together by mortar. I could tell this house had a strong foundation.

I really liked the place. I was already imagining how I would decorate it. I couldn't wait to tell Joe. We walked outside, to the back of the house where there was an unattached garage. Behind the garage were a few rows of fruit trees.

"This used to be an orchard," Regina said.

Looking back across the yard, I could see wooded areas on both sides of the house. The yard went far back butting up to a large open field. "How much land is here?" I asked.

"There's almost five acres," she replied.

"What kind of trees are those? Do they produce fruit?"

"There are apple trees, pear trees, a couple plum trees, and one cherry tree," Regina told me.

We walked around the yard, looking at the wooded areas. Her boys had a tree fort in one of the large trees. The old trees in the yard were massive, typical of an old farm yard. We walked around to the front of the house where I saw a stained glass window labelled 1862 above the entrance. I could see myself living here with Joe and our family.

"Thank you for the tour," I said to Regina as I headed back to my car. "I'm going to tell Joe, and hopefully he'll want to come over in a few days and look for himself."

"Bye," Regina called out as I drove away.

As I headed home my mind jumped from room to room, imagining how I could change the look. There was a lot of work to be done, and I wasn't sure if Joe would be up to it after working eight hours a day. I wanted to have a place we could move right into. Regina and Fran were packing things up, already in the process of moving out.

Joe got home and I sat him down, enthusiastically telling him what I had seen. "Joe, you'll have to see the place for yourself to make an opinion."

I made the call. "Regina, Joe said he could stop by after work tomorrow. Is that okay?"

"Sure, what time does he get done?"

"Around 3:30. I'll meet him there."

"See you tomorrow."

I finished telling Joe how the house was laid out. The kids heard us talking.

"Are we moving?" Kevin asked.

"We're looking for a house for all of us to live," I said. "The way this house is set up, if we decide to move there, everyone will have their own room. Sherry could be downstairs. You and Ryan could be upstairs. Tara is off at college, so she would only need a room when she comes home. It would be just right for the family. But,there's a lot of work to be done, and Joe will have to see if this is something he wants to tackle."

Joe and I went for our evening walk. He needed to be in bed by 10 p.m. so he could get enough sleep. Being a night person, I let him retire to bed and stayed up a bit with the boys and did some work around the house.

There was a young woman looking to rent Joe's place. They made arrangements for her to come over that weekend to check it out. I couldn't help but be excited that things seemed to be falling into place for us yet again.

The next day I met Joe at Regina's. We toured the house and stepped outside to the garage. "I have always wanted my own garage to work in," Joe told me.

We walked around the yard and stepped back to the field, where the sun was about to set. "Look at that beautiful sunset," I said. It was breath-taking.

We went back inside, taking one more look. Joe called Regina into the kitchen and asked her what she wanted for the house. She yelled for Fran to come and talk with Joe. They discussed the finances while Regina and I chatted.

"Carol and I will discuss this and get back with you. Thank you," Joe said.

As we climbed into the car, Joe looked at me. "I don't know if I want to do all that work. That house needs a lot of work."

"We can get ahold of a realtor and have them start looking for other houses for us," I said. Over the next two weeks, Joe and I looked at around ten houses. Nothing caught our interest. Most of them needed more work than Regina's place. A few months passed and I felt a pull in my spirit to go back and look at Regina's house. I finally told Joe.

"We can go back and look if you want," he said.

"I'll call Regina in the morning and see when we can come."

The next morning I called and Regina said we could come by. She was still getting the rest of their things out of the house and was ready to list it with the realtor.

"Joe and I'll be there around 3:30 if that's okay with you."

"Sure. I'll see you then."

That same day, I received a call from a woman who had driven by and saw the for sale sign in the window of my trailer. She wanted to know how much I wanted. I told her. I was asking close to the buying price I had paid for it. I would be breaking even, and we would have money to put on a down payment for whatever house we decided to buy.

I went to get some boxes in town. I was feeling compelled to start doing some packing myself. I had accumulated a lot of knickknacks and needed to pack them safely to prevent any breakage.

I met Joe at Regina's that afternoon, and we walked through the house. The walls were almost completely covered with dry wall, giving a whole new look to the house. There was less work that would have to be done now. We could move into the house immediately. Joe and I stood in the back room looking at each other.

"I really like this place, Joe."

"I have a peace about this place. I think this is it," Joe said.

"You need to call Fran back here and ask him what his bottom line is," I said. "Regina, can you and Fran come back here for a minute?"

We stood face to face with them and asked what the lowest amount they would take for the house was. Fran took a breath, looked at Joe, and told him what they could sell for. I looked at Joe.

"It's a deal," Joe said, shaking Fran's hand. "Get the papers together, Carol and I will work on getting her trailer sold to give you a down payment."

We left very excited this was going to be our new home. We told the boys when we got home. I was very happy they would be able to stay in the Chardon school system. I wanted Ryan to graduate from Chardon High School, and I didn't want to take Kevin and move him to a different school district. Joe called the girls to tell them.

I could not shut off my mind from all the decorating ideas I had for the house. I tried to calm down by packing some more.

The next morning the woman interested in my place called again, asking about the price and wanting to come take a look. We made arrangements for her to come over that day.

"I apologize for the boxes throughout my house. I'm getting ready for my move. We found our house," I told her.

"No problem. I'm looking to rent in this park. I need to move my daughter and me close to this school system," she said. We walked through and I showed her the rooms. I wasn't sure if she was just being nosy or if she was serious. We stood in the kitchen.

"Do the appliances stay?" she asked.

"Yes they do, except the washer and dryer," I told her.

"When do you plan to move?"

"As soon as possible."

"I want to give you cash so I'll have to get the funds together. I'll come back on Monday. I really like the place. I really want it," she said.

When she walked out, I thought to myself, she won't be back; she's just talking. No way does she have twenty-six thousand dollars. I told Joe about the woman when he came home. He thought the same thing. No one is going to just offer that much cash. We were sure we wouldn't be seeing her again.

We were putting together a rental agreement for the girl who wanted to rent Joe's place. She would be moving in on the first of the month and had agreed to pay so much a month that we would apply to her option to buy while she was waiting on a settlement that would allow her to afford to buy the trailer. She told us it would take close to a year to get all her finances in order, so we agreed to let her pay rent until then. Things were falling into place for our new home. The only thing we needed was a serious buyer for my trailer.

We spent that weekend packing and cleaning out the storage shed at Joe's place, getting rid of some things we didn't need. We piled the packed boxes up against the wall and did a bit of cleaning. We left for home and got Joe to bed early so he'd be well-rested for work early the next morning.

I continued packing the next day, this time at my place. There was a knock at the door. I was surprised to see the woman who had wanted to pay cash to buy my trailer. Oh no, I thought. She's going to bother me, and I really need to be packing.

"Yes, can I help you?" I asked, sort of snarling.

"I told you I was going to get the cash and come back. I have the money and I want to confirm the deal. I really want this place," she said.

I was shocked. She wasn't kidding. This was serious. I quickly recovered, "Come on in. Forgive me for being rude. I've been packing and I'm a bit edgy." I wasn't about to tell her I had thought she was a fake.

"Come on, we can sit at the kitchen table. I'll have to draw up a hand-written sales agreement."

"I have one already," she said, handing me the paper. I was surprised she was that thorough. "All we have to do is fill in the purchase price and I'll hand you over your cash. You can sign it and so can I, there are two copies. One for you and one for me."

I had judged this woman, but here she knew exactly what she needed to do. I looked over the form, making sure things were written correctly and I signed my name. She did the same. She reached into her purse, pulling out a white envelope with a bundle of cash. She started counting the hundred dollar bills, laying them on the table. For a quick second I thought, these must be phony bills. She kept counting. My eyes followed her hands as I counted along with her. She had exactly the right amount. I shook her hand and gave her the receipt.

"I'll call you tomorrow to let you know the exact date you can move in. I need to call the woman who owned the house we bought and ask her when we can move in. It'll be before the middle of September," I promised her.

"Bye," she said, walking out the door. "I'll talk to you tomorrow."

After I made sure she had driven away, I jumped up and down, thanking God for the sale of our place. I ran to the bank to deposit the money since I didn't want to have that kind of cash lying around. I held onto the deposit ticket waving it in the air as I continued to thank God for what He had done for us.

I called Regina to tell her that I sold my place. The paperwork was still at her lawyer's, and she wasn't sure how long it was going to take. I explained to her that the buyer needed to be in by no later than the middle of September and asked if we could start moving things into the house. I offered to pay rent for the month if we could start making the move. We would be giving her the down payment on Sunday in church, and the bank would continue to process the loan. We were friends, and she knew we could be trusted. I couldn't believe we were about to move into our new house.

When Joe arrived home from work, I sat him down on the couch to tell him the great news. I could hardly contain myself. He could see I was up to something since I was grinning from ear to ear.

"What are you up to?" he asked.

"What would you say if I told you we can start moving things into our new house this weekend?"

"How can we do that?" he asked. "Why are we doing that? Did you talk to Regina?"

"Yes, she knows. I'm going to give her a down payment on Sunday."

"With what?" he asked. I pulled the deposit slip from behind my back and flashed it in his face. "She came?"

"Yes, she bought the place. We have our deposit."

"That is crazy. She gave you cash?"

"I know," I said. "I thought for a moment she was wacky. But, Joe, she was serious. Maybe she was an angel."

"I thought I would sell my place before you, and here this woman comes and hands you cash," Joe said.

I leaped into his arms, "We are going to have our very own house, and I can start to decorate the way I want. I have all those boxes in my shed that I've been holding onto since I moved out of my house. I'll be able to pull things out to decorate. The kids will have their own rooms. Let's call them and take them over to see their new place." Tara was away at college, so she would have to wait until she came home on break.

Joe called Sherry, and I located the boys and we took a drive. Regina had given me a key in case we wanted to pop in on our own. We opened the door. Kevin ran through the house yelling how big it was and went to explore the yard. Ryan was sort of quiet. He looked around, but didn't have that much to say.

"We can get a basketball hoop and put it on the garage," Kevin said.

Sherry was quiet, walking through each room slowly. Joe and I held onto each other, amazed that we really were going to be calling this our home. As we walked from room to room, the kids told us which room they wanted.

The boys would be upstairs by us. Kevin had bunk beds so we could put them in the smaller room. Ryan was older, so he could have the bigger room. He had a single-size waterbed that my brother had given him although I was a little concerned the floor wouldn't hold it. Sherry would be in the room downstairs. Tara would be coming home next summer after graduation. Everyone appeared to like where they were going to be.

Regina was planning a garage sale over the weekend. I told her I would come and help. The table in the kitchen was an old library table. It was perfect for our large family. I hoped she was going to let me buy it.

There were a few other items at the garage sale that caught my interest. I could see them remaining as part of the legacy of the house. Regina told me to just take them. An old victrola with some 33 records were kept in the house from her mother. Some of the songs touched my heart, especially the old hymns I heard in church as a small child. I was thrilled I could place them back into this old home. I wanted to add antiques throughout the house, they would make a great addition.

Regina and I closed the sale and shut up the garage. She was trying to figure out what she was going to do with the things she didn't sell. I went through, picking out some more older things I could picture in the house. We decided to call a company and have them come and pick them up the rest. She wanted us to be able to move in the next week or the week after. Everything was falling into place—I was married to a godly man and moving into our very own house. Joe was so supportive of my decorating. I was not being controlled by anyone except the Holy Spirit.

The day of our move finally arrived. We rented a van and went over to Joe's place first to get the things out of his house. The van filled up quickly, and we made our first run. With help from so many of our friends, the work went fast. Joe stood in his empty trailer, half sad to be leaving the memories he had there. He had raised his daughters there. Sherry was emotional too.

We unloaded the first trip and went back for the second. We put a lot of the boxes in the garage to move them in the house later. Once we finished with Joe's place, we began to tackle mine. I was a pack rat and had four times the things Joe had. We would have more trips to make. We also still had to unload and get our beds up so we could sleep in them that night. Everyone was starting to get tired. The pressure was on, and it made us edgy. The boxes at my trailer were all packed and ready to move, so I stayed back at the house to start the unpacking. I moved the bed frames in the positions they needed to be in so all they would have to do is put them together. I tried to make it easy, but I was tired as well. It had been a long day.

I would have to go back in the morning to clean the trailers up so they would be ready for the new owners. I knew I was going to sleep well tonight, if only we could get our bed together. I was ready to sleep on the floor.

When we were finally in bed for the night, I took a moment to reflect on the day and on my life. I couldn't believe I was in my very own house with my husband and our children. God had truly blessed me. How different this was from when I had moved into a home with Owen. I had found God and with Him, I had found love and happiness.

In My Father's house are many mansions; if it were not so, I would have told you, I go to prepare a place for you. And if I go and prepare a place for you, I will come again and receive you to Myself; that where I am, there you may be also (John 14:2-3 NKJV).

CHAPTER THIRTY-ONE

Full Circle

Nine years later, Joe and I were headed back from South Dakota in the summer of 2003. We had been visiting Kevin at Teen Challenge, a Christian Center that helps young men get their lives in order by using God's principles. Kevin had been in trouble on and off with the law. He'd started using drugs and was way out of control. The court had sentenced him to go to Teen Challenge.

Ryan traveled with Joe and me to see Kevin. We were happy he went along. Ryan had been working closely with his dad, purchasing and selling stocks. Ryan would talk with Owen at prison on a regular basis. They were trying to build a business. I had never been able to share with Ryan all that went on between his father and me. He started talking about his father's release and going before the parole board. I knew Ryan really counted on his dad coming home so this trip was my chance to talk to him about Owen. I'd have his undivided attention since he couldn't run and would have to listen to what I had to say.

"Ryan, I've always told you that your dad won't be coming home until he gets right with God," I began. Ryan viewed me as a Jesus nut, thinking I didn't know what I was talking about. "There's another murder that will come to surface one day. Your dad thinks he will never be tried. They never found the body so he thinks he's free because they can't try the case."

I had always told the boys their father was involved in a second murder, but I never gave them the facts. Ryan was now at an age that he could handle the truth. It was time for me to tell him the story. I took a deep breath and started to share. I started from the day I met his father and ended with our divorce. He asked a few questions and as I answered, I was surprised to find understanding from him.

The rest of the drive home we talked about how he felt knowing about the murders. It was good Ryan finally opened up. It was a relief to me that it brought us closer together. Everything was now in the open. I had been so afraid of what Ryan would think of me when he grew up and learned about the kind of life I had led. And now he knew why I did what I had done. It brought a closeness to Ryan and me that we never had before.

We dropped Ryan at his place and hugged him goodbye. When Joe and I arrived home, I unloaded the car while Joe went to grab the mail that had accumulated from the past few days and put the pile of mail on the kitchen table. I sat down, rummaging through what I felt was important. One envelope caught my eye. It was from the Sheriff of Cuyahoga County addressed to Carol Kilbane Byler.

My first thought was, Oh gosh what did I do? It must be something from when I was with Owen. I opened the letter. My eyes skimmed down the page reading, "You are hereby ordered to appear in the common pleas before the grand jury." There was a business card with the name William Mason, Cuyahoga County Prosecuting Attorney at the top. In the middle of the card was Henry Tekancic, Investigator. My heart sank. What do they want me for? I couldn't think of anything I had done for them to call me to court.

I went over and picked up the phone, calling the number on the card. "May I speak with Mr. Tekancic?" I asked when a man answered.

"This is Henry," he responded.

"My name's Carol Byler. I received a subpoena to testify before the grand jury on July 19th. What am I testifying for?" I asked.

"Carol, do you remember the Arnie Prunella case?"

"Yes, what about it?"

"We've reopened the case, and we have new evidence to bring forward."

"This is so spooky. I just got back from visiting my son in South Dakota. I had told my older son, Ryan, on the way home today that this murder was unsettled. My boys have been told over and over by me that their father needs to come clean with what he did. You're putting me in a very difficult position though. I would have to testify against their father."

"Carol, we're only asking you to come to the grand jury," he said.

"I have to call my boys up and discuss this with them. I can't just testify against their dad without them knowing about it."

"You know, we can force you to come. You have a subpoena."

"I know, but you have to understand how I'm feeling. This is their father, no matter what he has done. I have to call them. I'll get back to you in the morning."

I hung up the phone and sat in the chair, stunned. I told Joe what had just happened.

"I have to call the boys and tell them," I said.

"What's up, Mom?" Ryan asked when he picked up the phone.

"Ryan, I need to call Kevin and get him on the phone. I have to ask you both something very important."

"Right now? Can't it wait?" Ryan asked.

"No. You will know in a minute. I'm calling Kevin, hold on."

I placed Ryan on hold and called Kevin. When a man answered the phone, I explained, "I need to talk to Kevin Kilbane. This is his mother. We have a family crisis."

"Hold on," he said. "I'll get him."

"Mom, are you alright?" Kevin asked with a trace of panic in his voice. "Did you make it home okay?"

"Yes. Kevin, I have Ryan on the other line. Hold on while I get him. Ryan, are you there?"

"Yes, Mom."

"In the mailbox today was a letter from the grand jury. I called to find out what it was about. I was sent a subpoena to testify against your dad at the grand jury on the Prunella murder. They have new evidence to reopen the case. You both know I was involved because I knew it happened. I don't want to go, but I have no choice. They will make me go. I went to jail years ago for contempt, and I won't go again. This means I have to talk against your dad. It could mean he'll never get out of jail."

"Mom, you need to do what you have to," Kevin said. "You can't lie. You have to tell the truth. Just be honest and tell them what you know."

"Ryan, what do you have to say?" I asked.

"This is crazy. We were just talking about this," Ryan said.

"I know. God is exposing it. He had me tell you about it so you would know He is working in our lives," I said.

"I have to go, Mom," Kevin said. "Do what you have to. Take care of yourself."

"Thanks, Kevin, for supporting me on this. I'm not happy that I have to do any talking to anyone."

"Bye Mom. I love you. Call me later," Kevin said as he hung up the phone. I continued talking to Ryan.

"I will be over in a bit," Ryan said. "We'll talk more then."

"Okay, bye," I said, hanging up. I turned to Joe. "I have support from the boys to tell what I know. They understand, so it makes it easier for me. I'll call Henry in the morning to tell him I'll come down. What is God doing? I can't believe the timing on this."

"Carol, God is just exposing the sin," Joe said.

"I don't like the fact I have to testify against their dad, but I will not go to jail for him ever again. I'll tell them all that I know. He never cared about Ryan in the first trial. I was separated from my baby because Owen only thought of himself. This time I am thinking about me and the boys. I will not look at a jail cell for him. He did this, and now he needs to come clean," I paused. "I hope I can tell Owen about this before I go down. I'll tell Ryan when he talks to him to have him give me a call."

Ryan came over and sat in my office while I explained some of what I knew. I opened the files I had saved from the case to show them. I had stacks and stacks of articles written about Owen. Ryan sat quietly, looking at the trial information written in the newspapers. He had never wanted to look at them before. It opened his eyes to what I had been telling him for a long time. Ryan was finally taking a good look at what his father was really about. I wasn't the bad person his father wanted him to believe. I was not the reason his father was away. Yes, I made a statement against Owen, but I wasn't the one who committed the crime. I was a victim, just like the rest, but I was lucky enough to still be alive. I had kept secrets for years, and I was not about to keep them anymore. Owen was guilty, and God was exposing what he had done.

I told Ryan about the day of the trial and how I had to leave him in his father's arms when I was charged with contempt of court. "I was breast-feeding you," I said. "Your father cared only about himself. He could have pleaded guilty, and I wouldn't have had to go to jail," I paused. "Hold on a minute. I'll be right back."

I walked upstairs to my bedroom to grab the pink teddy bear sitting on my shelf. I walked over to Ryan, holding onto the bear. "Ryan, when I was separated from you in the jail, some church ladies would come in with different crafts we could work on. There was a pattern of a little bear. There was only one color of fabric; it was pink. I sewed this by hand, stitch by stitch, thinking of you. I wondered when I would be able to see you again. I wanted to make it for you so one day I could give it to you and tell you where it was made and why. I have held onto it all these years. Today, I feel this is the time I can give it to you, and you will understand."

I reached down and gave him a hug. I could see the tears in his eyes. I had touched his heart. He took the pink bear in his hands.

"Ryan, I'm going to tell your father to come clean with this."

"I'm going to call his attorney in the morning to tell him I am dropping off all of Dad's papers and the money he gave me to buy the stocks," Ryan said. "I don't want anything to do with his business. I don't even know where this money is from."

"I'll let you know what happens when I go down to the grand jury," I said as I walked them out. "Goodnight, I love you."

"I love you too, Mom. Goodnight."

The next morning, I called the prosecutor's office. "Hello Henry. I talked to the boys, and they've given me their support. I will see you on the 19th."

"Carol, do you know who Ressler is?" he asked me. "He'll be there too."

"I hope I can talk with him. He knows how I've changed. We talked a few years back. He gave me a signed copy of the book that he wrote."

When I hung up the phone, I turned to Joe and said, "Isn't it amazing what God is doing? He's taking me back into the court system to some of the people who were there during the trial. They'll see the new person in me. I will be a testimony of God's love and mercy. They'll see how He changed my life. Will you take off work and go with me?"

"Sure, I'll be there to support you," he promised.

———◆◆◆———

The morning of my testimony, I could not calm my nerves as I walked into the Justice Center. The last time I had been there was when I did the remainder of my contempt of court charge. This time I wasn't breaking the law. I was helping the law. Joe and I went to the third floor to the Court of Common Pleas. I walked through the large wooden doors and on the other side stood a police officer and two gentlemen.

"I have a subpoena to appear here today," I told them, showing the officer my paper.

"I'm Henry," one of the men said. "Carol, you can come with me." We walked over to a wall of empty chairs. "Robert Ressler is in the courtroom right now. When he comes out, it'll be your turn to go in."

"Can I talk with Ressler?"

"I don't know. You both were called to the grand jury, and I'm not sure if they'll let you talk."

"I just want to say hello," I explained. "Someone can stand there and listen to our conversation. I'm not going to discuss the case."

Joe and I sat and waited for my turn. One hour went by, and we were still waiting. Finally, two men came out with Ressler behind them. I stood up and walked over to him. I wanted to shake his hand. The two men stood on each side as I faced him.

"How're you doing?" I asked.

"I'm great," he said.

"Thank you for the copy of your book. I read it. I'm working on mine right now, but I have a long way to go. I'll send you a copy when I'm done," I said. "Are you still working with the FBI?"

"I retired and am working on my own," he said.

"Robert, this is my husband Joe."

"Nice to meet you," he said.

They called my name, and it was my turn to go in. "Bye Robert. I'll talk with you soon."

Joe stayed in the hallway as I walked into the room. There was a large table in front of the witness stand with men and women on both sides. They stared directly at me, and I felt nervous again. I was instructed to walk to the front of the room and onto the stand. I was asked to place my hand on the Bible.

"I swear to tell the truth, nothing but the truth, so help me God."

The last time I swore in court, I had perjured myself. This time I refused to tell a lie. I would be convicted by God.

The prosecutors stood up and introduced themselves. I remembered William Mason. He had been working on this case for years. The questioning started with them asking me to state my name and where I lived.

"Do you know Owen Kilbane?"

"Yes, he is my ex-husband."

"Do you know a man name Arnie Prunella?"

"Yes."

"What do you know about him?"

"He was a pimp."

"Did you meet him through Owen?"

"Yes."

"When was the last time you saw him?"

"After he came back from Vegas."

The questions were intense, and I told them everything I knew. The jury kept their eyes on me. After more than an hour of questioning, I was asked to step down. A couple of the jury members nodded their heads at me. I had done my part. The case was in their hands now. They would decide whether or not to indict Owen.

The prosecutors thanked me for coming. Joe and I left the courthouse. It was over, I thought to myself, breathing a sigh of relief. Now I had to wait to see what the decision would be. Would there be a trial or not?

The Kilbane name was about to be dragged across the news media again and Ryan didn't want any part of it. The prosecutors called me before the news hit the airwaves. They got the indictment and the trial was set.

Owen finally gave me a call.

"Owen, I received a subpoena to appear before the grand jury," I told him. "This is your chance to make things right with God, to come clean and confess what part you had in Arnie's death. I spoke with the boys, and now they know the truth. Every time they thought you would be released on parole, I warned them you would not be freed as long as you have this murder hanging over your head. They're aware of your involvement, and they will do what they need to get justice for Arnie."

I tried so desperately to get him to realize the road he was heading down, but he was still trying to beat the system. He kept making up lies. He wasn't going to admit his involvement.

"You better keep your f***ing mouth shut and keep my name out of your mouth. You have done enough damage to keep me in here," he said angrily.

"You have done this yourself. Don't try and blame me for what you've done. I'm trying to warn you about what's going to happen, and you aren't listening. You're blaming me. You have been in there all these years, and you still are trying to fool the authorities. They know you did it. You can't win." I hung up the phone, thinking to myself, He's so stupid. He thinks he can fool them. They have the proof they need to convict him and he's still going to tell them he had no part in it.

He had been incarcerated for over twenty-five years, and he was due to approach the parole board. Even after all these years, he wouldn't come forward on his own to make it right. I couldn't help but think he hadn't changed and was never going to.

I called the boys to tell them about my conversation with their father. We all waited with anticipation to see if Owen would confess before the trial would take place. Once more he was putting himself before everyone else. He wasn't thinking of me or the boys. He knew the media would get ahold of the story again. Why would he want to put his grown children through the ordeal of a trial? Now he was going to try and smear their mother. He was asking me not to talk. Could he possibly be living in a fantasy world, thinking that I would get up there and lie for him again?

The boys and I put it out of our minds the best we could. I continued growing in my faith. I was busy going to the prisons to talk with the women. I knew in the back of my mind the day of the trial was approaching, but I hoped Owen would confess at the last moment so I wouldn't have to testify. What did he have up his sleeve this time? I wondered. He couldn't outsmart them.

August 16th arrived, and Owen still hadn't confessed. Joe and I drove to the Justice Center. I was so scared the media would be all over. I didn't want to deal with them. I didn't want the boys to have to go tell their friends or co-workers about their dad. We walked across the street, and I looked up at the large building in front of me, remembering when I walked out of it after testifying to the grand jury. I wondered who was going to be there this time. I walked up the steps entering the door and passing through security. I warned Joe ahead of time the procedure for entering the building. I only brought what was necessary so I could walk quickly through security. Joe emptied his pockets of his wallet and his keys. I placed my purse on the belt.

"Where are you going?" the guard asked.

"I am going to the third floor for a trial," I said.

I wondered if he knew I was here for the Kilbane trial. He pointed to the elevator, and we headed that way. I started to pray and ask God for strength. I hadn't seen Owen or Marty in more than twenty years and not only was I about to be face to face with these criminals, but I was going to snitch on them. The elevator stopped at the third floor, and as the door opened I could see people standing all around. I approached the desk and was greeted by a security guard.

"Can I help you?" the officer asked.

"Yes, I have a subpoena to appear in court."

"Have a seat over there, and you will be called."

I looked around to see if there were any familiar faces. The prosecutors came from behind a large door leading to the courtroom. As they approached, I noticed them talking to a gentleman I had seen before. It was Henry, the investigator.

"Carol, thanks so much for coming," he said. "We've been negotiating with the lawyers. Neither Owen nor Martin will take a plea bargain. They say they're not guilty and want to take it to trial. So I'm afraid you'll have to hang around to testify. We were hoping you wouldn't have to. I have a woman from the court that helps with victims of abuse, and she is assigned to help you through this difficult time. I'll have her come up shortly to talk with you. I'll be right back."

Outside, the courtroom was filling with spectators. I walked over to the window and looked out, to avoid making eye contact with any of them. Joe and I were eager to get this over with, especially me. A woman in her 40s approached me.

"Carol, I'm Annie. I've been assigned to support you today through this ordeal. I'd like us to go down the hall by ourselves and sit and explain a few things before we have to go into the courtroom. Is that okay with you?" she asked.

"Sure, can my husband come?" I asked.

"Of course he can. We can go right in here." We entered a small room outside the courtroom. She closed the door, and we all sat.

"I know this is going to be hard for you," she said. "When was the last time you saw Owen?"

"It has been years. Probably at least fifteen or more," I answered.

"Have you talked to him recently?" she asked.

"Yes, I tried to tell him he needed to make this right."

"I have to tell you that when you go in to the courtroom, the defendants will come in after everyone is seated. They will come in and sit to the far left of the room. You'll be taken aback when you see him. The prison keeps them confined where they are not exposed to the outside elements. Their coloring will be very pale, and some of them do not look very healthy. Your memory of what he looked like before is not what you'll see. So we try and prepare you for what you are about to see. Also, how are you feeling emotionally at this time about walking in there?"

"I think I'm okay. I won't know until I get in there."

"If at any time you need to stop and take a minute, we'll ask the judge to let you do that," she said.

"Thanks, that helps. I also have my husband here, and he's a big support."

"We need to go out now," she said. "I think they're going to start soon. We can stand over by the side so when the doors open, you won't be seen."

While we waited outside for my name to be called, I chatted with Annie.

"This is going to be so different than it was back in 1977, when I refused to testify," I said.

"I remember you being this feisty girl that we looked at. We realized that you'd been brainwashed, and there was nothing we could do. We wanted to help you, but we couldn't get through to you," she said.

"I know. I was so in love I couldn't rat on him."

"Are you afraid now?" she asked.

"No, not at all. There's nothing he can do to me now."

She was amazed at the transformation of my life. She must have known only God could have done this. I had been so enmeshed in a triangle of destruction. It had to be a higher power that intervened in my life to bring me out. I had been under the control of someone, in darkness, and now I was out in the open light, transformed into a person totally opposite of who I had been.

They came to get me, and I went into the courtroom. I sat in the last row of the room. Joe sat next to me, and I held on to his hand tightly. The defense came in and sat down at their table, and then the prosecutors came in. One of them walked back to me.

"Are you going to be okay?" he asked.

"The best that I can in these circumstances."

"We'll be starting soon. I'll call your name. Just come to the front by the judge, and you'll be sworn in. I'll then ask you questions."

"Okay," I said. "I can't wait for it to be over."

"All rise," the man shouted as the judge entered the room and sat behind his bench. He looked out into the room.

"Where are the defendants?" he asked.

"They're right outside the door waiting, Your Honor."

"Bring them in."

The door opened, and Owen and Martin walked in. I looked out of the corner of my eye. I wanted to look away, but I couldn't. I stared at them from head to toe. They were nothing like what I remembered. I was stunned at their appearance. They were white as ghosts. There was no color on their faces, and they were dressed in suits from the prison. Owen was completely bald. I didn't want them to see me staring so I quickly looked away.

"Joe, he looks so bad, sickly looking." I said, grabbing ahold of Annie's hand for support.

The guard waved for them to be seated against the side wall. The prosecutor motioned back at me, holding up his finger for me to hold on for one minute. The defense started their arguments, trying to get the case thrown out. They were quoting law. I glanced again and noticed that Martin had looked over at me. I looked away. Owen was so focused on the lawyer, he didn't seem to notice me. The judge ordered the trial to begin.

"Bring your witness to the stand," the judge ordered. The prosecutor waved me forward. I could feel Owen and Martin's eyes on me, willing me to disappear as I walked forward. I wasn't going to let anyone scare me. I reached the stand and was asked to place my hand on the Bible.

"Do you swear to tell the truth, the whole truth and nothing but the truth, so help you God?"

"Yes," I answered.

"You may take the stand."

"Can you state your name?" the lawyer asked me.

"Carol Byler."

"Where do you reside?"

"In Chardon, Ohio."

The questions went on and on. I wanted them to stop. I wanted to run out. The stares were getting harder to ignore. I wanted to slip under the stand and answer anything else they wanted, just as long as no one could see me. The defense was trying to make me look like I was a vindictive ex-wife that was out to keep Owen in jail. I would say anything to do so. The questions kept coming. Did I know this person and that person? Did I know of Arnie?

Finally I was asked, "Have you talked with Owen in the past year?"

"Yes, I have."

"When was that?"

"I asked Ryan, my son, to have him call me."

"Why was that?"

"I was given a subpoena to the grand jury, and I wanted to tell him this was his chance to get things right. He needed to make things right with God and tell the truth. I told him I told his sons the truth."

"What did he say to that?"

"He got very angry and started cussing at me, telling me I shouldn't be talking to anyone. That I need to keep his f***ing name out of my mouth, I have done enough damage."

The prosecutor walked away. I could see out of the corner of my eye Owen and Martin staring at me as if they wanted to shut me up right on the spot. I was running my mouth, and they couldn't stop me. I was on the other team this time. The prosecutor walked back to me, placing a tape recorder on the table in front of me. He pushed the play button. The conversation was there. It was Owen and I talking, exactly what I had just finished telling them I said. The conversation had been recorded by the prison. I couldn't believe it. Owen leaned back, and Martin laid his head back against the wall in defeat. They knew they were done telling their lies. It was on record. I was trying to tell him to get right. I wasn't the bad person here. I was still trying to help him, even after all that he had done to me. I was still trying to save his neck. He didn't care. I was the enemy in his, and especially Martin's, eyes. They were blaming me for all the years they had been locked up. They never did take responsibility for what they had done. I was just a victim in all of this. They were trying to use me as their scapegoat once more. Blame someone else long enough, and you will start to believe the lie yourself, I thought to myself.

"We need to take a short break," the defense said.

I was asked to step down off the stand. I wanted to run out of the courtroom. I was glad that they rushed Martin and Owen out immediately so I didn't have to face them. I went back by Joe, and the court counselor walked me out the door. I quit smoking years ago, but I felt like I could have used a cigarette at the moment because of how intense it was. I waited in the lobby for the prosecutors to let me know what was going on. The defense attorneys and the prosecutors walked into the hall and waved me to come along. We all went into another courtroom. I wondered what this was about.

"This is off the record. We want to ask you a few more questions about Owen and your conversation," they said. The prosecutors looked at me, nodding their heads that it was alright for me to answer. The two defense attorneys asked me their questions, one at a time. I looked them in the eyes and gave them the same answers as I did in the courtroom. I figured they were trying to see if I had been chorused into saying what I did, even after listening to the recording. They were making sure that the plea bargain Owen and Martin were about to accept would be worth it for them to take. They knew they would lose if they took it to trial. There was too much evidence against them.

One of the lawyers told me, "I hope things go well for you in the future." It was as if they knew what I had gone through, and it was their way of wishing me a better life. Joe had overheard one of them making the comment, "I wonder where she found him at," referring to Joe. They had no idea what God brought me through and how I was blessed with my great husband. They were looking at me in terms of my past, not the woman I had become.

We all walked back to the court for the plea. Owen and Martin were getting ready to plead guilty. They offered them a bargain, and it was now up to the judge to pass sentence on them. Everyone gathered back into the courtroom, and we were asked to rise as the judge entered. Then we were asked to be seated. Martin and Owen were brought in and taken to the bench in front of the judge.

"What do you plead?" he looked at Owen.

"Guilty," Owen said.

"What do you plead?" asking Martin.

"Guilty, your honor," he said.

The judge went on to lecture them, "You both were wrong for not coming forth before this time. The family of the victim has suffered. I am going to pass sentence on you both at this time. Do you have anything you have to say at this time?"

Owen apologized to the family for his part in Arnie's death. And Martin stood and said the same. After thirty-six years, Arnie was getting his revenge. The judge looked at them both.

"You are already incarcerated at this time, so I am going to run your sentence along with what you are doing. I am going to add five more years on to you, Owen, and four more years on to you, Martin. Take them away." As he pounded his gravel, Martin and Owen turned around and headed for the side door to go back to their cells.

I walked out of the courtroom with a sigh of relief. I was talking to the prosecutors when a young gentleman approached me.

"Carol, I want to thank you for your honesty. My brother and I have been following this case very closely. We don't want the Kilbane brothers to ever get out."

"Why do you say that?" I asked him.

"My mother was Marlene Steele, and they had a part in her brutal murder." I was silent. I couldn't speak. Here I was, face to face with this man. When he was a little boy, I couldn't stop his mother's death.

"I am so sorry," I finally said. "I wish I could have stopped it, but I couldn't. I was a victim, just like your mom was. They would have killed me. I pray that one day you will be able to forgive. You can't keep that bitterness inside; it will eat you away. You'll be letting them win if you get destroyed yourself. I just hope one day you will be able to find forgiveness in your heart." He walked away. I felt a deep sadness in my heart. I knew that he needed to let that go to find peace.

As Joe and I started to leave, the counselor approached me, asking if I would be so kind as to talk with Denise, Arnie's daughter. She was only three years old when her father had been murdered. She wanted to speak with me.

"Of course I'll talk to her."

"Carol, I want to thank you for your courage to come forth," she said. "I knew my dad had been murdered, and I waited all these years to have closure on his death. You have given that to me. I want to thank you for your honesty and for facing Owen the way that you did."

"Denise, my only regret is that I wish I would have had the courage to come forward a lot sooner. I guess God's timing is always on time."

"Carol, you take care now. I'm glad you're doing well."

"Thanks and I hope you have room in your heart for forgiveness one day."

She walked away, and I felt some closure in my own life. I didn't have to hold any more secrets. They were all exposed. All the skeletons were out of the closet. I could now move on and enjoy my life.

For in the time of trouble He shall hide me in His pavilion; in the secret place of His tabernacle He shall hide me; He shall set me high upon a rock (Ps. 27:5 NKJV).

Epilogue

To my many readers, as you took a journey through my life, you were able to experience the deep darkness in my life. As I became more transparent, I was able to allow the long-buried secrets to be uncovered.

My desire is that you will experience some type of emotion as you identify with the turmoil of my life, to help you develop awareness that you too can survive by pulling yourself to freedom as I have.

I want you readers to realize you are able to have the strength and courage to escape any situation as I did. As a survivor, I want you to be encouraged that no matter how dark or horrifying your circumstances may seem, there is always a way of escape.

The path of emptiness filled my life constantly. I was searching for many years to fill the large void in my heart that was empty. I grew up without my mom or my dad's nurturing love and guidance. I didn't have love. When love is not shown, how do you know what to look for? What do you compare it to? What does it feel like? I wasn't sure. What is love? Was it a touch? Was it sex? Was it a hug? I had no idea. I didn't know what I was searching for, but I was searching for something. I would attach myself to anything that would come my way to fill my emotional needs, even if it was temporary.

Through showing the pitfalls that I fell into, I now hope I can give you young women and girls some direction in your lives, something I never had. Perhaps you can relate to me with my poor relationships, especially with my mother and father. The lack of love and direction that should be in our lives and the effects that has on us is so important. We desire them, and when they are not filled, we go through life finding ways to fill the emptiness.

I strayed from God. He was always there, waiting with open arms to take me by the hand so He could begin to restore me back into a relationship with Him. The emotional damage in my life would only take a miracle to repair.

Like an earthy father should be, you can climb into the Heavenly Father's lap as a small child would, telling Him your heart's desire and all that is going on in your life. He is all knowing. He wants you to share the secrets you hold so dear. He already knows them before you even speak them. He will hold them close to His heart and never betray you. He is eager for you to share every detail of your life with Him.

I want you, my reader, to know about the Heavenly Father's love. He will be your best friend. He will never leave you nor forsake you. When we love on Him, He loves us right back. He won't turn on you. He loves us so much that it is hard for us to even fathom that kind of love. It is so deep, so wide—there is no word in our vocabulary that can explain how much He loves us.

Throughout all my years of searching for the right love, He was there the whole time. I ran from Him, but He never ran from me. He would gently take all the time I spent away from Him and heal the deepest areas in which I was so wounded. He will bind the wounds of the brokenhearted.

He can help you heal those deep wounds you carry in your heart. He just wants you to accept Him into your heart. It's that simple. It is by His grace we can turn our lives over to Him. I didn't do a thing. I came with my soiled life, and He cleaned me up. He has intensive care for the hurting.

The desire to move forward needs to be greater than the memories of past pain. When that desire comes back into your spirit and begins to live in you again, you will find release for your pain. There was nothing I could do or say for Him to want me; all I did was surrender to that grace. He is not a religion; He is a personal friend.

People with a past have always been able to come to him. He makes us into someone wonderful and marvelous. I would love to share my Heavenly Father, my personal friend with you, if you give me that chance. He is all about restoration; He knows how to take a mess and turn it into a miracle. If you are in a mess, don't be upset about it because God specializes in fixing up messed-up lives. He will take your mess and turn it into a message to help others who are hurting.

So as I end the horror of a once lived life, I open my heart to help others find the same freedom I now have.

Write me at caroljbybook@gmail.com

Visit my website at http://caroljbyler-kilbane.com

With His Love,

Carol J. Kilbane Byler

I will restore to you the years which the swarming locust has eaten (Joel 2:25 RSV).

Where They Are Today

Owen Kilbane has served over 30 some years. He is presently serving time in the Grafton, Ohio, prison.

Martin Kilbane has served over 30 some years. He is presently serving time with his brother in the Grafton, Ohio, prison.

Martha Kilbane has divorced Owen and is living in another state.

Phil Christopher has been released from prison, and a book has been written about him.

Robert Steele died in prison from cancer.

Barb, his secretary that he married, died of a brain tumor while he was in prison.

The Steele boys are in Florida with their grandparents that raised them. I talked to them a few years ago and told them I was sorry for my involvement with their mother's murder. They keep fighting to keep the Kilbane brothers in jail with no parole. I told them that one day I hope they can have forgiveness so they can heal their wounded hearts.

Arnie Purnella's daughter talked to me at the trial, thanking me for her to be able to have closure on her father's death. Arnie's mother went to her grave not knowing what happened to her son. His daughter thanked me for my bravery for coming forth with the truth.

Rick Robbins was given a new identity under the witness protection act with his family. Some day I hope that he and I can talk. I pray that he does ask God to forgive him.

Karol has accepted Jesus and is living in California. She wrote me many years ago, telling me that she is a born again Christian. I hope to hear from her again someday.

Sonja and I lost contact, and I have no idea where she is at right now. I hope to hear from her again someday also. I hope she is still following Jesus.

My boys are doing very well and have moved on in their lives with the healing process of what their Mom and Dad have put them through.

Joe and I live in Chardon, Ohio, in our century home and breed Rottweilers.

My mother is living with us. She is 90, and it is by the grace of God that I can even take care of her. We are still not close. She is like a stranger in my home.

I once thought all these things were so very important, but now I consider them worthless because of what Christ has done. Yes, everything else is worthless when compared with the priceless gain of knowing Christ Jesus my Lord. I have discarded everything else, counting it all as garbage, so that I may have Christ and become one with Him. I no longer count on my own goodness or my ability to obey God's law, but I trust Christ to save me. For God's way of making things right with himself depends on faith. As a result, I can really know Christ and experience the mighty power that raised Him from the dead. I can learn what it means to suffer with Him, sharing in His death, so that, somehow, I can experience the resurrection from the dead! I don't mean to say that I have already achieved these things or that I have already reached perfection! But I keep working toward that day when I will finally be all that Christ Jesus saved me for and wants me to be. No, dear brothers and sisters, I am still not all I should be, but I am focusing all my energies on this one thing: Forgetting the past and looking forward to what lies ahead, I strain to reach the end of the race and receive the prize for which God through Christ Jesus, is calling us up to heaven (Phil. 3:7-14 NLT).